I AM MARRIED ON PURPOSE

I am MARRIED *on* PURPOSE

Jordi Bostock

Copyright © 2016 Jordi Bostock
All rights reserved.

No part of this book may be reproduced, stored in retrieval systems, or transmitted by any means, electronic, mechanical, photocopying, recorded or otherwise without written permission from the publisher. No part of this book may be reproduced, stored in a retrieval system, or transmitted, in any form or by any means, electronic or photocopy or otherwise, without the prior written permission of the publisher except in the case of brief quotations within critical articles and reviews. You must not circulate this book in any format. This book is licensed for your personal enjoyment only. This book may not be resold or given away to other people.

Although the author and publisher have made every effort to ensure that the information in this book was correct at press time, the author and publisher do not assume and hereby disclaim any liability to any party for any loss, damage, or disruption caused by errors or omissions, whether such errors or omissions result from negligence, accident, or any other cause. The information provided is on an "as-is" basis and any examples used are intended for practice or test environments and should not be used in your production systems.

The author/ publisher is not engaged in rendering legal, accounting, medical or other professional services. The information and opinions presented in this book are intended for informational purposes only.

Calibri & Garamond typefaces used with permission from Microsoft.
Bergamot Ornaments typeface used with permission from Emily Line.
(www.emilylimedesign.etsy.com)

ISBN:9780998600109

CONTENTS

Introduction   vii

SECTION ONE - Now That You've Said 'I Do' ...

Chapter 1	1
Chapter 2	13
Chapter 3	23
Chapter 4	47
Chapter 5	65

SECTION TWO - Order In The Court

Chapter 6	87
Chapter 7	99
Chapter 8	109
Chapter 9	125
Chapter 10	141
Chapter 11	153

SECTION THREE - It's Getting Real

Chapter 12	177
Chapter 13	187
Chapter 14	195
Chapter 15	217
Chapter 16	231

SECTION FOUR - The Truth About Love

Chapter 17	241
Chapter 18	251
Chapter 19	261
Chapter 20	273
Chapter 21	297
Chapter 22	307
Purpose Principles	313
Index	319

INTRODUCTION

I AM NOT a relationship expert…there, I said it! As I write this book, I'm keenly aware that most married readers may wonder how I can speak on marriage if I've never been married. That's a legitimate question, one I would even ask. To answer your question, it was by the divine brilliance and will of God. Because I'm not tainted with a personal perspective or objective, God used me to be a modern-day scribe, to prophetically share His revelation regarding marriage to the body of Christ *according to* the Word of God (not the personal words of Jordi).

How to have a great marriage? It is simpler than you think! I said simple, not easy. I can sum it up in four words; *purpose, covenant, order,* and *love*. You could be in love and covenant but out of order. Anything that's out of order doesn't work properly. Without purpose you have no drive, no reason *to* drive, and no direction. Consequently, love is built into the covenant. If you thought the affectionate Eros love for your spouse is enough to keep your marriage together, you are seriously fooling yourself. There's no true love relationship without God. God must be the third cord keeping your marriage together. That means the Word and reverential fear of God should govern your decisions, feelings, perceptions, perspective, finances, and every aspect of your marriage. Things must be done HIS WAY. Although the husband is the head of the wife, God is the head of the husband!

The *I AM* portion of the title represent the covenant agreement with The Great I AM (God) and *you*. It's about personal accountability and allowing God a place in your marriage through your vow and obedience. When people struggle in their relationship, their behavior and choices are usually predicated on how their spouse treats them. However, when you say I AM Married on Purpose, you are making the decision to honor your covenant by remaining faithful, loving, obedient, and righteous even when your spouse is not doing any of the above. You are committed to trusting God to be part of your marriage and I AM declaration. Knowing that he will never leave you or forsake you.

Most books you read will share great ideas on how to be a good wife or husband, or to have a great marriage *according to their experience*. That may be good for someone in a similar predicament but the dynamics of your relationship is exclusive to you and your family (different people, different issues). What do you do when your problems are unique and strange? Whom do you turn to? There has to be consistency somewhere to get the help you need. And you don't want to be judged while getting information! There is a difference between judgment and conviction. The latter is to lead you to repentance and deliverance.

What makes *I AM Married on Purpose* different from most publications on the subject is this: I share revelation according to the scriptures and deal with the core issues instead of the symptoms or manifestations of your problems. The reason many marriages fail or struggle is we keep putting a band-aid on a samurai sword wound! You're hemorrhaging to death because the root of the problem has not been addressed. Most people are aware of the core problem but do not want to deal with it because of fear—fear of loss, backlash and future consequences. It's very real and natural to feel this way. However, whether you acknowledge it or not, our being is not natural, it's spiritual. We should not be governed by feelings but by our spirit.

Carnality deals with fleshly, worldly feelings. God is a Spirit, He is also love. If He is in you and your marriage, then His word will take preeminence over your feelings. I'd like to say this is the easy part but it's not. It's probably the most challenging thing you'll ever do in your life but the rewards far outweigh the sacrifice. The problem then, is most people have not figured out the purpose of their marriage. Why should they have to sacrifice anything? Isn't my love enough? It should be but not love as a feeling but love as a being. This is a prime example of accessing the core problem to reach the divine solution.

Some couples are in a marriage where they really love each other but things are not working out. There are reasons why that may be, which we will address. There are spiritual laws and statutes that we unconsciously violate, which then detonates curses and judgments in our lives. It could be as simple as being out of order. God has established the family to function through the patriarchal *system*. Is your marriage under a matriarchal system? Do your children take precedence over your wife or your husband? Does your parents/in-laws have too much influence in the marriage? If you are out of order, God doesn't curse or judge you, it's already built into the disobedience. When things are in order, there's a continuous flow but discord causes blockages.

Other marriages suffer from financial pressures. Bad money issues are a manifestation of a deeper problem. Somewhere along the line, a spiritual law has been violated. No matter how deep you may be in debt, it can be remedied. There is an effective system in the word of God that can help restore your finances, marriage, and your home. However, *it is a process*, one that has many components but it's very effective on several levels! First thing I want you to do is throw words like *easy, quick,* and *instant* out of the window. That is unless you're using the scripture, 'My yoke is easy and my burden is light." Even with that, there's still a yoke and a burden. It doesn't go away but it does get better…much better! But you must mentally prepare yourself for the spiritual fight of your life. There is so much more on the line than you can imagine which is why the enemy attacks marriages so ferociously in this area.

Of course, you have marriages that have been plagued with infidelity. There's a lot to be said here because there are so many components to each situation. Sometimes you have one spouse that has not committed adultery, who is willing to stay and work on the marriage. At the same time, the other spouse still has one foot in the marriage and the other out. What do you do? Or perhaps the spouse guilty of having the affair is sorry, has left the other person and now wants to do the right thing, do they take them back? Some spouses have taken partners back but have a hard time recovering from that devastating blow. How do you recover? God has left instructions for how to handle these things but it usually tastes like bad medicine. You know it works but you just don't want to take it. The choice is always yours.

I may not have mentioned the specific challenges you're facing. However, God has already addressed them all. Unfortunately, we're so trained by the world's influence and system that we don't readily apply the principles in God's Word that will help us. Most people don't even know what those principles are! *I AM Married on Purpose* is going to show you through Scripture how to have an anchor, referee, judge, mediator, counselor, father, protector, financier, whatever you need to be fruitful, multiply, replenish, and subdue. You'll know why your marriage has or hasn't worked and how to make it better.

If your marriage is dying, the Word will define what's going on spiritually and guide you to the truth and the answer. Some marriages won't make it and the Word tells us why. If that should be the case for you, God will instruct you and cover you through the process but you will have a better understanding of what's going on. God only wants the best for you. Sometimes we've put ourselves in things that God did not ordain. The choice is always yours but there are consequences to the choices we make. No matter what you're going through, you can make it if you decide to.

> Matthew 19:8
>
> *He said to them, "Because of your hardness of heart Moses permitted you to divorce your wives; but from the beginning it has not been this way.*

Jesus said because of the hardness of your heart, Moses permitted divorce. Therefore, it's a heart issue and God can give you a new heart, especially to replace one that has been broken.

SECTION ONE

Now that you've said "I do" …

CHAPTER 1

Love & Marriage

WHAT IS THE purpose of marriage? I mean, why legally bind yourself to someone for the rest of your life? Wouldn't it be easier to just never get married, stay in a relationship as long as it feels good, and just leave when it doesn't?

I'm sure at one point or another, you may have pondered this question…we all have. The answer is simple yet complex. Marriage is all about you, not two. Your personal sacrifice and surrender to another, in *LOVE*. Terms like *us* and *we* are actually manifestations of an absolute *you*. It is the ability to love *God* so much that you keep His Word as your own (in character and spirit being) no matter what your spouse or anyone else does to you, or how good or bad they treat you.

God *is* love and He *NEVER CHANGES*. He said if you love Me, you will keep My commandments. When you keep your covenant with God by loving another like yourself at all times, you become the embodiment of Christ on earth accomplishing what He did in the spirit, in your flesh. It's the *ONLY WAY* to truly become one. Commitment to surrender your individual will and body for the sole *purpose* of being fruitful, multiplying, replenishing, and subduing is *your assignment*. That mandate cannot be accomplished alone. Marriage covenant is one of the vehicles God uses for us to accomplish His will on earth. The ultimate purpose of marriage is to produce godly offspring.

Jesus was the perfect living seed that God planted into the earth. It is through our covenant relationship with Him we have the ability to multiply His seed on earth. Jesus is King of kings and Lord of lords. When men get born again, they become sons of God. However, in order for Him to rule on earth, He must be a king. He becomes a king when He gets married to a daughter of Zion. That's one of the reasons why the scripture says, "He that findeth a wife, finds a good thing and *obtains favor from the Lord.*" In other words, he doesn't just receive a beautiful, prudent wife. He gets a major status change from being a son to a king!

What's curious about the scripture, *he that findeth a wife, finds a good thing*, is if a woman is unmarried how is it possible for her to be a wife when the man finds her? She becomes a wife through her *covenant relationship* with God. Upon being born again, she accepted Jesus as her Lord and Savior. She then enters a covenant agreement (a marriage) with God and devotes herself to Him. God and the woman become one. Therefore, she is no longer who/what she was but now is a new creature - though her body of flesh remains the same, her inner man is one with God.

Spiritual knowledge of how two become one is paramount in discovering how to be married on purpose. Our physical bodies are houses and our spirit man is the actual person. Your body is a geographical location, a territory. It's a building—one in which everybody wants to occupy, including you/self. In order for a spirit, (whether God or a demonic spirit), to take over your body, you must surrender yourself or open the door to it. There are spiritual laws and principles that exist (whether you know or acknowledge it or not) that must be honored and respected or else there will be dire consequences. Accepting Jesus as Lord and Savior legally gives God access to the use of your body. He becomes your head, the brains of your operation. We understand that the brain sends messages to the body and tells it what to do and where to go through words. Whomever you listen to and believe will be the one who governs the body.

PURPOSE PRINCIPLE

Whomever you listen to and believe will be the one who governs the body.

After you've accepted Christ and have given Him legal access, you, your body, and God's spirit (mind) become one body, as in a marriage. The reason why God uses the marriage covenant institution is that it is a permanent legal agreement that stipulates what your responsibilities, rights, and inheritances are. You and your spouse (if you are born again) are both God in the flesh. Once married, you and your spouse became one in spirit and in covenant. In other words, your marriage license is not the covenant, your agreement to each other, your oath, and the Word of God is.

Whether you're born again or not, when you marry someone you form a soul tie. However, being tied is not the same as becoming one. The spiritual law of marriage requires two to become one. Therefore, much of the tension you may be experiencing is your spirit trying to become one but cannot. As a result, you both become bound (tied up).

Ultimately, it's all about you (each individual), what you choose and allow. Every day, God expects you to let Him have control over your body. Even though the scripture says the husband's body belongs to the wife and wife to the husband. It all ends up with two being one because both of you should have given up yourselves, not for your spouse but for God's use of YOUR BODY.

Covenant understanding leads to the purpose for marriage. God's kingdom comes on earth, through you. We cannot control another person, only ourselves. Oftentimes in marriage, people complain about what their spouse did or didn't do. But the question is ALWAYS, what did YOU do, how did you respond? Did you pray? Did you find godly counsel? Do you put on the full armor of God? Are you wrestling with your spouse when the Word already told you that we wrestle NOT with flesh and blood? No matter what the circumstances may be, God expects YOU to ALWAYS remain in covenant with Him! If both spouses would always fulfill their covenant obligation to *God* regarding their relationship, they will ALWAYS be *IN LOVE*.

The answer is not in emotions, experiences, or observation. Rather, it is founded in the Word of God. Understanding why God has brought you and your spouse together, why He cares about marriage in the first place and the purpose of it will become the rock on which your house will be built, rather than information that comes from people telling you *their* story. It may or may not match your life.

Many people would argue that communication is the secret to a great marriage and to a degree, it is. Although it's clearly a necessary component, it is *not* the key factor but rather a result of it. Contrary to popular beliefs, *the way* to a great marriage is right in front of us, just rarely considered. Do you realize that the only thing that God asks of us is to obey Him? If you would just stick to the covenant agreement (the Word of God), it would rule *how, when, and to whom* you communicate.

Unfortunately, most people in life and marriage are governed, controlled, and influenced by their *emotions* instead of their *spirit*. *Feelings* of love might have been the reason why you married but feelings will not keep your marriage together. Knowledge, wisdom, understanding, and the fear of the Lord are what you'll need for your marriage to endure, honoring your covenant (til death do you part) and your oath.

The covenant I speak of is not only your marital covenant but also your individual, personal covenant to God. Therefore, it's safe to say your challenge in staying married is learning how to govern YOURSELF by staying in *position* as husband or wife regardless of how you feel. It is possible (happens all the time) you can love and communicate with your spouse and still *feel* like getting a divorce. Your marriage was not founded on feelings (feelings and emotions *change*) but on a covenant agreement and sealed with an oath (*your* word).

God is a spirit. Emotions and feelings come from the flesh, not the spirit. As a matter of fact, the most successful people I know have learned to take their feelings out of business and just look at what's best for the company. Marriage relationships should be governed and managed the same way. Feelings change but the Holy Spirit/LOVE does not. He's perfect, solid, and eternal. That is the foundation on which you should build and expand your marriage/family.

PURPOSE PRINCIPLE

Money, power, and sex can form a bond but it's your word and spirit that makes you one.

Why is that relevant? Your word is spirit *and your bond*—not just to your spouse but also to God and your family. It's what makes you one. Words have power, so when you promise, swear, and go into a covenant, a spiritual agreement takes place. God looks for His Word in righteousness to perform it. So when you make your oath before God, entering into Holy Matrimony, *God will be with you to perform His part of the covenant* and that is to do what His Word says when *you do* what the Word says. That's why your individual covenant as a believer is equally important as the covenant you have with your spouse. Furthermore, God no longer sees two people but one. In its simplest terms, marriage is about *personal accountability*.

> Jeremiah 1:12
> *Then said the LORD unto me, you have well seen:
> for I will hasten my word to perform it.*

Even during the times when your feelings are beyond articulation and comprehension (pleasant or unpleasant), your oath to keep covenant will help your marriage survive. If you no longer like or respect your spouse and *feel* like you're in love with someone else, your covenant, knowledge, wisdom, and the fear of the Lord will still keep you.

Knowledge of what it means to truly be in Love and Covenant is widely misconstrued because *Love (God)* is a *person* and *covenant* is a legal *body*. Marital covenant is not so much about feelings and emotions (i.e. happiness and romance) but about love. How much do you love God that you can love another beyond yourself in order to do His will? When both parties are in agreement, happiness and romance is inevitable in most cases but contentment and satisfaction will be in all.

> John 14:21
> *Whoever has My commandments <u>and keeps them</u> is the one who loves Me. The one who loves Me will be loved by My Father, and I will love him and reveal Myself to him."*

> John 14:23
>
> *Jesus replied, "If anyone loves Me, <u>he will keep My word</u>. My Father will love him, and we will come to him and make Our home with him.*

> John 15:10
>
> *If you keep My commandments, you will <u>remain in My love</u>, just as I have kept My Father's commandments and remain in His love.*

Funny, when Jesus talks about love, He doesn't require affection. The manifestation of true love according to Love Himself (God) is the keeping of His commandments. In other words, if you really love me, then you will do what I say. Sounds controlling, right? It is. Remember, we have given our bodies to God and spouse; and whomever you listen to and obey, controls the body. When you live according to the Word of God, you are living out God's will on earth. Giving up your life for another is the supreme act of love.

Both love and marriage are directly connected to God's divine assignment for His kingdom on earth. Your marriage and the family you produce is the nation God has ordained for you to birth and govern as an expansion of *His kingdom*. Society suggests that building your marriage on affectionate love (Eros) and happiness, is the criteria for a satisfying union. Howbeit, they're quite wrong because love without purpose, solely built on emotions, will be erratic and unstable because feelings change.

Society today perpetuates a message of "do as thou wilt." Whatever you do to make yourself happy is okay, and the rest of the world should just accept this. This is callous, reckless thinking of the future, and God doesn't move like that. He's strategic and, as a good father, He arranges marriage according to *His purpose*. In other words, God knows the life ingredients needed from each spouse such that when brought together, would produce what He intended. The purpose of marriage is to produce godly offspring.

> ### Malachi 2:15
> *And did not he make one? Yet had he the residue of the spirit. And wherefore one? That he might seek a godly seed. Therefore take heed to your spirit, and let none deal treacherously against the wife of his youth.*

It's through your offspring (spiritual/natural) that God creates a nation. That nation is to expand the Kingdom of God on earth. Unfortunately, many marriages are not thriving because their relationship is only on the elementary level of receiving. It's all about you and your spouse and how much you love each other. God desires for you to exercise perpetually the act of sowing and reaping. When you love your spouse, you empty yourself and fill the other. If both are obedient to this system, they will find that no one is lacking. However, oftentimes, one spouse is pulling more of the weight than the other does. God sees all this and, if you continue to obey His will, He will satisfy you and deal with your spouse for you. Remaining on the self-serving "romance only" level will only produce babies, not godly offspring. That's where purpose and work come in. At some point, you have to leave the bedroom and get to work.

Let's begin adjusting the lens by expressing the obvious, *God is love*. Of course, you know that but do you really *know* that? In other words, how intimate are you with Love? Is God actively considered in your marriage? I'm not talking about going to church. What I'm referring to is a covenant relationship with God. If you don't have that, then you're not *really in* love. No matter how deep in your marriage you may be, sometimes you have to go back to basics to get in realignment.

In essence, love and marriage are states of *being*. Your marriage covenant should be an agreement to love your spouse by becoming the actual embodiment of Love through behavior and conversation according to the Word. Each and every day should be a step towards becoming more of a loving person, not being fake trying to force feelings, but rather allowing God to make you like Him (the embodiment of LOVE Himself). That actually IS part of your covenant which is why the covenant overrides how you feel and think about your spouse, be it good, bad, or indifferent.

PURPOSE PRINCIPLE

The marriage covenant overrides feelings and what you think about your spouse, be it good, bad, or indifferent.

Although we know purpose is the key to a successful marriage, it's not to be confused with the ideal of a "happy marriage." You probably haven't noticed but, in the scriptures, the word happiness is never mentioned in association with marriage. We've actually seen glimpses of people in the Bible who were married and at times very unhappy (e.g., Leah & Jacob, Abigail & Nabal, to name a few) and they couldn't leave. I'm not saying this to discourage you because those marriages and countless others were *still* married *on purpose*. You'll find that the Bible speaks more of joy and peace than happiness because *happiness* is *not* the foundation on which a great house/marriage is built. Happiness is an emotional response, a feeling from external stimuli which can be subject to change. This point is sooooo important because many marriages are strained or end simply because they're unhappy or don't *feel* as good with their spouse as they did before. God is a spirit and is immutable (He never changes), which means we are spirit as well.

So what is God's purpose for marriage? He's looking for you and your spouse to produce a godly seed. In other words, God is expanding His kingdom through your family here on earth. And the purpose of this family is to become a nation…a Holy Nation. We were created in God's image and likeness. He created us to exist in this world and dimension, on *His* behalf. Understanding that the seed is in the man, when *he knows* his wife, *he imparts* this seed into her. He then re-produces children who are born with that seed in them. Notwithstanding, godly seed is not limited to the production of children only but also spiritual multiplication. Thus carrying out God's will and mandate of Genesis 1:28 and Malachi 2:15 of being fruitful, multiplying, and filling the earth. However, the second part of the mandate is to subdue and rule it. This is the purpose of marriage in a nutshell—God's kingdom coming through you and your family.

> Genesis 1:28
>
> *God created man in His own image, in the image of God He created him; male and female He created them. God blessed them; and God said to them, "Be fruitful and multiply, and fill the earth, and subdue it; and rule over the fish of the sea and over the birds of the sky and over every living thing that moves on the earth."*

When God wants His will executed on earth, He does it through people. Marriage to your spouse should be the *express image* of your first marriage (covenant between you and Jesus Christ) on earth, by which you're managing His kingdom on earth. This is why it's so important to learn how to view your spouse in their respective position properly and treat them accordingly. Your husband is a king, priest, and prophet over your home. Your wife is a vessel, your helpmeet, and daughter of the King of kings. Both are powerful positions of purpose that God takes very seriously. Violation of either party produces serious implications, problems, and curses. Obedience to God's will and way is paramount to producing and enjoying all the blessings He has in store for you, your family, and legacy for generations to come.

I know this is a lot to take in if you're not familiar with the spiritual aspect of marriage. Consequently, everything that has been created, birthed, or seen began in the spirit realm first. Therefore, we cannot build strong marriages or get to the core of marital problems without addressing the spiritual aspect of your purpose. You need a spiritual blueprint from the master builder for a solid foundation. There must be a standard of living to abide by, aspire to, and measure yourself with or to simply be the referee in your relationship! As we continue, I'm going to share this standard. Sometimes you will live up to the standard; other times, you will fall short but the point is to know *there is a standard*, a point of reference to help you find your way back home to what's right.

Jesus said:

> ### Hebrew 10:5-7
> *Wherefore when he cometh into the world, he saith, Sacrifice and offering thou wouldest not, but a body hast thou prepared me: In burnt offerings and sacrifices for sin thou hast had no pleasure. Then said I, Lo, I come (in the volume of the book it is written of me,) to do thy will, O God.*
>
> *In the earth realm, the only way God's kingdom comes is through you and the covenant. This is why the enemy fights against marriage so hard. Satan doesn't want God to reclaim the territory that Adam lost.*

CHAPTER 2

Covenant

MARRIAGE IS AN agreement formed between man, woman, and God. This agreement is pledged in the form of a covenant. Unlike a contract that can be cancelled, annulled, or breached, a covenant bonds you for life. Covenant is a more secure, stable entity as it is only dissolved through death and sealed by blood and an oath. Unfortunately, when people hear terms like "bound for life," they feel suffocated and locked in, unconsciously resulting in fight or flight. In actuality, marriage covenant bonds you, not binds you. You and your spouse naturally become one for life—very much

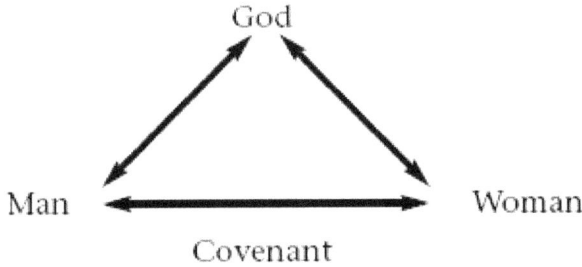

like the existence of your spirit within your body, both are one. Your spirit is not an interruption to the body but the very life source. The same goes for your spouse.

Why not common law? The difference between common law and covenant is that the marriage covenant requires agreement, an oath, and blood. A sacrifice must be made, that's why people use the term "we *cut* covenant." Common law is a marriage of convenience and disobedience created by the law. The common law husband did not agree neither did he make an oath to seal his covenant. There is no real love in this union because love *fulfils the law*. If you really love someone, you don't have to be forced by law to do the right things to them. Real love gives, covers, protects, and provides - willingly. Common law is not honored because it lacks formal commitment. It's your word, your oath that sets you apart and seals your covenant. You have consciously chosen to marry your spouse, not because the law forced you but because you love them.

> Hebrews 7:28
>
> *For the law maketh men high priests which have infirmity; but the word of the oath, which was since the law, maketh the Son, who is consecrated for evermore.*

The question is, when you got married, what exactly did you agree to? What does your marriage covenant entail? What does God expect from you?

- Produce godly offspring
- Become a holy nation
- A peculiar people
- A royal priesthood

> ### Genesis 1:27, 28
> *So God created man in his own image, in the image of God created he him; male and female created he them. And God blessed them, and God said unto them, Be fruitful, and multiply, and replenish the earth, and subdue it: and have dominion over the fish of the sea, and over the fowl of the air, and over every living thing that moveth upon the earth.*

In order for you and your spouse to accomplish the responsibilities of your covenant, God expects you to become one with Him in order to become one with each other. To **become** is a process that happens over a period of time.

PURPOSE PRINCIPLE

God expects you to become one with Him in order to become one with each other.

Acknowledgment of your marital covenant, taking FULL RESPONSIBILITY for YOUR OATH (til death do you part) should settle your spirit, adding a sense of purpose in regards to your role. You're not boyfriend and girlfriend! You have entered into a completely different institution with greater purpose and responsibility. That role is not defined by society standards or your own personal concoction of what a husband or wife is supposed to do or be. Everything that you are to be, become, govern, and establish is already written in the covenant, which is the Word of God. Without God, it is virtually impossible to accomplish a successful marriage. There's just too much to contend with. If you have not developed a relationship with the Holy Spirit, you would probably identify God's voice as your conscience but it's more important to know Him as God in person. When we adhere and execute *His word*, GOD PERFORMS whatever it is that He said He would do. And unlike a contract, you're in covenant, which is bound by blood, sealed with an oath and until death do you part.

You may not *feel* like you're in a covenant but that's just it, there's nothing to *feel*! It's not about your feelings but all about what you've agreed to—much like when someone mortgages a home. Once you sign and agree to the terms, the bank gives you the money to purchase your home. From the moment you close, the bank expects you to fulfill your obligation of paying the mortgage even if you don't like the house anymore. After you purchase your home, you may find a bunch of problems the appraiser didn't tell you about or you didn't notice. You might have been one of those new homebuyers that made the ghastly mistake of purchasing a money pit where the repairs are very expensive with one problem leading to the next. Your dream home has become a nightmare, nothing like what you expected or envisioned and you want your money back.

The bank doesn't care at all about your dream becoming a nightmare, that's not their problem. Bankers have a job to do as well and that is to make money for the bank that hired them. So for them, it's just business. They entered a covenant with you so that when problems arise (which they inevitably do), emotions don't govern the outcome. The outcome was established in the beginning with the agreement. Therefore, regardless of your series of unfortunate events, they expect you to be responsible for all repairs and damages. The bank doesn't care if your house has gotten old and doesn't excite you as it used to. If you lose your job, the bank personnel may feel sorry for you but the institution will still expect you to fulfill your part of the agreement. Basically, the bank is saying, you made the decision to purchase this house, we gave you the money to purchase it, and you agreed to pay us the money back with interest at the allotted time.

No emotions, just business. The good feelings and emotions come when you handle your business! Anything that goes on with that house whether it ages, breaks down, needs repairs or refinance is all your responsibility. The same goes for the vows you made to your spouse in the presence of God.

PURPOSE PRINCIPLE

You will feel good about your spouse when you handle the business of your marriage and they will feel good about you.

Covenant mindset dictates and establishes in your heart that divorce is not an option. It's a whole different (mature) state of mind. A contract can be broken but a covenant is bound by blood and is only terminated by the death of one of the parties. The worldly concept of being in love and married is more like, "I like you a lot until you tick me off and I'm out!" That's contract thinking. Covenant says, "I don't like you right now but I'm not going anywhere, so we're just going to have to work this out." God in the form of love and commitment to HIS WORD is the one who fortifies you to commit on this level.

PURPOSE PRINCIPLE

Contract thinking says, "I love you until you tick me off, then I'm out." Covenant mindset says, "I don't like you right now but I love you so I'm not going anywhere."

~

PURPOSE PRINCIPLE

Change your vision/perspective/perception by putting on the mind of Christ.

In covenant marriage, there's a male and a female. Both have their own personal thoughts, ideologies, philosophies, history, and experiences that have made them who they are today. Neither person became who they are overnight. Character traits, persona, habits, and idiosyncrasies were forged through years of programming. Information, data from parents, educational systems, family, friends, and environment all collaborated consciously and unconsciously. Those imparted thought processes that may be acceptable to you might be completely foreign to your spouse. Although a couple may love one another, their thoughts and views about what's acceptable, how things should, could or would be done can vary drastically. So how do two adults, with years of separate programming bridge the gap and become one? Part of the answer lies in this scripture:

> Genesis 1:27
> *So God created man in his own image, in the image of God he created him; male and female created he them.*

When God created man, He made a *"them."* Remember, God said, "let *us* make man." Who is *us*? The Father, Son, and the Holy Spirit. Man was created in His image and likeness, so the *them* God is referring to is also three-in-one…you, your spouse, and God equals *them*. In order to fulfill your purpose as a nation, you have to leave your former being of individuality and become one… *them*.

Theoretically, this sounds simple but it's virtually impossible to deprogram years of psychological, cultural, and emotional consciousness and behavior overnight and on your own. If you've been trying to make your spouse "better," they probably silently resent you or openly can't stand you for it. No doubt, various thought patterns and behaviors are the cause of many troubled marriages for a number of reasons. In one person's family, shouting to get your point across is normal. If the other spouse was raised in a quiet environment where each person waits patiently for each person to make a point, a shouting match all the time could really be disturbing. On the other hand, the more vocal spouse may not trust their quiet partner because they don't express themselves verbally and passionately. They may feel like they never really know what they're thinking and feeling. Each spouse could be guilty of making the fatal mistake of trying to change their partner or they try to referee the situation according to what was culturally correct *to them* growing up. Both are right in their own eyes because of what they've been taught. Consequently, when a couple is at odds in communication like this, they're being themselves …not a *them*.

Arriving to the status of oneness requires both parties to lose themselves and become *like* God. In order to accomplish that goal, you have to put on the mind of Christ. That means, both parties have to do things and behave the way the Word of God instructs us to do. Being like God creates love, a beautiful atmosphere and power like you wouldn't believe because God/LOVE is governing you and your marriage. You have perfection *Himself* working on your behalf. It's through the mind of Christ that your thoughts shall be established, and agreements are formed in the process. Once agreement is established in the mind, the body will follow and movement occurs.

> Amos 3:3
>
> *Can two walk together, except they be agreed?*

There are some interesting things about that scripture. Notice it says, *be* agreed. He's talking about a state of *being*, your very nature has to be established in order to make moves *together* successfully. Let's talk about your nature. Understanding the manifestation of the nature that is inside of you will help you go from things being all about you to *being* a *them* (one in Christ). Sometimes because of our emotions, delusion, arrogance, or sin, we don't see ourselves. Your spouse may be trying to become one with you but in order to become one, you must be of the same spirit. If one spouse has the sin/flesh nature, you will experience a person who is a perpetual, repeat offender. They will treat you badly or offend you, apologize about the same things over and over. Why? Because if you have a sin/flesh nature, you may have the mind to do good but your nature (like a default setting) will cause you to continually violate because IT IS WHO YOU ARE!

> ### Galatians 5:16-26
> *This I say then, Walk in the Spirit, and ye shall not fulfil the lust of the flesh. For the flesh lusteth against the Spirit, and the Spirit against the flesh: and these are contrary the one to the other: so that ye cannot do the things that ye would. But if ye be led of the Spirit, ye are not under the law. Now the works of the flesh are manifest, which are these; Adultery, fornication, uncleanness, lasciviousness, Idolatry, witchcraft, hatred, variance, emulations, wrath, strife, seditions, heresies, Envyings, murders, drunkenness, revellings, and such like: of the which I tell you before, as I have also told you in time past, that they which do such things shall not inherit the kingdom of God. But the fruit of the Spirit is love, joy, peace, longsuffering, gentleness, goodness, faith, Meekness, temperance: against such there is no law. And they that are Christ's have crucified the flesh with the affections and lusts. If we live in the Spirit, let us also walk in the Spirit. Let us not be desirous of vain glory, provoking one another, envying one another.*

Who you are as a person is not your physical body. You cannot physically take two people and make them one person. So what is God talking about? Where is your spirit located? In your mind! Think about it, if you want to stand up and walk, unconsciously, your mind gives your body the command and your body gets up and respond…that is when you are in your RIGHT mind. If you lose your mind, you lose cognitive control of the body. If your mind could not give your body commands, your body would be erratic or would not move at all. Matter of fact, in time not only would your body become immobile, it would begin to lose its composure.

The husband is the head of the wife, but Christ is the head of the husband. What that means is the thoughts of the husband regarding governing the body cannot be ruled by his own carnal desires, ideas, or feelings. Many a man misuses and even abuses his power over his wife and family because he forgets that he has a governing head that he must submit to. Abuse of power causes the growth and movement of the family to stagger or stop. Just as the wife is to submit to her own husband because he is the head, the husband has to submit to the Word of God which IS THE MIND OF CHRIST.

It's the spirit within the body that makes it live, walk, and breathe. Both spouses have to practice the Word of God in their lives, individually, until Jesus becomes alive in them. He is the one who makes you and your spouse one. The goal is to lose the old *you*, so much so that the behaviors and former ideologies that were developed through your family, environment, culture, and opinions (that were in error or counterproductive) will no longer have preeminence in your life, communication, and marriage.

Amos 3:3 also uses the word *agreed*, which is past tense. In other words, if you have already agreed, whatever you agreed to is established. When you and your spouse make the decision that the bottom line of EVERYTHING you do will be founded on God's way of doing things, you are now in agreement. God's way is the fine print to your covenant and should be forever foundational because this is how you will be able to endure to the end.

> Psalm 37:5
>
> *Commit thy way unto the LORD; trust also in him;*
> *and he shall bring it to pass.*

> Proverbs 16:3
>
> *Commit thy works unto the LORD, and thy thoughts*
> *shall be established.*

Most people fail to understand God's purpose for us. He desires to have an intimate relationship with us—one where we offer ourselves to Him with reckless abandon! We ought to give Him our bodies so that He may come in and tabernacle with us. Without a body, a spirit cannot physically touch or feel. That is one of the reasons why Jesus had to come in the flesh so that He can feel what we feel. God will not enter our bodies without our permission.

You may be thinking why would you want God in your body. There are countless answers but, in a nutshell, God *is love*. You want the spirit of love inside of you and your marriage at all times. It is through love that you can do extraordinary things. Not only that, when you and your spouse say yes to Him, your marriage will be able to withstand anything because anything coming against you is coming against God and it will not stand a chance!

You're no longer walking alone. In order for your marriage to grow and prosper, two have to become one. If you don't become one with the mind of Christ, you will end up dealing with a two-headed monster.

CHAPTER 3

Treat Your Husband Like God!

> 1 Peter 3:6
>
> *Even as Sara obeyed Abraham, <u>calling him lord</u>: whose daughters <u>ye are</u>, as long as ye do well, and are not afraid with any amazement.*

I HAD TO laugh to myself as I began to write this chapter because I know what you're probably thinking… oh, no she didn't! Oh, yes she did! Relax; it's not what you think. In no way, shape or form am I suggesting that you make your husband your god. That would be idolatry.

However, the Word is telling us that God has left the husband in charge over you in His stead. Therefore, you are to submit to him as if it were God standing there Himself.

> ### Ephesians 5:22
> *Wives, submit yourselves unto your own husbands, <u>as unto the Lord</u>.*

Now that's a tall order! Submission to God is easy because…well you know, He's God! When He gives an instruction or command, He expects us to do it out of love, faith, and obedience.

Of course, we oblige simply out of reverence and respect for who *He is*. Following commands and instructions with your spouse with that same reverential respect is exactly what God requires wives to do. But why?

The wife's submission to the Word in this manner releases the power of God *on her behalf*. Do you know that one of the hardest things for women to do is to be still? God Himself says, "Be still and KNOW that I AM GOD."

For many women, submission is unfathomable because they don't believe their husband deserves this kind of treatment, they think he's weak, irresponsible, etc. or they feel more secure doing things themselves.

Others were raised in a matriarchal environment where the wife/mother/woman knows and controls everything and bosses/controls the husband. Some women are aware that submission is the right thing to do, even want to do it but don't think their husband will be responsible with that kind of power over them. Unfortunately, you do have that other group of men that seem to refuse to step up and take the leadership role, so the women go ahead and take the helm.

Whatever the case may be, you must apply the Word to your marriage to make it work. Treating your husband like God in this manner provokes, ignites, and inspires the God in your husband! This is how you inspire him to greatness:

> ### 1 Peter 3
> *But let it be the hidden man of the heart, in that which is not corruptible, even the ornament of a meek and quiet spirit, which is in the sight of God of great price. For after this manner in the old time the holy women also, who trusted in God, adorned themselves, being in subjection unto their own husbands*

PURPOSE PRINCIPLE

Your husband will do his job when you stop doing it for him.

Basically, wives simply need to stay faithful to God and His Word. Christ is the hidden man of the heart. God will move heaven and earth for you when you walk in obedience. He knows how to get your husband's attention *for you*. Submission to your husband when he knows that you don't agree (though out of a meek and quiet spirit) ACTUALLY GETS HIS ATTENTION.

Remember, the devil is a liar. The devil uses society to tell women that they need to yell, scream, manipulate, nag, and even hit men to control them and acquiesce to their will. Even worse, some women will use their children or family to manipulate or control their husbands. Everything the devil says is a lie and is contrary to the Word and will of God.

Therefore, it becomes more evident that the truth of the matter is your husband will listen to you more, when you say less. He will do more, when you do less. When you submit to him and his will, just like with God, you put the pressure on him to deliver. This type of pressure brings out the best in men. That may seem strange but it is the true wisdom of God.

PURPOSE PRINCIPLE

Your husband will listen to you more when you talk low and say less.

When two believers come together in marriage, the standards by which they live are different from familiar, worldly convictions. Both man and wife, because they have accepted Christ, are new creatures that have become one with Him. Naturally, you cannot put two physical people together as one person. Therefore, it is clear that transformation of our being is spiritual. In other words, on the outside, they have their regular suits of flesh but the person that resides inside is Jesus.

With that in mind, your husband is no longer just a man. He is the embodiment of Christ…whether you see the full manifestation or not. Our walk in God is a journey of becoming, however, God doesn't operate in *becoming*. He instructs us to speak things that *be*, not as though they *were*.

> ### Hebrews 1:3
> *God, who at sundry times and in divers manners spake in time past unto the fathers by the prophets, Hath in these last days spoken unto us by <u>his Son</u>, whom he hath appointed heir of all things, by whom also he made the worlds; Who being the brightness of his glory, and <u>the express image of his person</u>, and upholding all things by the word of his power, when he had by himself purged our sins, sat down on the right hand of the Majesty on high.*

PURPOSE PRINCIPLE

You already are who you are going to be, as you're becoming it.

> **Romans 4:7**
>
> *(As it is written, I have made thee a father of many nations,) before him whom he believed, even God, who quickeneth the dead, and calleth those things which be not as though they were.*

So who exactly is your husband? He is the express image of Christ—Priest, King, and Prophet. To be scripturally sound about that, I decided to research the Word to see if there were any references to support this statement. Initially, I couldn't find anything specifically confirming the husband to be King, Priest, or Prophet, not until God revealed to me who we *are and become* through Christ. Jesus is the King, High Priest, and Prophet of His bride, the Church. He became the High Priest *in the order* of Melchezidec and so did your husband.

> **Hebrews 7:1-3**
>
> *For this Melchisedec, king of Salem, priest of the most high God, who met Abraham returning from the slaughter of the kings, and blessed him; To whom also Abraham gave a tenth part of all; first being by interpretation King of righteousness, and after that also King of Salem, which is, King of peace; Without father, without mother, without descent, having neither beginning of days, nor end of life; but made like unto the Son of God; abideth a priest continually.*

There is a saying, "familiarity breeds contempt." This quote probably couldn't be truer especially when it comes to wives in relation to their husbands. Wives see their husbands at their best and most certainly their worst. Sacred secrets are shared between you and your spouse, thus creating a sense of trust, security, and stability. However, being in such constant close proximity day in and day out oftentimes facilitates negligence, subtly unconsciously creating an atmosphere of disrespect. You begin to see him, address and even talk to him as if he is…common. All of this, in most cases, is unbeknownst to the wife because she doesn't see a king…just the man she married.

A few years ago, I was in a relationship with a well-known pastor, whom I adored and highly respected. He was a prophet, educated, and spoke all over the world. Because of my personal access to him, after a while, I began to treat him in a common manner, so much so that God Himself convicted me and corrected me. It was at that moment when I took a step back and remembered that I wasn't dealing with just any man, I was dealing with God's anointed. I literally had to call him and apologize for treating and addressing him in a common way. Now, there's nothing wrong with being relaxed and comfortable around your spouse, that's how it should be. However, there should always be a reverential esteem that governs how you communicate with your husband because he is a king.

Your husband is so much more than some guy you married, he's God's anointed. *As a prophet*, he speaks to you on behalf of God. *As a priest*, he speaks to God on your behalf and pronounces blessings over you and your house. He's greater and more important than you can ever imagine because he is an appointed *king* who can make decrees over your life and children's lives. He's the man in position to build a nation with you and rule over you.

> ### Genesis 3:16
> *Unto the woman he said, I will greatly multiply thy sorrow and thy conception; in sorrow thou shalt bring forth children; and thy desire shall be to thy husband, and he shall rule over thee.*

Did you just read what I read? God said that your husband should have RULE OVER THEE. Our carnal mind wants to ignore this portion of scripture. But if you're battling poor communication, lack of passion, or conflict in your marriage, is it possible you're experiencing that because you've been trying to rule over *him*? Or have you *refused* to let him rule you? That's something to think about.

As an ambassador for the Lord, your husband's various roles and purpose as king, priest, and prophet will require certain things from you. Although he is your husband, he is not just a man. If he was just a man, you could refuse, argue with, and defy him. Acknowledging and referencing your husband according to the Word of God should change everything (communication, tone of voice, and timing), believe it or not, for the better. It is so important that you follow God's instruction because it is through the wife that the husband is reminded of who he is because you are a reflection of him. Sometimes, he may forget or might not even realize who he is until the hidden man in you, speaks to his inner man through reverential love, kindness, and submission.

When you genuinely begin to treat him like God and see him as king, it will change your demeanor and your perception of your husband. More importantly, addressing him as king will eventually make the king in him respond. It will even change what you allow…how your children, family, friends, and people in general talk to him around you. Never allow anyone to disrespect him. In time, not only will he become a believer and start manifesting god-like quality, you will believe in him too. He *needs* you to believe in him.

Remember, it's not what you say that makes most of the difference but how you say it and even more so your behavior. Establishing your home and relationship around *his leadership* **by faith**, making what he says law, will build up the king in him.

HUSBAND DEFINED:

1. a male partner in a marriage
2. manager, steward
3. a frugal manager
4. *Occupier and tiller of the soil*

A husband defined in Webster's dictionary is as a partner in marriage and a manager/steward. The Hebrew word for husband is "ish." Interestingly, the Hebrew word for wife is "ish-shaw," which is the feminine form of ish, thereby suggesting that the wife is the extension of the man. Ownership requires stewardship. It is the husband's responsibility with the help of the wife to manage what God has given him. God made man in *His image*.

God has put your husband in charge of your family (a Holy Nation). The law, vision, and word come to him first to govern the family. This is a huge responsibility because God holds the husband accountable for what He has given that man charge over.

Also, that same vision God has given your husband…newsflash…God may not have given you. He gives it to your husband *to give to you* so that you can help him with the vision that was already given. For some women, this is hard to receive or comprehend, not out of conscious rebellion; rather they may simply not understand their husband's vision. Or, the wife has her own vision or desire for the family that seems to her like a better idea and will persist in trying to convince him to "come to his senses." Thus, she resists the leadership of her husband. Either way, for wives, it is considered rebellion when you do not submit to your husband.

One of the hardest things to do as a manager is manifest your vision through a team that doesn't believe in you or will not follow instructions. Wives understand, your husband carries the burden of a manager and God is expecting a return on His investment through your family. Men are genetically predisposed to fulfill the capacity of the assignment, just as you are genetically inclined to help.

Many marriages are failing simply because the roles have been reversed. Wives act like the head while husbands submit!

That even sounds wrong!

What's required here and in every area of your marriage is unconditional love and faith. Wives, your husband is a man that makes mistakes, and may get overwhelmed, frustrated, and even scared sometimes. He may or may not show it. This is where your obedience comes in and helps him. God did not design the work involved in marriage to be done by one person. When you obey God's Word, God is obligated to intervene.

In a lot of cases, women can be very effective at whatever they're trying to accomplish. However, wives that supersede their husband's leadership and authority often fail to calculate in their equation the destructive ripple effect that goes throughout their entire family as a result of their superwoman complex. Yes, super wife saved the day… at the expense of her husband's now lost sense of purpose. You stole his job. He didn't have the opportunity to show and prove to you that he could actually do what he said he would, nor did he have the opportunity to *fail*. Sometimes, God will allow him to fail to show him where he is weak and what he needs to strengthen. It's also an opportunity for the husband to discover how supportive his wife is during tough times. Failing and recovering is an important component to bonding and growth.

Consequently, the wife also stole the moment God could have used to show both of them that His way works and if you walk with Him together, you can do amazing things. Lastly, your children and all onlookers just witnessed and learned how to be insubordinate, weak, and disrespectful to your husband.

> Genesis 2:15
>
> *And the LORD God took the man, and put him into the garden of Eden to dress it and to keep it.*

Your husband's nature is also to provide and protect. The very word *husband* is defined as an occupier and tiller of the ground. In other words, he is supposed to work. Everything about his makeup has prepared him to be fruitful, multiply, replenish and subdue on this planet. In order to do so, he has to manage all that both of you have and make it produce. The ability to multiply is a blessing that God has promised him through the promise made to Abraham. Thus, faith in God regarding manifesting increase has to be in place. You and your husband are one, so if he believes in a certain idea/project/business and he sows into it, the wife must submit to his leadership, the reason being that the husband has to be in alignment with God's word to avoid failure and hindrances.

According to the order of the Word, this blessing goes to the head first (the husband) down the beard and on to the skirt. The wife is a beneficiary.

> **Hebrews 6:13**
>
> *For when God made promise to Abraham, because he could swear by no greater, he sware by himself, Saying, Surely blessing I will bless thee, and multiplying I will multiply thee. And so, after he had patiently endured, he obtained the promise.*

In most cases, a man who appears hostile, angry, or despondent is usually inwardly frustrated because he hasn't successfully been able to be fruitful, replenish, multiply, replenish, and subdue. Not being able to lead the family the way he sees fit is debilitating to him. God instructed him to oversee the family. When his spouse doesn't submit to who he really is, he begins to feel unsure of himself or unhappy because he doesn't know how to balance doing what he knows to do without backlash from his spouse. Wives, the best thing to do is help him accomplish the vision God has given him through submission and intimacy, because that's what you're created to do. If you don't believe in him, pray for wisdom on what to do and ask God to intervene on your behalf.

> **1 Corinthians 11:3**
>
> *But I would have you know, that the head of every man is Christ; and the head of the woman is the man; and the head of Christ is God.*

Although at times you may or may not feel it, he is also your covering/protector. This assignment is not limited to physical presence and protection. He's a spiritual covering, your eyes and ears. Adam and Eve fell because Adam allowed Eve to persuade him to go against what he knew God had told him directly. Adam did not manage his wife well enough. He should have known who she was talking to and stopped her. Surely, he shouldn't have partaken of the fruit either. Interestingly, it's clear to see how obedience and order is built into the position. When Eve ate the fruit, nothing happened. It wasn't until Adam ate that *their eyes* were opened. Again, in this situation, Eve *thought* the vision she had was better than doing what God instructed her to do. She was guilty of *insubordination to management*.

> Genesis 3:16
>
> *The LORD God commanded the man, saying, "From any tree of the garden you may eat freely; but from the tree of the knowledge of good and evil you shall not eat, for in the day that you eat from it you will surely die."*

KING:

Definition of *king*

- a male ruler of a country who usually *inherits his position and rules for life*
- a boy or man who is *highly respected* and very successful or popular
- a boy or man who is awarded the *highest honor* for an event or contest

You are the daughter of the King of kings, which is one of the reasons God allowed you to marry His son in the first place. When your husband married you (a born-again believer), he went from sonship to kingship. God made your husband a king over the nation that you two are to produce on earth in His name. Since we are created in His image and likeness, the way that you and your husband are to govern is according to the Word. Like a king, God expects your husband to speak things into existence.

CHAPTER 3 | TREAT YOUR HUSBAND LIKE GOD

> Romans 4:17
>
> *(As it is written, I have made thee a father of many nations,) before him whom he believed, even God, who quickeneth the dead, and calleth those things which be not as though they were.*

> Proverbs 18:21
>
> *Death and life are in the power of the tongue: and they that love it shall eat the fruit thereof.*

Since God is King of kings, guess who is the king with a little "k"? You guessed it, your husband! Therefore, God expects your husband to rule with full authority and power. Once a king makes his final decision, it is final. Everyone else, including his wife, should submit to his sovereignty within the home and family. That doesn't mean a man should not meet and consult with his wife (that would not be scriptural). It means that he has to lead the family *ahead* of his wife by making a final decision in the direction he believes they should go. His decision may require major sacrifice from you, be prepared.

A king rules and governs his kingdom/nation. He has the responsibility of managing, expanding, conquering, and producing. As a ruler that is subject to a higher authority, he has to get his instructions from above. King-to-king relationships are special and personal in their own right—ones that wives will never be privileged to experience the fullness thereof. The husband/king must walk by faith according to what God has spoken or shown him. There are some things that God will reveal to your husband and not you. This could be very confusing to some wives because they may have good ideas and the God-given idea doesn't sound so great at first. The God-given idea is designed to be challenging because it requires faith to manifest it. Sometimes, this vision is so great and beyond him that it may take a while for him to even grasp what God has shown him.

It may take a lifetime to fulfill; therefore, he can only show a portion to you in increments. As women, we often want to know all of the details. Your husband may very well want to share those details but when you ask him *how* he's going to do this or that, he may not have figured it out yet. At the same time, he doesn't want you to lose confidence in him so he might not speak at all. In cases like this, he's not trying to leave you out of the loop. His silence—or what you would call lack of communication—is wisdom. He's not saying anything until he is certain about his plan of action. Don't press him, just pray. The same way God will give you a vision or a dream but hasn't given you the how yet, you have to be prayerful and patient. That's how you should consider your husband's leadership.

Kings have a lot to consider—their spouse, children, the kingdom, expansion, enemies and last but not least, themselves. Most men internalize the magnitude of their thoughts and fears because they understand that they are the anchors. That's why you may feel like your husband is not a great communicator. Understanding his kingly mandate and position should help you communicate with *him better*. He is the king, you have to conform to him and meet him where he is.

Prior to approaching your king, consider everything, as much as possible! In real life, if you were privileged to visit a king in a palace, there would be people who would tell you the rules on how to approach the king, what to do, how to do it, what to say or not say, and when to speak. That attention to detail and reverential fear is how you should approach your king. When he comes home from work and looks tired, that is not the time to start talking…about anything! Let him invite you into conversation. Assess his mood, and then create a comfortable environment. A good wife is always prepared to work and serve her husband. If you need to talk about something important, don't ramble. Be prepared with facts and information, in order. Watch what you wear, how you smell, look, your body language, and watch your tone. Preparation is key. If you are self-centered, your focus will be on satisfying and pleasing yourself. Proof of narcissistic behavior in a wife will manifest itself through manipulation, nagging, forced conversation, neglect, and the like. The wife only does this when she is fighting to be heard and understood, or when she lacks attention. What she is considering most is how she feels and how she thinks her husband should respond to her needs. Granted, he should respond to her needs but the king has the power and authority to do so *when he is ready*. If you want more from him and he's not listening, talk to God about it in prayer.

Esther and Vashti are two queens in the Bible that were married to a king. Vasti was banished from the kingdom, lost her crown and position because she went with how she felt instead of acquiescing to the responsibility associated with her position. When the king summoned Vashti, she wouldn't come. She didn't go because the king and his friends were drunk and she didn't want to be paraded around in front of a bunch of men like that. She was a queen and that kind of disgrace was well beneath her dignity. As understandable as that may be, her job and purpose as queen was to *serve the king*. In other words, when he calls, she is supposed to come no matter what! When the king's council advised for Vashti to be exiled, they determined her fate to be harsh because if they let her disrespect slide, she would influence women in all nations to dishonor their husbands. In other words, her actions were not considered just a personal faux pas but a tremendous negative influence on the entire nation!

On the other hand, Esther, was implored by her uncle to talk to the king on behalf of her people when they were facing destruction. During those times, even Esther his wife, could not just walk up to the king unless he held out his scepter (symbolizing that he authorized her visit). She considered everything before she approached him. First, she invited him to dinner, to set the stage for her request. Then she invited him to another and then she made her request known. Esther didn't take her position for granted. The fact is she hadn't seen her husband in about a month prior to her visit. Now, I'm not saying that you have to wait a month to communicate with your husband. Your approach, timing, and attitude should be humble and patient. This may not be your natural temperament. Either way, the Bible is giving you a mandate and strategy on how to communicate with the king in your husband.

To some women, what I'm saying may come across as chauvinistic or condescending. If that's how you feel, you're not abiding by your covenant vow. Whether you like it or not, your husband is a king. You can talk either to the king in him or to the fool in him. Whomever you talk to the most is the one that is going to respond. A king is not impressed with random words and conversation as women are; as a matter of fact, it's terribly annoying because he has so much on his mind. It's so important that you understand this. Your husband/king loves you so much that most of his day is spent figuring out how to be the best king for you. If you don't SEE him for who he is, that's insulting to him and it won't yield the results of love and affection you desire.

Don't take what the king says and how he says it personally…take for what it is and take it to heart. Actually, listen to what he's saying. Men don't waste words like women do, they often say what they mean and mean what they say. Don't try to read between the lines. Read the line! What did he say? If he says he doesn't like fat women, don't take that personally. It doesn't mean he doesn't love you, he just doesn't like fat on women. He simply *prefers* slimmer women. You can argue the validity of his desires and preferences on what you think is right or wrong or you can try to please the king. If you love him like you love yourself, you want to make you happy, right? Then on a diet and to the gym you go! (Of course, this is just an example). Personal responsibility, not taking things personally is key. If he says something like, *I'm not ready for kids right now*, he meant that. He has his reasons that he has already considered because he has more to consider than you do. Don't make it your mission to change his mind directly through conversation. Win him over through prayer and your behavior. Pray to God about your concerns because God is the only one who can change the mind of the king. You don't have the heart of the king, God does.

> Proverbs 21:1
>
> *The king's heart is in the hand of the LORD, as the rivers of water: he turneth it whithersoever he will.*

Understanding his kingly nature will explain why he doesn't follow your lead. He's not designed to do so. You will also notice how much more he will treat you like a queen when you address the king as a KING. Children are also watching your marital dynamic, how he rules over those he loves along with all that he's responsible for and how you follow. It's important that we do things God's way so that we can reproduce godly seed. Every day, your children learn sowing and reaping techniques from your kingdom practices. They will observe either obedience or disobedience. If the queen will not acquiesce to the king, she strips his power and the children will learn dysfunction.

PURPOSE PRINCIPLE

He will treat you more like a queen when you address him like a King.

~

PURPOSE PRINCIPLE

The wife serves the King

> **1 Corinthians 7:34**
>
> *There is difference also between a wife and a virgin. The unmarried woman careth for the things of the Lord, that she may be holy both in body and in spirit: but she that is married careth for the things of the world, how she may please her husband.*

What if I feel like my husband is incompetent?

Some wives feel their husbands are incompetent. However, there are few variables to that situation. For one, God instructs us not to be unequally yoked. Some women are suffering within their marriage because they're unequally yoked. Unfortunately, you were the one that got yourself in this situation and it will take you and God to get you out or through it. This is what the Bible tells you to do if you're in that situation:

> **1 Peter 3:1**
>
> *In the same way, you wives, be submissive to your own husbands so that even if any of them are disobedient to the word, they may be won without a word by the behavior of their wives, as they observe your chaste and respectful behavior.*

The Bible is telling the wife here that her behavior is the remedy. Not just any kind of behavior, the Bible is specific: RESPECTFUL behavior. Now, I'm not married but I was once in a relationship with a man that I was physically attracted to BUT I didn't find him to be very competent in dealing with real life and business affairs. Awh, come on, don't judge me! You know it's those cute ones that get you! LOL, back to my point. Deep down inside, although I liked him a lot, I didn't respect him because I always felt uncovered. I felt like I had to pick up all of the slack and that all he was worth to me was a good time and after a while…let's just say it wasn't much fun at all.

My lack of respect for him manifested in ways that I was conscious of and ways (he said) I was unaware of. On the surface, you may say, "I respect my husband." You say this because you have choked his voice and bullied him into a "yes dear" so things appear to be peaceful. But the Bible says "out of the abundance of the heart the mouth speaks."

I never said out of my mouth to my ex, "I don't respect you." My tone of voice told him. My body language told him. My facial expression told him. My lack of trust in his ability to lead told him. Treating him like a child when he tried to take the lead, requiring him to need my approval to operate at the capacity he should be functioning in—all of these and many more told him! Many times, I embarrassed him (unknowingly) in front of his friends and family by BOSSING him around. This, my sisters, is disrespectful behavior.

Fortunately for me, he was just a boyfriend. You, on the other hand, are bound to a covenant. If you're committed to the covenant, then you're committed to doing things God's way. Trust me; there will be many times it feels unfair. You're like, "God you know he always drops the ball," "You know he doesn't know what he's doing," "he needs me to tell him what to do." Listen, that's not God's way. God honors position. Let me explain why.

Faith without works is dead. We think that when we talk about "work," we do all the work. God revealed to me another layer to that mindset. It's true that faith requires work. However, the work that is required from us is one of positioning. In other words, I was thinking (I'm sure many of you were too) of work as something you do. However, God told me to think of work as defined in physics. Take a look:

In physics, a force (this would be God) is said to do **work** if, when acting on **a body (You)**, there is a displacement of the point of application in the *** direction of the force.***

Basically, in order for you to endure and change your marriage for the better, you need to change your behavior BY FAITH! You cannot do so on your own. That would be YOU doing the work. That's why God says "faith without works is dead." Therefore, when your husband doesn't come through for you, or he drops the ball and makes things worst or embarrass you by sounding stupid, don't address the fool in him. Why? It's counter-productive.

God is a Spirit, He's not sensual. In the grand scheme of things, it's not about your feelings; it's about His power through His word. Remember that your husband is in the king, priest, and head position and by faith, treat him as such. So when you get in position through submission, GOD INTERVENES! HE DOES THE WORK!

Ironically, women who disrespect their husbands because they feel their husbands do not love them like Christ loves the Church, usually begin to feel justified in resorting to disrespectful and unloving behavioral lifestyles. This is disobedience to God and insubordination to the husband; not to mention that your position as a wife requires you to help HIM. Nowhere in the Bible does it say to help your children, family, friends, or even your church *before* your husband.

It is a natural proclivity to love those who love you and be nice to those who are nice to you. That's easy. How excruciating to have a husband that ignores you, takes you for granted, disrespects, insults, and disappoints you, then you have to turn around and help him?! Most wives just turn around and give the love they really wanted to give to their husband and give it to family, friends, or anybody in the world who appreciates them.

That actually makes sense. However, God is not sensual. There is a power at work that we cannot see in the natural. God is telling us the secret to a successful marriage. Wives, the key is, by faith, return to your position as a helper and help your husband wherever you can. Even if it cost you something (and it will) and even if it hurts[1] (and it will), help him. Treat him like God—a king, a priest, and leader—regardless, if he's treating you right or not. And watch God go to work! When you stop being the answer, judge, jury, and executioner, there is a debt in the spirit realm. You sowed faith. God will not owe any man and He's not a man that He should lie, so if He said that the man would be changed by your behavior, HE WILL BE. Don't expect it overnight, though that could happen.

Men sometimes can be insecure just like women. Believe it or not, he thinks the world of you. There were millions of women out there and he chose you, one out of a million, to give his name a meaning. He trusts you. With that in mind, when you think he's stupid, he feels it. And if he had any insecurity, your ACTIONS just fed it.

God told me, whatever you focus on expands. If you focus on the king in him, that's who is going to arise. You speaking into his spirit and SHOWING him respect inspires him to be greater because he doesn't want to let you down. You help him by supporting him if a plan falls through. Look at it as a learning curve for him.

I know, I know you're like, "Oh, that's cute and all but if we lose our life savings on this dumb idea or our house etc., I will be done with him because I KNEW IT WAS A BAD IDEA FROM THE BEGINNING!" Now hold that thought…whatever you focus on

---

[1] I'm not talking about physical abuse, that's another topic.

expands. If you find yourself in this position, submit to YOUR HUSBAND. That doesn't mean you submit to the idea. That means you support HIM and HELP make the vision come to pass. You do so practically as well as spiritually. This is where prayer is key and you invite God to be the Head of your head and do the work.

Do you know your behavior could be the very thing that is weakening your husband? When the woman with the issue of blood touched Jesus, He turned around and said, "Who touched me?" He said so because He felt virtue leave His body. In other words, she extracted power out of Him to heal herself. Her faith gave her access to make this withdrawal from God. In Proverbs 31, the Bible talks about the virtuous woman. Another word for virtue is power. She was a powerful woman. Her husband was in his rightful position and he sang her praises. Why? Because instead of draining him to accomplish her desires, she simply *feared the Lord, submitted.* God said in His Word that the woman who does this EXCELLED them ALL!

> Proverbs 31:25-30
>
> *Strength and honor are her clothing; and she shall rejoice in time to come. She openeth her mouth with wisdom; and in her tongue is the law of kindness. She looketh well to the ways of her household, and eateth not the bread of idleness. Her children arise up, and call her blessed; her husband also, and he praiseth her. Many daughters have done virtuously, but thou excellest them all. Favour is deceitful, and beauty is vain: but a woman that feareth the LORD, she shall be praised.*

> 1 John 2:5
>
> *But whoso keepeth his word, in him verily is the love of God perfected: hereby know we that we are in him.*

> ### Ephesians 4:1-3
>
> *I therefore, the prisoner of the Lord, beseech you that ye walk worthy of the vocation wherewith ye are called, With all lowliness and meekness, with longsuffering, forbearing one another in love; Endeavouring to keep the unity of the Spirit in the bond of peace. There is one body, and one Spirit, even as ye are called in one hope of your calling; One Lord, one faith, one baptism, One God and Father of all, who is above all, and through all, and in you all.*

CHAPTER 4

Treat Your Wife Like The Holy Spirit

> 2 Timothy 1:14
> *That good thing which was committed unto thee keep by the Holy Ghost which dwelleth in us.*

I'M SURE YOU enjoyed what I had to say to the wives concerning treating their husband like God. It's so nice to be treated like a king, right? It's even nicer to have someone to completely submit to you as the king you are.

As appealing as that may be to the male ego, those instructions are strategically in place to edify both of you in order for you to be effective in operating, managing, and multiplying your family/nation. Your wife IS NOT SUBSERVIENT TO YOU. You and your wife are joint heirs.

HEIR DEFINED:

- A person who has the legal right to receive the property of someone who dies.
- A person who has the right to become a *king* or *queen* or to claim a title when the person holding it does.

For the sake of order, God has instructed the wife to submit unto her husband. Prior to you, she has had a lifetime of thoughts, experiences, education, adventures, revelations, and so much more. She has proven that she could survive *without you*.

However, her divine mandate requires her at times to silence all of what she has learned, understood, and known to acquiesce to you. This is not a light thing and it should be considered and respected. Her submission is an act of love, surrender, and obedience… *to God.*

With that being said, the Bible instructs the husband to *love and consider her with honor* as a fellow heir.

> Colossians 3:19
> *Husbands, love your wives, and be not bitter against them.*

> Ephesians 5:25
> *Husbands, love your wives, just as Christ loved the church and gave Himself up for her.*

CHAPTER 4 | TREAT YOUR WIFE LIKE THE HOLY SPIRIT

> ### Hebrews 1:3
> *God, who at sundry times and in divers manners spake in time past unto the fathers by the prophets, Hath in these last days spoken unto us by <u>his Son</u>, whom he hath appointed heir of all things, by whom also he made the worlds; Who being the brightness of his glory, and <u>the express image of his person</u>, and upholding all things by the word of his power, when he had by himself purged our sins, sat down on the right hand of the Majesty on high.*

Husbands are the express image of Christ as the son, head, king, priest, and prophet on earth in the flesh. A wife is like the Holy Spirit as she is on the inside of you (your inner circle/soul mate) and she's the vessel used to aid in multiplication.

Jesus came as God in the flesh for the purpose of our salvation (like the husband). In other words, Jesus got us through the doors of the Kingdom of God. But in order to multiply Himself on earth, He had to do it through the Holy Spirit and the woman.

Likewise, you cannot multiply your seed alone in your flesh, for you need your wife to be the vessel in which your seed is multiplied. Jesus could not multiply Himself in the flesh; that was the function of the Holy Spirit. Yet, God the Father, Jesus, and the Holy Spirit are all one. Your marriage is a reflection of that formula. God the Father, the Husband and your wife are all one.

> ### Mark 3:24, 25
> *And if a kingdom be divided against itself, that kingdom cannot stand. And if a house be divided against itself, that house cannot stand.*

Your wife is a vital key to your wealth, prosperity, success, and expansion. It is for this reason that if you don't treat your wife right, your prayers will be hindered. Why? God will not go against Himself. You and your wife are one and God is looking for godly seed and multiplication. If you don't serve His purpose, you hinder your own progress.

Therefore, if you mistreat your wife, God will ignore your request because you have broken rank and disobeyed the covenant. God is obligated to keep His word with you when you keep your word with Him.

PURPOSE PRINCIPLE

Your wife is priceless. You can produce a seed but you cannot reproduce without her!

Remember, you're created in His image and likeness. You and your wife are one and you cannot function and move if you're divided against yourself. Your wife represents the body but the body is only able to move and have its being through the Spirit of God. You are the head and the head gives the messages to the body regarding the direction the body is to move.

Therefore, although your wife's body may be physically moving in the natural, when you disobey God's order on how to treat her, she won't respond spiritually because God is your head and you cannot control God who is ultimately controlling the body. This is a major cause of stagnation because many husbands want the wife to do the work and sacrifice of submission but refuse to die to self *for her*, which is the ultimate act of love.

Death to self HAS TO OCCUR! Jesus is the example for how a husband should treat his wife. He is long suffering with us. He had to maintain the divine vision (that He alone had) despite persecution of the Church (His bride). It was through *purpose* He was able to maintain His focus. It wasn't until Christ died to self (the flesh) that the Holy Spirit was able to come. When you got married, that was the day you went to the cross and died to the single man that you once knew. It was at that moment you and your wife's spirit became one.

PURPOSE PRINCIPLE

Your wife is your God-given help.

> ### John 15:16
> *But when the Comforter is come, whom I will send unto you from the Father, even the Spirit of truth, which proceedeth from the Father, he shall testify of me*

Your wife was sent from the father to help you, she is your comforter and her very being should testify daily of God. Now, your wife is NOT THE HOLY SPIRIT. Again, she is the *likeness* of the Holy Spirit.

> ### John 14:16
> *But the Comforter, which is the Holy Ghost, whom the Father will send in my name, he shall teach you all things, and bring all things to your remembrance, whatsoever I have said unto you.*

> ### Proverbs 19:14
> *House and riches are the inheritance of fathers: and a prudent wife is from the LORD.*

> **Proverbs 18:21,22**
> *Death and life are in the power of the tongue, And those who love it will eat its fruit. He who finds a wife finds a good thing And obtains favor from the LORD.*

The Holy Spirit is also referred to as an advocate or a counselor. Your wife is your help meet, which means you must meet with her in counsel regarding decisions for your marriage, family, along with the direction you're leading her to. When she asks you questions, she is not questioning you. She is meeting with you to see how she can help. Her very nature is designed to help you.

There are times men feel overwhelmed with their own personal pressures or agenda that they deal harshly with their wives because they just want them to be seen and not heard…just submit. That is not biblical. Her very existence, nature and DNA is formulated to help! She cannot help it! lol

God created her to help *you*; and in order to do that, she has to be *informed* about your vision and direction, to understand her role in that plan. Since her vantage point is different from yours, she may not see things the way you do. What you consider nagging could simply be her trying to bring awareness to the king on important issues you may be missing. Like the Holy Spirit, she will bring to remembrance all God has said concerning you.

Always keep in mind that she is a part of YOU. Nobody wants to hurt themselves. She's on your team. She is your spiritual eyes and ears. She's trying to do you a favor! That doesn't mean you have to agree with her all of the time but it's important to hear her out (in love). God created her to meet with you. To shun her from meeting with you is to disobey God.

CHAPTER 4 | TREAT YOUR WIFE LIKE THE HOLY SPIRIT

ad·vo·cate defined

A person who publicly supports or recommends a particular cause or policy.

COUNSELOR DEFINED:

1. A person who counsels; adviser.
2. A faculty member who advises students on personal and academic problems, career choices, and the like.
3. An assistant at a children's camp, often a high-school or college student, who supervises a group of children or directs a particular activity, as nature study or a sport.
4. A lawyer, especially a trial lawyer; counselor-at-law.
5. An official of an embassy or legation who ranks below an ambassador or minister.

As an advocate, your wife represents a public display of support. It is her job to make recommendations to you that would enhance, empower, or improve your life. She is a fellow heir to the inheritance, which is your nation and kingdom of God here on earth and it's her job to counsel with you. And she's qualified to do so because she knows your secrets and the innermost parts of you.

> **1 Peter 3:7**
>
> *Husbands, in the same way, treat your wives with consideration as a delicate vessel, and with honor as fellow heirs of the gracious gift of life, so that your prayers will not be hindered.*

The relationship between husband and wife is a series of checks and balances. The husband (like Christ) is the savior of the body (your wife being the body). He washes her with the water of the word, which is a form of baptism. It is your job to cover, protect, and deliver her through the Word of God, not just by speaking it but by being a physical manifestation of it (which is real Love). Getting your wife to become who she is to be, who you desire her to be, requires a character assessment of yourself. When you learn to love her more than yourself that is when you have adopted the character of Christ. It's imperative this transformation occurs because the head gives the body commands on how to live and move. Like Christ, we are a reflection of him. If you do not act like Christ, she is prone to reflecting the nature of whatever YOUR character ACTUALLY IS (good, bad or indifferent).

PURPOSE PRINCIPLE

When you love your wife more than yourself, that's when you know you've adopted the character of Christ.

> **1 Corinthians 7:4**
> *The wife hath not power of her own body, but the husband: and likewise also the husband hath not power of his own body, but the wife.*

Molding your wife to become more like you is a process, one in which you have to go to the upper room in prayer to see manifested. Remember, she's not a girlfriend, mistress, or side chick; this is your wife. She is literally one with you. It is part of your marital purpose to find ways to please her and to dwell with her with understanding. This is a work in progress! Understand that she had an entire life and thought process ingrained in her long before you came into her life. She had her own visions and dreams that may be contrary to the direction you desire to go. Unraveling those old thoughts and patterns take time (sometimes years), prayer and the gentle washing of the Word that YOU have to administer. Husbands are the savior of the body! Remember, when you talk to your wife, you're talking to yourself. In the beginning, God said let us make man in our own image. That *us* is himself in three persons. Consulting with your wife is the same thing...you, your wife, and God in conversation.

No one else can have this prestigious position in your life other than your wife—NOT YOUR MOTHER, children, parents, pastors, prophets, no one! Your wife, like the Holy Spirit, knows all of your intricate workings and keeps them in the covenant.

I emphasized the mother relationship because many marriages are strained today as some men have a hard time distinguishing guidelines between their spouse and parents (mothers in particular). The mother/son bond is an incredible one; I mean, after all, your mom brought you into this world. She is your first love and the one woman that offered you unconditional love. Many men, therefore, feel obligated and loyal to the influence and presence of their mothers to the detriment of their marriage.

Letting go may be especially difficult for a man whose mom was a single parent. Oftentimes, single moms make their sons a companion of sorts. You became the man of the house. As a result, some mothers feel betrayed when their son gets married and will try to either break up his relationship, interfere all the time, oppress the daughter-in-law or try to control him and his marriage. Many wives complain about this because her focus is to please her husband but she cannot focus on doing so if there's another woman that has the attention of her man.

Some men feel like they cannot choose between their mother and wife and just let them fight it out. Or they may tell their wife to just work it out or ignore it all. Both is wrong. The Bible instructs men to LEAVE their mother and father and cleave to their wife. Nowhere does it say for the wife to have to work ANYTHING OUT with your mother. Your wife is one with *you*, she is not your mother, but she has taken the role of pleasing you. In order for you and your spouse to bond and become one, everyone else must be moved out of the equation. No one is saying forsake your mother. But the Bible does say to leave and cleave for the sake of oneness. You're not just one in spirit but one body and joint heirs.

> **Genesis 2:24**
>
> *The man said, "This is now bone of my bones, And flesh of my flesh; She shall be called Woman, Because she was taken out of Man." For this reason a man shall leave his father and his mother, and be joined to his wife; and they shall become one flesh.*

Understand that your marriage is not an extension of your immediate family. God is creating something *new* through your family. In other words, your new immediate family is your new nation that is going to go in the direction of your leadership—your leadership, not your parent's leadership. And your wife is JOINT HEIR to the kingdom with YOU.

She's also the weaker vessel. Your wife is a delicate flower in so many ways. Even if she is strong and independent; deep inside, there is a frailty when it comes to emotions and stability. She's soft and feminine by nature. Therefore, you cannot treat her like one of the guys, rough housing her, teasing, taunting her, yelling, (never beat her) all the time. Even if she is cool with that kind of behavior, if it's done too much or too long, she'll begin to resent it because her femininity is being distorted.

Do you know that blaspheming the Holy Spirit is an unpardonable sin? Although coming against your wife won't bring that condemnation on you, God doesn't take kindly to you abusing His daughter! The Bible says your prayers will be hindered. God will not hear you. That means, your business deals, finances, personal endeavors will go unheard. You'll see what you want right in front of you but God will not allow you to obtain it. In other words, if you shut her down, He will shut you down where it hurts!

The Bible instructs you to consider her. Watch your wife, study and listen to her, feel her. You will learn where her frailties are. Remember, you are the savior of the body not the abuser. Whatever you do to her is being done to you. You are one. If you don't open her doors, carry her bags, carry the heavier burdens, it is a bad reflection on YOU. Trust me; people won't say anything to you but THEY NOTICE. If you don't treat your wife like a lady, it makes you look like less of a man.

Women in general are more emotional, we need lots of attention and affection. That doesn't mean sex all the time but rather, intimacy, romance and sensuality. It's no different from how women like sex but men NEED SEX. Yes, men crave attention, romance and affection but women NEED attention, affection and romance. Even your protection as a man, the extra care you give her when you lay down your life (your desires) for hers, is considered beautiful affection and attention to her. Being preferred and acknowledged above all (except God) is also equally important to her.

Your wife doesn't want anybody or anything else when she wants you. That is her nature and God-given instruction to please you. Don't make the mistake of condemning her for being a wife to you because her needs may come at an inconvenient time. Lay down your life for her. You will be blessed for doing so. It's no different if the Holy Spirit instructs you to give or do something you weren't very excited about doing, you did it anyway because you love and trust God. You know that the Holy Spirit is only setting you up for a blessing. Consider your wife in the same light.

Some men may have grown up in an environment where the males disrespect the females. These men teach each other to just take what they want from women and don't give anything in return because they are afraid of being played or ridiculed. For instance, if you open doors and pull out chairs for your wife, your boys may say things like, "you're weak" or "you're hen pecked" or "whipped". They may even go as far as to say she's just using you. If this is you, you're living in error. Your wife IS YOU. You won't deprive yourself, would you? You give yourself the best, right? You are a priority to *you*, right? Would you let your friends influence what you buy, do, or spend time for yourself? Then don't let that outside influence or gold digger fear/mentality cause you to dishonor your wife. She always should come first. You are her king, always be that for her. Here's a scripture to consider:

> Proverbs 25:2-7
>
> *It is the glory of God to conceal a thing: but the honour of kings is to search out a matter. The heaven for height, and the earth for depth, and the heart of kings is unsearchable. Take away the dross from the silver, and there shall come forth a vessel for the finer.*

Your wife is a vessel and you are the savior of the body. Take away the dross from the silver (silver represents truth) and there shall come forth a vessel for the finer. In other words, you have to search out what God has concealed about your wife. Anything that you find that is not right, help her to make it better. Doing so is credited to YOUR HONOR!

Vessels are used to contain things. Just as we need to be filled with the Holy Spirit, you need to fill your wife (the weaker vessel) with love! Don't pour hatred, domination, control, fear and intimidation, rather speak the Word of life into her, she needs to hear it from you. Fill her heart with words of reassurance, your presence, affection, attention, resources, and time. When you love her for real, it fills her heart with joy. It's strength and life to her bones. As with any vessel, once it's full, you must empty out in order to fill again. In other words, when she is full of love, she'll pour it out on you!

When your wife is on empty, she has NOTHING TO GIVE! Emotional emptiness for a woman is like a slow and painful death.

That deficit creates space for the enemy to creep in. It's your job to keep your body alive, as this is part of your covenant agreement. A man is nothing if he doesn't keep his word. You swore to love her. God commands that you love her, as Christ loved the Church and gave His life for it. He gave His life so that He could pick His life up again. That is what will happen to you when you love your wife. She will pour life back into you! If you don't feed her love, you're starving YOURSELF to death!

Loving your wife this way is something you should always do naturally. Not because of what anyone else says you should do, but because of who you are and who she is to you. Remember, you need her just as she needs you because a body without the spirit is dead. It is love (God) that gives us life.

> **James 2:26**
> *For as the body without the spirit is dead, so faith without works is dead also.*

Your affection and attention makes her feel safe and assured. Consider, you may not need that kind of reassurance but most women do. Sometimes, your presence (without you saying a word) is sufficient. Coming to her defense, whether it's against a real threat, a family member or friends, fills her heart with peace knowing you are covering her.

ABOUT YOUR WIFE..

She is a helper:

> Genesis 2:18
> *And the LORD God said, It is not good that the man should be alone; I will make him an help meet for him.*

MEET DEFINED:

1. to see and speak to (someone) for the first time : to be introduced to or become acquainted with (someone)
2. to come together in order to talk : to go to a place to be with someone else
3. :to come together formally : to have a meeting : to come together for a discussion

HELPER DEFINED:

- To give assistance to (someone); make it easier for (someone) to do something; aid.
- To contribute to the effectiveness or improvement of (something).
- To ease the pain or discomfort of; relieve: medication to help your cold.
- To be of service; give assistance: I made a cake, and my friend helped.
- To be of use or provide relief.
- The action of helping; assistance: Do you need help with that package?
- One that helps.

CHAPTER 4 | TREAT YOUR WIFE LIKE THE HOLY SPIRIT

Submits to her husband:

> Ephesians 5:22
> *Wives, submit yourselves unto your own husbands, as unto the Lord.*

> Colossians 3:18
> *Wives, submit yourselves unto your own husbands, as it is fit in the Lord.*

> 1 Peter 3:1
> *Likewise, ye wives, be in subjection to your own husbands; that, if any obey not the word, they also may without the word be won by the conversation of the wives; While they behold your chaste conversation coupled with fear.*

> Ephesians 5:24
> *Therefore as the church is subject unto Christ, so let the wives be to their own husbands in everything.*

Is a good thing:

> Proverbs 18:22
> *Whoso findeth a wife findeth a good thing, and obtaineth favour of the LORD.*

> **Genesis 2:18**
> The LORD God said, "It is not good for the man to be alone. I will make a helper suitable for him."

> **Proverbs 19:14**
> Houses and wealth are inherited from parents, but a prudent wife is from the LORD.

> **Proverbs 31:10**
> A wife of noble character who can find? She is worth far more than rubies.

Her body belongs to you:

> **1 Corinthians 7:3-6**
> Let the husband render unto the wife due benevolence: and likewise also the wife unto the husband. 4The wife hath not power of her own body, but the husband: and likewise also the husband hath not power of his own body, but the wife. 5Defraud ye not one the other, except it be with consent for a time, that ye may give yourselves to fasting and prayer; and come together again, that Satan tempt you not for your incontinency.

> **1 Corinthians 7:12-14**
> But to the rest speak I, not the Lord: If any brother hath a wife that believeth not, and she be pleased to dwell with him, let him not put her away. And the woman which hath an husband that believeth not, and if he be pleased to dwell with her, let her not
>
> *cont/d...*

> *leave him. For the unbelieving husband is sanctified by the wife, and the unbelieving wife is sanctified by the husband: else were your children unclean; but now are they holy.*

> ### Genesis 2:24
> *Therefore shall a man leave his father and his mother, and shall cleave unto his wife: and they shall be one flesh. And they were both naked, the man and his wife, and were not ashamed.*

CHAPTER 5

Sexual Healing

PLEASE, FORGIVE ME but I find it hysterically ironic that when women are single, they find time to work, do charity, shop, travel, hang out with friends, and date several men all at the same time. As exhausting as that may sound, they were never too tired for sexual encounters. Once these women cleaned up their lives and the pastor or someone tells them they have to wait until they're married, it's like, "Well, why don't you just put me in a straight jacked and throw me in an asylum!" During those single days, you were never too tired to look cute, smell nice, and have sex if you could…lots of it. I'm not condoning fornication but it was a fact of life for a lot of women.

So WHY when they finally get married with an official green light from God to be as sexually active with their husband as they want, they act like the virgin Mary?! You already know it—putting your husband on a once a week or longer ration? No, my sister, (if this is you), you're in error! Not only are you sinning against your husband, you're sinning against God and yourself.

****Newsflash: Sex is part of your Purpose and Assignment.

It's your job to help your husband! For him, sex is not a want, it's a NEED! God said in the scriptures that I shall supply all of your need. You are an answer to your husband's need and he is the answer to yours. Seriously, you may need it but he REALLY needs it! He literally has a biological, physiological need for sex. The presence of testosterone in the man's body triggers strong desires to release sperm that builds up within his testicles. Although he may be able to control these urges, it can be painful and cause discomfort to his overall well-being until he is able to release. God understands he created man this way and told him that it is better for him to marry than to burn. Therefore, it is the job of the wife to help her husband in this way.

The purpose of sex, aside from pleasure, is to physically come together as one and conceive, though it's not limited to conception of a baby. Sometimes, when there is friction in the marriage, having sexually intimate moments can actually be a spiritual avenue where you both are relaxed enough to resolve problems and soothe each other.

Sex is very powerful as it has tremendous benefits for the couple. Now, by nature, men are depositors and women are receptors. Sexual intercourse is more than a physical activity—it goes into the emotional and psychological spheres. Therefore, when the husband releases his sperm, he is saying, "I'm for you, and this is my token of the covenant, even my blood." Each time you come together sexually, you are strengthening the bond. In sex, men release power and virtue when they release their sperm—a token, their blood of the marriage covenant. The wife releases some fluid—her token of blood—or egg (if she is in a fertile condition). What is usually referred to as SOUL TIE is formed through sex. That's why after wedding, the couple is said to CONSUMMATE their marriage through their first sexual encounter. The bond (til death do us part) is formed, and that exchange of blood seals the vows they made before God and witnesses.

Psychologically, after a good round of sex, the man will feel recharged. He also rests better, which literally helps him recharge physically. Even studies have shown that sex, if done the right way, can help boost self-esteem. Imagine your husband going to work feeling great for the day, all because you served him well in the bedroom. You too, as the wife, will feel fulfilled. This is mutually benefitting. When you're always satisfied in the bedroom, you will have good mental and emotional health, and your body will resonate with that. This is sexual healing.

However, recharging through sex only works best in the confines of marriage. God designed it that way. It doesn't work the same outside of marriage. Matter of fact, men and women deteriorate over time when they fornicate and commit adultery. Ever notice how prostitutes and whoremongers begin to look dark, sucked out, and worn? Why? God is not involved in their sexual activity. Spiritually, they are dying because they are robbing God of His place in marriage. I can't make this stuff up folks; think about it, you've seen it.

> ### John 10:1
> *Verily, verily, I say unto you, He that entereth not by the door into the sheepfold, but climbeth up some other way, the same is a thief and a robber.*

God created marriage to be a self-contained unit that functions on His behalf, for His purpose. The husband manages this operation and when he is tense or overwhelmed, the wife is the only one that should give her husband this kind of release. Listen, sex is too powerful to falter in this area! Entire nations have been brought down over it. Don't let your nation become a casualty because you just don't *feel* like it. There are so many women that would love to "help" your spouse however, whenever and wherever they like. Don't let disobedience open the door to the enemy who is *willing* to help out.

Sex when you want it can be pleasurable but if you don't want it, it can be downright miserable for some people. It's imperative that you treat your marriage like a job because you have work to do. When you have a regular job, no matter how you may be feeling, you don't bring your negative feelings to work. You just do the assignment to the best of your ability. The same goes for your marriage. When your spouse desires sex and you don't want to, you must get into *character* and *act* like you do. You must walk by faith during these times. God will give you the grace and anointing to perform. As a wife, your aim is making sure that your husband is at his best so that he will remain focused and accomplish the goals set for the family.

Wives, I know you don't want to hear this but if you will accept God's divine strategy, the mystery of His wisdom will unfold right before your eyes. Your husband is mandated by God to love you till death. Whether he actually does, this is between him and God. God will hold him accountable for how he treats you. But I'm communicating with you here for self-examination. Consider this; it is clear in the scriptures that God compared wives to slaves, servants, and Himself.

> ### 1 Peter 2:13-25
> *Submit yourselves to every ordinance of man for the Lord's sake: whether it be to the king, as supreme; Or unto governors, as unto them that are sent by him for the punishment of evildoers, and for the praise of them that do well. For so is the will of God, that with well doing ye may put to silence the ignorance of foolish men:*
>
> *cont/d…*

> *As free, and not using your liberty for a cloke of maliciousness, but as the servants of God. Honour all men. Love the brotherhood. Fear God. Honour the king. <u>Servants, be subject to your masters</u> with all fear; not only to the good and gentle, but also to the froward. For this is thankworthy, if a man for conscience toward God endure grief, suffering wrongfully. For what glory is it, if, when ye be buffeted for your faults, ye shall take it patiently? But if, when ye do well, and suffer for it, ye take it patiently, this is acceptable with God. For even hereunto were ye called: because Christ also suffered for us, leaving us an example, that ye should follow his steps: Who did no sin, neither was guile found in his mouth: Who, when he was reviled, reviled not again; when he suffered, he threatened not; but committed himself to him that judgeth righteously: Who his own self bare our sins in his own body on the tree, that we, being dead to sins, should live unto righteousness: by whose stripes ye were healed. For ye were as sheep going astray; but are now returned unto the Shepherd and Bishop of your souls.*

> 1 Peter 3
>
> *<u>Likewise, ye wives</u>, be in subjection to your own husbands; that, if any obey not the word, they also may without the word be won by the conversation of the wives.*

He didn't say that you were a slave but he used the term *likewise* after describing slaves in the previous chapter. What I believe God is saying to wives is that your devotion to your husband should be so unwavering and selfless, that your wants and needs *submit to his needs*. God created men and He knows what inspires them. Men admire and respect humility and loyalty, whether they tell you or not.

Therefore, you may be thinking that you have the right to refrain from sex because of how you feel ("I'm tired, I don't want to have sex," "I'm not attracted to him anymore," or worst, "he doesn't deserve it, when he acts right, then he will get it"). Servants/wives do not have such options. They simply do as they are told even if they're tired. That is the level of devotion GOD HIMSELF is expecting you to give your husband. It is your service TO GOD.

> **1 Corinthians 7:4**
>
> *The wife hath not power of her own body, but the husband: and likewise also the husband hath not power of his own body, but the wife. Defraud ye not one the other, except it be with consent for a time, that ye may give yourselves to fasting and prayer; and come together again, that Satan tempt you not for your incontinency.*

When men cheat, women are fast to come down on them but when you actually hear both sides of the story, I often hear that the wife did not perform her sexual duties. No, it's not your fault that he cheated but it is your fault that you gave *place* to the enemy through disobedience.

> **Ephesians 4:26, 27**
>
> *Be ye angry, and sin not: let not the sun go down upon your wrath: Neither give place to the devil.*

> **1 Corinthians 7:5**
>
> *Defraud ye not one the other, except it be with consent for a time, that ye may give yourselves to fasting and prayer; and come together again, that Satan tempt you not for your incontinency.*

Husbands, Be Knowledgeable:

> 1 Peter 3:7
>
> *Likewise, ye husbands, dwell with them according to knowledge, giving honour unto the wife, as unto the weaker vessel, and as being heirs together of the grace of life; that your prayers be not hindered.*

In 1 Peter 3:7, we see God giving husbands explicit instructions. Husbands, did you know that there are reasons why women often lose interest in sex? One of the main reasons is that you *didn't know her*. Whenever the Bible talks about sex and intimacy, it says "he knew her."

Notice, the Bible NEVER says "she knew *him*." On the contrary, it clearly declares how the husband *knew the wife* and that was when conception occurred. When you're intimate with your wife by getting to know her, she opens her soul to you. If you touch her soul, she will give you her body. It's within this sanctuary that God meets with both of you in a special way. Her very body will speak to you when you actually get to know her.

PURPOSE PRINCIPLE

If you touch her soul, she will give you her body.

Consequently, the word *know* is the root word for knowledge and *knew* means to already *know*. And now, we see God instructing husbands to dwell with their wives *according to* knowledge. Remember, you (husband) are one with God, making *you* God in the flesh when you are in agreement with him and His Word. The Bible says, "before I formed you in the belly I *knew* thee".

Believe it or not, you *already knew* your wife but you forgot. Everything we see in the natural realm began in the spirit. Therefore, you and your wife were one before you even became a living being. Information about your wife is already inside of you because she is of you. However, because she had been the part of you that were removed (your rib), you have to re-discover that side of you. Revelation of who your wife is will unfold as you begin to love her like you love yourself because that's exactly what you are doing.

***sidenote to wives**

Wives, the Bible instructs the husband to dwell with his wife according to knowledge. Once your marriage was consummated (sexually) it is said that the husband *knew* (past tense) you. However, the actual knowing wasn't sexual, rather spiritual. The only reason why he married you was because he saw himself in you. The physical act of sex was the manifestation of what was confirmed in the spiritual.

Now it's up to you to *receive* that oneness with you and your husband by faith by *knowing* that he really loves you. It's equally important that you *know* your marital purpose according to your individual covenant with the Word of God, *sealed with your oath* submit to your own husband.

Don't let the world, your friends and family fool you. No matter how you feel about it, God has given your husband authority over you and your body.

> **1 Corinthians 7:4**
> *The wife hath not power of her own body, but the husband: and likewise also the husband hath not power of his own body, but the wife.*

We have faith in God because we *know* him, (his flawless character, righteousness and faithfulness). That's how wives should be with their husbands. Knowing that their husbands request is his desires and wives should fulfill those desires because it is the will of the king (never refuse the king). When God speaks and commands, let there be…things manifest. In order for there to *be* a *let*, someone or something has to *allow*. Your husband, being made in the express image and likeness of God, will behave in that same likeness by speaking and commanding his desires. When God does it, the entire universe bows down, moves out the way and allows the word to go forth and manifest.

As a wife, when your husband speaks or makes a request, just the same as if God would you must *allow* him to have his way. That means although you as a person have the free will to resist and say no, out of obedience to God you will submit to the will of your husband by allowing him access to *whatever he desires* (as unto the Lord).

Disobedience to Gods way in this matter is you NOT ALLOWING God to His will through you. Remember, God instructs you to submit YOURSELF unto your own husband AS UNTO THE LORD! That includes your husband's sexual desires. If you don't like his desires, go to the Father in prayer. If he abuses you, run to safety (God doesn't want you to suffer this way). The Holy Spirit will deliver you out of that situation and hinder his prayers.

> Ephesians 5:22
> *Wives, submit yourselves unto your own husbands, as unto the Lord.*

God, King of Kings, Lord of Lords, Savior Husband/King does this:	Obedience to God's Word and way is how you *make love!*	The Church/Bride/Servant/Wife/Help Meet does this:
Command		Obey
Desire		Faith
Let		Allow
Know		Know
Give		Receive

To get an even more precise understanding of where God is going with this, let's look at the full definition of the word *dwell* and *knowledge*:

Dwell defined:

- to live as a resident
- ***to keep the attention directed***
- to remain for a time
- to speak or write insistently

Knowledge defined:

- information, understanding, or skill that you get from experience or education
- awareness of something : the state of being aware of something

Getting to know your wife on a natural and spiritual level is an investment, an ongoing process not a one shot deal. God instructs husbands to *dwell* with her, which means not just to live in the same house with her. It means to continuously, consciously think about her and her needs. Your wife's needs are unique to her. In other words, you may have had past relationships where certain things didn't bother any of your ex-es but does to your wife. She may need constant reassurance of your love through verbal communication, or physical touch. Other women may need space and don't like a man being too clingy. Whatever her nuances are, (which will be unique to her) you need to learn them and respond according to that knowledge. God is saying, live, love and treat her according to all of the *Intel* that you have gained from living with her and consciously thinking about her.

Men are great at analyzing things, especially big things. Sometimes, a husband is so accomplished with big things—like paying all the bills, purchasing a home, and affording material things—that he thinks he has done his job and his wife should be satisfied. Although some wives hold that in high esteem, other women would trade all that in for more of your time and attentive affection. Consider your wife as a lifelong project you must figure out and conquer. Learn her rhythm, her mood swings, what makes her happy, what ticks her off, what makes her feel secure or insecure. Pay attention to her and listen to what bothers her because she will surely tell you. If you respond *accordingly*, she will not only be happier with you, she will love you more. Attention to detail in this area is definitely *a sexual turn on*! And we all know a happy wife makes a happy life!

Study every part of her body as to how it responds to your touch. Listen to her sounds, moans, and tone of voice. Her body will speak what her mouth cannot say. Although your body may be raging with testosterone and passion, her body has a different level of estrogen, which causes variations in energy and emotions. As a result of that influx, she may not be in the mood. Understanding your wife creates a greater bond of intimacy because you now *know* that her lack of drive has nothing to with her feelings for you or your performance. She's not rejecting you; so don't take it personal.

If you don't take the time and effort to get to know her, sex will just be mechanical, which will not be pleasurable for anyone. Men can survive off just physical sex for much longer than a woman can because, in most instances, he just needs to ejaculate. For women, the act of sex is not just physical but emotional, and spiritual in the respect that this is the environment in which you both become one. At that particular moment, she has you all to herself. For her, she not only opens up herself physically, she does so spiritually because she's a receptor. If you're not showing her love through consideration, you two will not be in agreement and that is the only way to become one. Her body may go through the motions but she will feel nothing but resentment, and all you will get is a good night sleep.

The Bible says that the husband *sanctifies* the wife, which means she is anointed and set aside specifically for a purpose. You are not just her protector and king, you're her savior… not oppressor or dictator. Her very body and soul is waiting for you to pour life into her and she cannot become one with you if you don't know her.

Women are beautiful creatures that men have adored, lusted after, and even killed for, from the beginning of time. Unfortunately, because of their femininity, many women have been raped, molested, abused, and rejected. This is so important for husbands to know because your wife may have been one of those women. Sometimes, women will share that information, many will not—not because they are deceptive but for a thousand psychological reasons. I'm bringing this to your awareness that some of the drawbacks or hindrances coming from your wife could be stemming from that.

Some women didn't have a father around or the one that was physically there wasn't a good one. So when the husband enters her body sexually, he has to contend with and defeat ungodly soul ties, generational curses, demons, and strongholds. She may not be aware of some of these, but because you're the savior of the body, YOU SHOULD KNOW. It's her job to help you to release and it is your job to save her. Pray that God reveals to you every demonic stronghold, mindset, hindrance, and soul tie. Ask the Lord for wisdom on how to contend with that particular situation.

**Sidenote:

Many men have been through the same thing. Therefore, both of you should pray together and ask God to reveal any spiritual hindrances.

Husbands, in order for you to know your wife, you must consider her. It is through gentle, thoughtful consideration that a woman gets aroused and motivated to please you. When you keep your wife in mind, you won't just treat her like a piece of meat. If something hurts her or offends her sexually, it should be considered.

This is a BIG ISSUE for many marriages. Although the Bible is silent as to sexual conduct in the bedroom, the scripture does say to honor your wife as the weaker vessel. To honor means to hold in high esteem. There are some sexual requests that are offensive, painful, and dishonorable. That is something that husbands are to *consider* because she is the weaker vessel. In other words, you must handle her with care.

> ### 1 Corinthians 10:3
> *All things are lawful for me, but all things are not expedient: all things are lawful for me, but all things edify not.*

> ### Romans 14:19
> *Let us therefore follow after the things which make for peace, and things wherewith one may edify another.*

> **Romans 15:2**
> *Each of us should please his neighbor for his good, to build him up.*

Let's go back to your covenant instructions where it says to love your wife as Christ loved the Church and gave His life for it. In other words, instead of indulging in your pleasure at your wife's expense (just because you have the authority to do so), lay down your desires in order to save her the humiliation, pain, suffering, or --- (you fill in the blank). She is you and you are her; both are one. Love her as you love yourself. You don't want to have to do what you don't want to or hate to do, now would you?

> **Ephesians 5:25**
> *Husbands, love your wives, even as Christ also loved the church, and gave himself for it; ²That he might sanctify and cleanse it with the washing of water by the word, That he might present it to himself a glorious church, not having spot, or wrinkle, or any such thing; but that it should be holy and without blemish.*

Take into consideration that her body is a vessel designed to receive. Physically, sex for her could be painful at times. Some women have a lower cervix than others, which is more prone to sexual discomfort especially if her husband is well endowed. Women also menstruate, which means during that time, she's may need a break. Women are often sensitive, not just emotionally but physically, which makes them prone to infections like yeast infections and common discomfort.

Most of these scenarios you may already know but God instructs husbands to *consider* all these things about their wife. If she's noticeably tired because she has been working, cooking, cleaning, and dealing with the children, consider her. If you've been having sex a lot and she is swollen or irritated, consider her. The act of consideration is a manifestation of love, wisdom, and kindness, which is an aphrodisiac for women and a commandment from God towards her husband.

> ### 1 Peter 3:7
> *Likewise, ye husbands, dwell with them according to knowledge, giving honor unto the wife, as unto <u>the weaker vessel</u>, and as being heirs together of the grace of life; that your prayers be not hindered.*

If you want to get her in the mood, consider her! Buy or cook dinner, clean or do something that she would have to make time for and spend energy on so that you can clear her schedule. Run her a bath, so that she can be relaxed. I'm not your wife, so I have no idea what will make her relax or happy. You should know and if you don't, find out! Set that atmosphere according to what you know about her!

Listen, Satan desperately wants to separate you in any way that he can because together, you are unstoppable. Sex in the sanctity of marriage is an act of worship. It is a powering station for both of you to recharge, connect, and release. If you do not obey God's instruction in relation to you and your spouse, **your thought process** will become a demonic **stronghold** that will give **the devil access and authority** to cause havoc in your relationship, home, family, and life!

PURPOSE PRINCIPLE

Married couples, don't withhold sex from your spouse.
Have sex…lots of it and have fun doing it! God has given you the green light!

This leads me to my next point. The scriptures do not dictate what you can and cannot do in the bedroom, neither should you allow your parents, pastor, best friend, family; nobody can tell you what to do when it comes to intimacy between you and your spouse. The idea is to become one with each other, paying close attention to the needs of your partner. If they have freaky desires, indulge out of love and according to knowledge. Matter of fact, have fun with it! Sex is a gift from God that is only licensed to married people, so exercise your privileges. If you do not like what he wants you to do, go over his head and pray about it. I guarantee God will help you. It's a hard thing when you are not used to certain sexual behaviors that make you uncomfortable.

****If your spouse is physically abusive, separate from him or her for a while with plans of reconciliation. You are only separating to get safety while they get help but reconcile after they do.

> Ephesians 2:16
> *And that he might reconcile both unto God in one body by the cross, having slain the enmity thereby.*

God is strategic, it's no accident He created us to be sexually intimate beings. You will find not only are there spiritual benefits to intimacy but there are many health benefits as well. Here's a few:

Helps Keep Your Immune System Humming

"Sexually active people take fewer sick days," says Yvonne K. Fulbright, PhD, a sexual health expert. People who have sex have higher levels of substances that defend the body against germs, viruses, and other intruders. Researchers at Wilkes University in Pennsylvania found that college students who had sex once or twice a week had higher levels of a certain antibody compared to students who had sex less often.

Boosts Your Libido

Longing for a more lively sex life? "Having sex will make sex better and will improve your libido," says Lauren Streicher, MD. She is an assistant clinical professor of obstetrics and gynecology at Northwestern University's Feinberg School of Medicine in Chicago. For women, having sex ups vaginal lubrication, blood flow, and elasticity, she says, all of which make sex feel better and help you crave more of it.

Improves Women's Bladder Control

A strong pelvic floor is important for avoiding urinary incontinence, something that will affect about 30% of women at some point in their lives. Good sex is like a workout for your pelvic floor muscles. When you have an orgasm, it causes contractions in those muscles, which strengthens them.

Lowers Your Blood Pressure

Research suggests a link between sex and lower blood pressure, says Joseph J. Pinzone, MD. He is CEO and medical director of Amai Wellness. "One landmark study found that sexual intercourse specifically (not masturbation) lowered systolic blood pressure." That's the first number on your blood pressure test.

Counts as Exercise

"Sex is a really great form of exercise," Pinzone says. It won't replace the treadmill, but it counts for something good to keep the body fit. Sex uses about five calories per minute, four more calories than watching TV. It gives you a one-two punch: It bumps up your heart rate and exerts workout pressure on various muscles. So get busy! You may even want to clear your schedule to make time for it on a regular basis. "Like with exercise, consistency helps maximize the benefits," Pinzone says.

Lowers Heart Attack Risk

A good sex life is good for your heart. Besides being a great way to raise your heart rate, sex helps keep your estrogen and testosterone levels in balance. "When either one of those is low, you begin to get lots of problems, like osteoporosis and even heart disease," Pinzone says. Having sex more often may help. During one study, men who had sex at least twice a week were half as likely to die of heart disease unlike men who had sex rarely.

Lessens Pain

Before you reach for an aspirin, try for an orgasm. "Orgasm can block pain," says Barry R. Komisaruk, PhD, a distinguished service professor at Rutgers, the State University of New Jersey. It releases a hormone that helps raise your pain threshold. Stimulation without orgasm can also do the trick. "We've found that vaginal stimulation can block chronic back and leg pain, and many women have told us that genital self-stimulation can reduce menstrual cramps, arthritic pain, and in some cases even headache," Komisaruk says.

May Make Prostate Cancer Less Likely

Going for the gusto may help ward off prostate cancer. Men who ejaculated frequently (at least 21 times a month) were less likely to get prostate cancer during one study, which was published in the *Journal of the American Medical Association*. It's not clear that sex was the only reason that mattered in that study. Lots of factors affect cancer risk. But more sex won't hurt.

Improves Sleep

You may nod off more quickly after sex, and for good reason. "After orgasm, the hormone prolactin is released, which is responsible for the feelings of relaxation and sleepiness" after sex, says Sheenie Ambardar, MD. She is a psychiatrist in West Hollywood, California.

Eases Stress

Being close to your partner can soothe stress and anxiety. Ambardar says touching and hugging can release your body's natural "feel-good hormone." Sexual arousal releases a brain chemical that revs up your brain's pleasure and reward system. Sex and intimacy can boost your self-esteem and happiness, too, Ambardar says. It's not only a prescription for a healthy life, but a happy one.

SECTION TWO

Order in the court

CHAPTER 6

The Royal Priesthood

CLEARLY, THE WORLD system, which is led by Satan, has given us a false impression of the idea of marriage. We've consulted each other about what it takes for a great marriage but have you consulted God on what His plans were in the first place? You and your spouse are part of a royal priesthood. You are heirs to the kingdom.

Each married couple have a territory to govern and their assignment is unique to their family, which is why it is unwise to compare your relationship to other marriages and equally unwise to consult with unbelievers. You and your spouse have been selected and chosen for a specific assignment, which is to be:

- A chosen generation
- A royal priesthood
- Holy nation
- A peculiar people

> **1 Peter 2:9,10**
>
> *But ye are a chosen generation, a royal priesthood, an holy nation, a peculiar people; that ye should shew forth the praises of him who hath called you out of darkness into his marvelous light: Which in time past were not a people, but are now the people of God: which had not obtained mercy, but now have obtained mercy.*

Read between the lines and you will see that God is telling us that we have responsibilities, royal obligations to His Kingdom. Most couples NEVER consider this. Those marriages are *governed* by feeling and feelings don't matter much when it comes down to the bottom line...your purpose as a couple to be fruitful, multiply, replenish, and subdue.

In the Old Testament, initially, each man would sacrifice unto God for himself, as Cain and Able did in Genesis. Then later on in scriptures we see the father serving as priest over his home, making sacrifices on behalf of himself and his family.

We see this particular order with Noah, Abraham, Isaac, and Jacob. As we continue further, God instructs Moses to set up the tabernacle, a place of worship, meeting, sacrifice and atonement for the people. According to the Levitical arrangement, the office of the priesthood was limited to the Levites and out of that tribe, God called out a *family* to serve...Aaron and his sons.

The priesthood was considered a people and a lifestyle. There were specific instructions for how they were to dress, handle the various articles of the tabernacle, and how/when to approach God on behalf of the people. The high priest would perform various sacrifices unto God to atone for the sins of the people.

Duties of Priests and Levites

> Numbers 18:1-7
>
> *And the LORD said unto Aaron, Thou and thy sons and thy father's house with thee shall bear the iniquity of the sanctuary: and thou and thy sons with thee shall bear the iniquity of your priesthood. And thy brethren also of the tribe of Levi, the tribe of thy father, bring thou with thee, that they may be joined unto thee, and minister unto thee: but thou and thy sons with thee shall minister before the tabernacle of witness. And they shall keep thy charge, and the charge of all the tabernacle: only they shall not come nigh the vessels of the sanctuary and the altar, that neither they, nor ye also, die. And they shall be joined unto thee, and keep the charge of the tabernacle of the congregation, for all the service of the tabernacle: and a stranger shall not come nigh unto you. And ye shall keep the charge of the sanctuary, and the charge of the altar: that there be no wrath any more upon the children of Israel. And I, behold, I have taken your brethren the Levites from among the children of Israel: to you they are given as a gift for the LORD, to do the service of the tabernacle of the congregation. Therefore thou and thy sons with thee shall keep your priest's office for every thing of the altar, and within the vail; and ye shall serve: I have given your priest's office unto you as a service of gift: and the stranger that cometh nigh shall be put to death.*

The tabernacle itself had various components which required special authorization, which if not obeyed could cost you your life (even if you were the high priest). Order and reverential fear was paramount. The same is true of your responsibilities and commitment to God and your spouse. Service in your marital sanctuary, order, and reverential fear of the Lord should be ultimately considered. God especially expressed how the stranger that "cometh nigh" shall be put to death. In marriage, the stranger generally represents extramarital affairs, strange women, evil men, and strange doctrine. Of course, you won't physically kill anyone. However, you are to kill that relationship AS IT APPROACHES before it starts.

The Levites served by helping to move the tabernacle articles when it was time to go to another location and they also worked at the tent of meeting. In other words, God has gifted some men and women of God to help you care for the tabernacle. These believers are anointed and appointed to serve alongside of you, ministering to you, consulting, and advising at times to help keep your marriage moving along. Understand they have a place in ministry with you but there are limits. Although God ordained them to enter the tabernacle at this capacity, it was not an all access pass. They were not allowed to enter the Holy of Holies where the Ark of the Covenant was. Only the High Priest was allowed there. Your private marital business, secrets and the heart of your marriage is private and exclusive only to your spouse.

As husband and wife, you are the High Priest of the tabernacle (which is your physical body as well as the body of Christ). This is possible through your acceptance of Christ and you becoming one with Him. You and your spouse are chosen to be part of the Royal Priesthood. The scriptures say that you bear the responsibility for *offenses* connected with the priesthood. We are talking about sins and trespasses that go on within your marriage and family. As priest, you must make the necessary *sacrifices* to make your marriage better. It is also your job to care for the sanctuary and the altar.

There were two altars in the tabernacle, which are very significant in the spiritual and overall purpose of your marriage.

- The brazen altar: it was located outdoors in the courtyard outside of the Holy Place or Tent of Meeting. This was where sacrifices were burned. On this altar, a perpetual fire was to be kept burning.

- The altar of incense: it was located inside the Holy Place in front of the veil that served as a partition between the Holy of Holies which contained the Ark of the Covenant. At this altar, incense was burned daily with coal taken from the brazen altar in the morning and the evening. The incense had to be made specifically the way God instructed, NO OTHER WAY OR INGREDIENTS WERE PERMITTED.

As previously mentioned, both spouses are High Priest through Christ. Although Christ fulfilled the law and became the perfect sacrifice, the Old Testament priest was a type and shadow of Him. Therefore, the instructions of the temple were not abolished but *now reside within us*. As a royal priesthood, our mandate is the same as the priest of old. It is our purpose and assignment to maintain the temple and tabernacle. The priest, before he even approached the brazen altar to commune with God to make a sacrifice, worship or make atonement, he had to first inspect himself and cleanse himself.

> 1 Corinthians 3:16
> *Know ye not that ye are the temple of God and that the Spirit of God dwelleth in you?*

You are the temple of God. But wait, the *you* referenced here is not just you as an individual, rather you *including* your spouse. Therefore, the same is true that before you approach God today, you must make things right with your spouse first. Notice, the brazen alter is at the Place of Meeting. Your wife is a helpmeet. There is a place where you both should meet and that would be at the brazen altar. That's where the blood sacrifices are made, its flesh was burned and sins were forgiven. Forgiveness has to occur in order to move forward into God's presence. This is a place of purging.

Your marriage is a ministry. People are watching and learning from your example. How can you be a royal priest with unforgiveness in your heart? How can you teach your children forgiveness if you refuse to forgive your spouse whom you say you love? God is love and He never changes. Therefore, your love shouldn't change. Unforgiveness is not of God but directly connected to emotions, which are carnal. Love conquers ALL, including the flesh. It's impossible to manage the tabernacle properly if it's unclean with the stain of unforgiveness.

At the brazen altar, there's a perpetual fire burning. What is that fire? For us, it would be the Holy Spirit, the Spirit of truth. Always be honest with your spouse. It is in the fire of truth that iniquity is purged. Harboring secrets and sins, haunts and invades the integrity of your relationship like a ghost. Your spouse can feel its presence but cannot touch it because it is hidden from them. The whole point of the tabernacle is to have a place to meet with, worship and commune with God in love, light and truth. Another way to say it is that the tabernacle is the place to make love. Love is pure, perfect, without blemish, and forgiving. No matter what your past may be, be as transparent and vulnerable with your spouse as you would with God because they are representatives of God in the flesh. Loving and living honestly and in righteousness creates heaven on earth, a place for God/Love to reside.

Priests are not only responsible for keeping the brazen altar; they're also responsible for the altar of incense. However, before they entered the sanctuary, they had to wash their hands and feet of dirt. They did so at the laver of washing. For us, the laver of washing is in the Word. It's not enough to just forgive but we must cleanse ourselves of unrighteousness. This is in reference to how we live and treat others. Self-reflection and introspection on a constant daily basis ACCORDING TO THE WORD (not your own righteousness) makes you worthy of the priesthood. It also keeps peace in the sanctuary.

Husbands are the priest of their home and body which is his wife. He cleanses his wife with the washing of the Word to present her to *himself* as a glorious Church! Remember, man was created in God's image and likeness. The Church is the bride of Christ and God is going to present the Church to *Himself* without spot or wrinkle. Your marriage should mimic the same process. That's why it matters what you say to your wife and how you treat her. Everything you do to and for her, you are doing to yourself.

The spouse that loves, forgives, sacrifices their pride to be honest, true and righteous, that will humble themselves before their spouse, is worshipping God daily in the temple. That is the procedure for the altar of incense. Every day, you must confess and purge your sins before the Lord and your spouse. Every day, you must wash with the water of the Word over you and your spouse. Doing so is a sweet-smelling savor to God and to your marriage. This is the secret, if you will, behind a special romantic bond because doing these things leads you to the Holy of Holies, the presence of God.

Past the veil of the Holy place is The Holy of Holies which contains the Ark of the Covenant (the presence of God). Within the inner most part of you and your marriage is the Ark of the Covenant. The covenant is the agreement you have with God to live according to His will and that He will be your God. This is so important because the idea of God being Lord over your marriage somehow gets lost in translation. It's lost in part because no one is managing and serving in the tabernacle. No one wants to endure the process of keeping the fire and incense burning; no one wants to cleanse him or herself. As a result, we never reach the innermost part of God, which translates to us as real love and intimacy.

Furthermore, it is important to note that only the High Priest is allowed in the Holy of Holies. Whenever someone entered the Holy of Holies unauthorized, they were struck dead. If a priest approached the presence of God without cleansing himself, he too would die. Today, as a priest/spouse, you must not allow people into your sacred Holy of Holies. Don't share the innermost parts of you marriage with people. Don't approach your spouse if you are unclean. Illegal access causes death/separation.

Keeping yourself clean, righteous, and holy qualifies you for a relationship with God. When you enter His presence, your prayers will not be hindered. It is through prayer that your marriage with thrive and survive. The enemy cannot stop you from praying but he will try to distract you so that you won't want to pray for your spouse or pray at all. And if he cannot distract you, he will attempt to make you disqualify yourself through connection with sin. This is why it is your responsibility to keep the fire burning for the Lord in love, truth, and righteousness.

The Priesthood

The priesthood is more than just you and your spouse maintaining the tabernacle. It encompasses your entire nation, your family, and all that you are connected to (work, church, etc.). The more you become like God, the more you will produce and the more opposition you will encounter. Opposition comes because the enemy wants to kill your seed because it is Holy. Your children are destined to continue the lineage of the Royal priesthood.

In order to reproduce godly offspring (which is the purpose of marriage), you must first be godly. Your marriage is not just about you and the love of your life making cute little babies that look like you. This is serious business! If you and God are one, the family that you produce will be like you, which in actuality should look like *Him*. The business is reproducing offspring with the characteristics of Christ. Likewise, if you're not one with God, you are one with the enemy by default and will reproduce that seed (i.e. generational curses). Either way, whatever you birth will eventually grow, marry, and reproduce a family in your likeness as well. God's intention is for us to continue to produce godly offspring, thus creating a Holy Nation.

Marriage is ministry. You may be saying to yourself right now, I don't want to hear this entire spiritual stuff; I just want my marriage to work. If you're saying that to yourself, it means you don't fully understand and believe the power of the Word, love and covenant. You're focused on self, how you feel, how hurt or disappointed you are or how *satisfied you are*. If that mindset continues unchecked, it could be the demise of your marriage because love without purpose is not love, *it's like a lot*.

PURPOSE PRINCIPLE

Love without purpose is not REAL Love.

Priest/Overseer/Head

> Titus 1:1-7
>
> *This is a faithful saying: If a man desires the position of a bishop, he desires a good work. A bishop then must be blameless, the husband of one wife, temperate, sober-minded, of good behavior, hospitable, able to teach; not given to wine, not violent, not greedy for money, but gentle, not quarrelsome, not covetous; one who rules his own house well, having his children in submission with all reverence (for if a man does not know how to rule his own house, how will he take care of the church of God?); not a novice, lest being puffed up with pride he fall into the same condemnation as the devil. Moreover he must have a good testimony among those who are outside, lest he fall into reproach and the snare of the devil.*

There is a standard and lifestyle God requires of all priests. The way that he instructs us to go is the way of righteousness. Its not about laws and restrictions but more so about doing what you know in your heart to be the right thing. The Bible tells us that the law is written on our hearts and that Jesus has fulfilled the law. What that means to you is that *the way* both priest are to go is according to God's Word and instruction.

No longer do priest wear robes and ephods, etc.. but we are to be clothed in righteousness. Husbands who lead the family in righteousness not only direct his family the way God wants them to go, he also sets the order for generations to come.

Your lifestyle of righteousness teaches your children what is right. It also perfects your marriage. If both husband and wife are clothed in righteousness, God will always be there. He *ALWAYS* delivers the righteous! Another way to say it, love will always abound in your relationship.

> Isaiah 61:10
>
> *I will greatly rejoice in the Lord, my soul shall be joyful in my God; for he hath clothed me with the garments of salvation, he hath covered me with the robe of righteousness, as a bridegroom decketh himself with ornaments and as a bride adorneth herself with jewels.*

> Psalm 34:15
>
> *The eyes of the Lord are upon the righteous and his ears are open unto their cry.*

> Romans 13:14
>
> *But put ye on the Lord Jesus Christ and make not provision for the flesh to fulfill the lusts thereof.*

Righteousness is something you put on and should never take off. It is your priestly garment. Doing what's right is a choice, one you must make daily. Your righteousness is what sets you apart from the world and will make your household/nation great.

The priest in your husband should have the character of the Christ but he may not have come into the fullness of his being yet. Needless to say, as a priest, he's one of God's anointed. That means he's endued with power and is selected for the assignment at hand on behalf of the Lord. Therefore, God commands us not to oppress them, *(touch not my anointed ones and do my prophets no harm)*. In other words, there should be a reverential care and approach in the way His anointed ones are handled or there will be consequences.

Some of the consequences for violating God's way in this regards can be a detachment of the husband from the wife. He can lose his motivation and attraction to his wife. Another could be that the wife opens the door to the destroyer through disobedience. That could be a financial destroyer, health problems, spiritual setback, and seducing spirits, which could lead to divorce. Disobedience/Sin/death=separation.

> 1 Chronicles 16:22
>
> *He permitted no man to oppress them, And He reproved kings for their sakes, saying,* <u>*"Do not touch My anointed ones, And do My prophets no harm."*</u>

> Genesis 20:7
>
> *"Now therefore, restore the man's wife, for he is a prophet, and he will pray for you and you will live. But if you do not restore her, know that you shall surely die, you and all who are yours."*

> ### Hebrews 6:16
> *For men verily swear by the greater: and an oath for confirmation is to them an end of all strife. Wherein God, willing more abundantly to shew unto the heirs of promise the immutability of his counsel, confirmed it by an oath: That by two immutable things, in which it was impossible for God to lie, we might have a strong consolation, who have fled for refuge to lay hold upon the hope set before us: Which hope we have as an anchor of the soul, both sure and steadfast, and which entereth into that within the veil; Whither the forerunner is for us entered, even Jesus, made an high priest for ever after the order of Melchisedec.*

What is the anointing?

It is empowerment from God that allows you to do an assignment with supernatural ease.

CHAPTER 7

The Blueprint Order

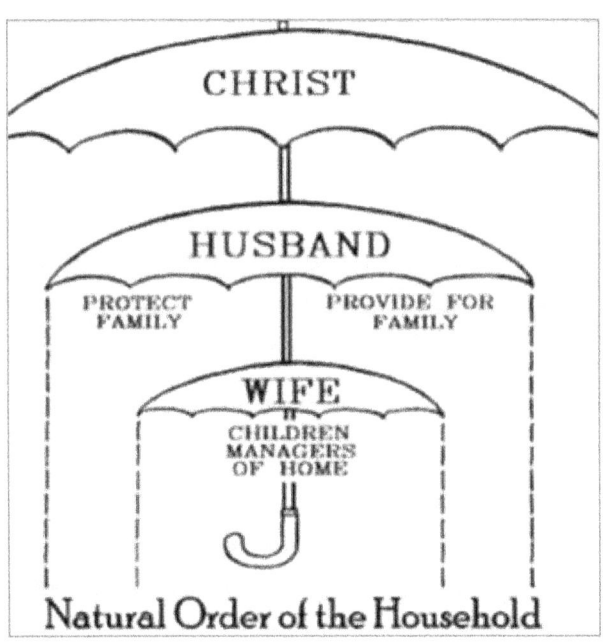

ORDER

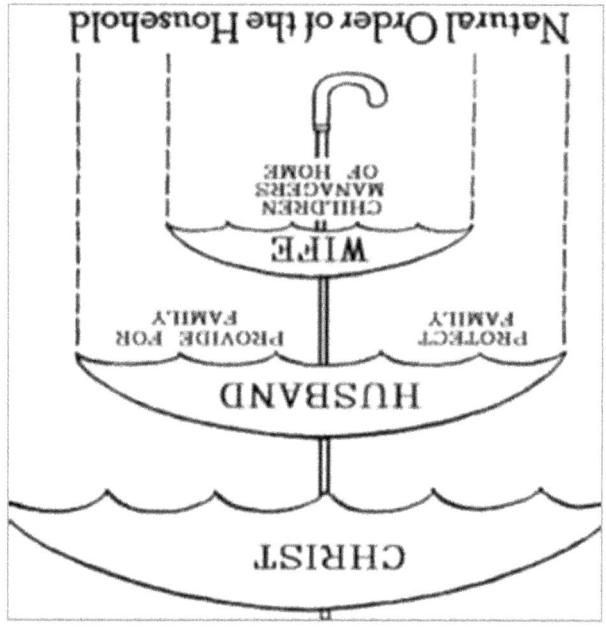

OUT OF ORDER

ESSENTIALLY, FOR ANY organization to work properly there must be order. God has established the institution of marriage, where Jesus is the Head of the husband, the husband is the head of the wife and together they raise the family and establish a nation.

> Ephesians 5:3
> *For the husband is the head of the wife, as Christ also is the head of the church, He Himself being the Savior of the body.*

As mentioned in the previous chapter, Jesus is our example on what a marriage and husband should look like as well as the purpose. We see here in Ephesians 5:3, just as Jesus was the Savior of the Church, likewise *the husband* is the savior of the *body*. The body encompasses not only the wife but the children as well. The magnitude of the responsibilities for each spouse is incredible and surprisingly seldom noticed or respected by the other.

The role of the husband is a divinely strategic position. Maintaining this order is critical to maintaining the flow of the anointing of God and prosperity on your marriage. If you take a look at the above illustration, you see the umbrellas' covering hovers in a downward direction so that the water can flow while you remain dry. There is no collection of stagnant water but a continuous flow of protection. That's what happens when things are in order.

The husband's umbrella is larger than the wife's because he's uniquely designed and ordained to cover her. It's not bigger because he's better rather he was created to manage more than himself. That includes wife, kids, work, church, everything.

Notice also that the Bible refers to the husband as the head. The head contains the brain, eyes, nose, mouth, and ears. As a prophet of the Lord, he is eyes, mouthpiece, as well as intercessor. He is Priest, King and Prophet. Yes, he may not look, sound or move like it right now, but he is. That means he can speak and decree a thing and it shall be done. He can name a thing and it will be what he has decreed.

This is powerful information. Much of what is going on in your marriage/family has to do with what the man has or hasn't said and the authority he is or is not walking in. As much as women like to talk and rationalize everything, women do not have the same vision or *spiritual authority* as men. Unfortunately, when a woman cannot see the vision, she is prone to undermine her husband with *her* logic.

Thus, as to the order expressed in the scriptures, the wives are to submit unto their own husbands as unto the Lord. Wow! Who can argue with God? Who can tell God no and it still goes well with them? Well, you have it right here, no matter if your husband is smart, dumb, rich, poor, sick, you name it, God *still* instructs us to submit. It's not the type of submission you do to just shut someone up but the submission you give God with reverential fear.

As believers, not only are our marriages and families under a patriarchal order, it is also under a Theocracy not a Democracy. Americans enjoy the liberties and the backlash of a democracy. We vote people in and out of office. People have freedom of speech and can debate just about any issue they choose whether male or female—not so in Theocracy.

Theocracy Defined:

A system of government in which ***priests rule in the name of God*** or a god.

Democracy Defined:

Control of an organization or group by the majority of its members.

The husband is the priest that rules in the name of God in your home. He also functions as a prophet being a messenger of God. The Bible says: *touch not my anointed and do my prophet no harm.*

Disturbing the divine order is one of the major causes of divorce today. Wives often usurp the authority of the husband and the household, dominating with control and manipulation. When the wife does so, it's like the illustration above where the marriage is out of order. The umbrella is no longer covering the family. Everyone gets wet, as the water collects and builds up inside the umbrella, and then spills and overflows.

We all know I'm not talking about water. In your marriage, when you silence the head, resentment, discontent, anger and hostility builds up. Even if the wife appears effective at getting what she wants, it's ultimately an illusion because she shut the mouth of God and removed the covering over her home. The negative price for that is astounding!

> **1 Peter 3:7**
>
> *Likewise, ye husbands, dwell with them according to knowledge, giving honour unto the wife, as unto the weaker vessel, and as being heirs together of the grace of life; that your prayers be not hindered.*

We perish for lack of knowledge. Wives that would like to effectively support and submit to a husband they don't believe in have to rely on God by faith. God never told wives to trust their husbands.

The Word says, "It's better to trust God than in man." Remember, the husband is the head of the wife but God is the Head of the husband! Submission and prayer is your defense and protection from a husband that is out of order.

What if your wife is out of order? Well, there are a few interesting things that I have found regarding this situation. For one, it is interesting to note that nowhere in the Bible will you find a woman putting away a husband. However, you do see the husband put away the wife. It's about reproduction and expansion. The husband deposits the godly seed but the wife is the vessel. The vessel can be changed but the seed cannot.

You see God is concerned with His divine order because the entire kingdom is watching and at stake.

A great example is found in Esther with Queen Vashti:

> **Esther 1:15**
>
> *What shall we do unto the queen Vashti according to law, because she hath not performed the commandment of the king Ahasuerus by the chamberlains? And Memucan answered before the king and the princes, Vashti the queen hath not done wrong to the king only, but also to all the princes, and to all the people that are in all the provinces of the king Ahasuerus. For this deed of the queen shall come abroad unto all women, so that they shall despise their husbands in their eyes, when it shall be reported, The king Ahasuerus commanded Vashti the queen to be brought in before him, but she came not. Likewise shall the ladies of Persia and Media say this day unto all the king's princes, which have heard of the deed of the queen. Thus shall there arise too much contempt and wrath.*

The king's advisers basically said, that Vashti's disrespect to the king's command would be contagious and harmful throughout the *entire kingdom*. It's better to get rid of her than to destroy the order. But before you use this as an excuse to justify leaving your wife, hold on! Consider a few things, the Bible instructs the husband to dwell with his wife according to knowledge and treat her as the weaker vessel. You also have to be doing what you are supposed to do as king, priest, and prophet; otherwise, God will not hear you! You can fool some people but you cannot fool or manipulate God. Getting things in order begins with the head. You don't have to put your wife away. All you have to do is what you are supposed to do as a husband and if she doesn't come in alignment with your leadership, she may eventually leave.

The outline of the tabernacle of Moses also provides insight on the order of things.

CHAPTER 7 | THE BLUEPRINT ORDER

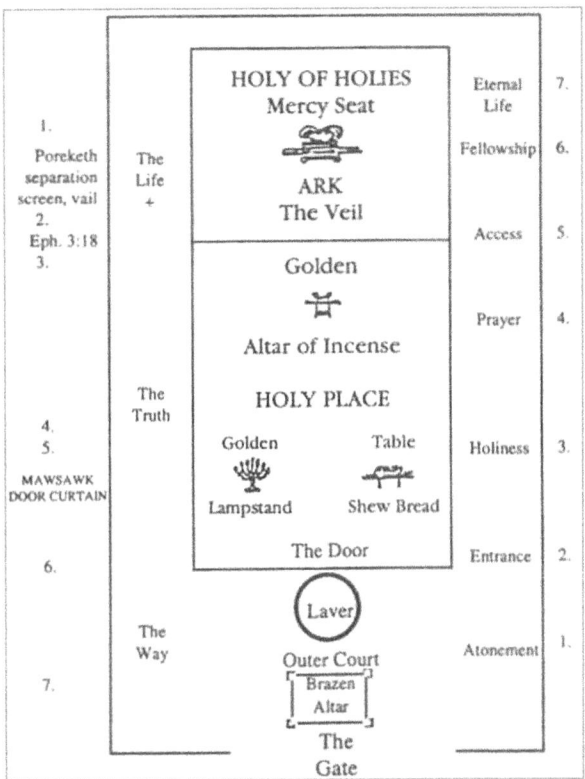

The Divine Order:

Holy Place & Holy of Holies

- You, God and your spouse

The outer court:
- Issues
- Work
- Children
- Church
- Family
- Enemies

- Friends
- Society
- Government

Above is the floor plan of the tabernacle of Moses. This diagram is really an illustration of your spiritual body, who you are. The largest box and the space within is the outer court. For us, that represents our bodies/flesh, the external part of us. It's also the area of our lives (in relation to marriage), where everyone outside of your spouse should go. The people I'm referring to are children, in-laws, church folks, friends and work relationship.

The Holy Place is where your soul resides. The Holy of Holies is where the Ark of the Covenant is. When you get married, the two of you become one; meaning, the veil separating the Holy Place and the Holy of Holies is torn down. It is now all one. This area is to be accessed only by the High Priest. NO ONE ELSE EVER!

Who is the High Priest? You, your spouse, and Jesus! All three of you have become one and are the only ones that are supposed to access this sacred part of you. You are not your flesh; you are a spirit. It's in the Holy Place and Holy of Holies where you find whom you really are. This order is interrupted with tragedy when this law is violated by allowing someone outside of your spouse gain access to this part of you.

Your body is the Ark of the Covenant. Inside of you resides the covenant agreement between you and the Holy Spirit. In Him, we live and have our *being*. God is still talking about order. The actual Ark of the Covenant from the Old Testament contains the following:

- Aaron's staff that budded
- The ten commandments
- Manna

Aaron's staff represents the royal priesthood. Aaron was chosen to be the High Priest, so was your husband through Jesus (our High

Priest). The Bible is revealing to us the order within, along with instructions of who has the POWER AND AUTHORITY to be on the inside.

The Ten Commandments, also found in the ark, represent your covenant agreement. In essence, the Word of God, which is His commandments, is your core value system on how to live. For the children of Israel, this was the Mosaic Law. Today, the Bible tells us that the law is *WRITTEN ON OUR HEARTS* and *love fulfills the law*. In other words, your spirit tells you what's right and what's wrong even if you cannot explain it, see it or understand why, that law on your heart should govern you. You know the difference from right or wrong and you don't need a warden to tell you what's right, you already know it/feel it in your spirit.

For example, a spouse is at work when a co-worker starts flirting with them. If the spouse starts flirting back because no one is around, that is a problem. You can lie to your spouse and people because your tactics were covert and no one was around, but God and your spirit knows that the conversation had was inappropriate and your spouse would be offended.

The wife could be wearing a dress that is way too revealing and past age appropriateness. No one has to tell her the dress is too short and tight, her spirit tells her by making her feel uncomfortable. Although she could actually fit the dress, SHE KNOWS it's not right!

Manna, the final item located inside the Ark of the Covenant represents provision from heaven. It is God's reminder of who your source is. In your marriage and life in general, it is paramount that you never forget that God is in covenant agreement with you to be your source and provider. When the children of Israel were in the wilderness, they didn't know what to do for food. God knew their situation and made provisions. The translation for the word Manna is "what is it?" When you find your marriage in a wilderness and you cry out for help, His provision/answer may appear as manna (what is it?). The provision may be unorthodox but God reminds us that He will provide no matter what; and the provision is always inside of you through the declaration of His Word and Holy Spirit.

> ### Proverbs 5
> *Drink waters out of thine own cistern, and running waters out of thine own well. Let thy fountains be dispersed abroad, and rivers of waters in the streets. Let them be only thine own, and not strangers' with thee. Let thy fountain be blessed: and rejoice with the wife of thy youth.*

PURPOSE PRINCIPLE

Nothing works right when it's out of order.

CHAPTER 8

Establishing Your Home

The Foundation

WHAT IS YOUR house built on? Not just your literal house, rather what are the core principles that keep your marriage stable? Foundational support is vital because it is the anchor that holds your house together as you grow and expand throughout the years. Early placement and fortification of a sound base will ensure that your home will be able to withstand just about anything.

> Luke 14:28
>
> *For which of you, intending to build a tower, sitteth not down first, and counteth the cost, whether he have sufficient to finish it?*

Before you build anything, you must count the cost. Assess what you need and make a plan of execution. What does your home need?

Write down your needs, pray, then write the vision. God will give you the wisdom on what to do if you have the faith to follow. Writing the vision is the first step in the planning before the foundation is laid.

Foundations are intended to be permanent. Whatever you lay down in the beginning for what the standard of living will be in your family will be established. Don't rush the process but allow God to govern the way you do it.

In order for your marriage and family to withstand the twist, turns, and challenges of life, the Word of God has to be your foundation. The Word is where you go for your bottom line in the way you should go and how you should be.

Our roles are clearly defined but often ignored because the flesh tries to put the spirit under subjection instead of the other way around. Our flesh represents our feelings, emotions and senses which all are subject to change. You will notice that at the core of most disagreements, fights, and confusion, emotions/feelings (the flesh) is the most prominent. The Word of God will challenge your flesh by instructing us to resist it by yielding to the power of God.

Build according to pattern

> Exodus 5
>
> *According to all that I shew thee, after the pattern of the tabernacle, and the pattern of all the instruments thereof, even so shall ye make it.*

Many people were not raised in Christian homes, didn't have a father present, and there was no structure, order or discipline. Although, as an adult, you may now understand how important these things are, you may not know how to build a solid home and foundation. There may be some people who've had those things and still don't know how to do it. No worries, the Bible tells us to simply build according to pattern. Christ has set the pattern for us through His words. He also uses people as an example.

Observe and consult with seasoned Christian married couples whose life reflects the application of the Word. Do things the way God says to do it, period! You will find, if you really pay attention, just about every problem you've created for yourself occurred when you disobeyed God's word (consciously or unconsciously).

Unity: A house divided cannot stand

> Luke 11:17-23
>
> *But he, knowing their thoughts, said unto them, Every kingdom divided against itself is brought to desolation; and a house divided against a house falleth. If Satan also be divided against himself, how shall his kingdom stand? because ye say that I cast out devils through Beelzebub. And if I by Beelzebub cast out devils, by whom do your sons cast them out? therefore shall they be your judges. But if I with the finger of God cast out devils, no doubt the kingdom of God is come upon you. When a strong man armed keepeth his palace, his goods are in peace: But when a stronger than he shall come upon him, and overcome him, he taketh from him all his armour wherein he trusted, and divideth his spoils. He that is not with me is against me: and he that gathereth not with me scattereth.*

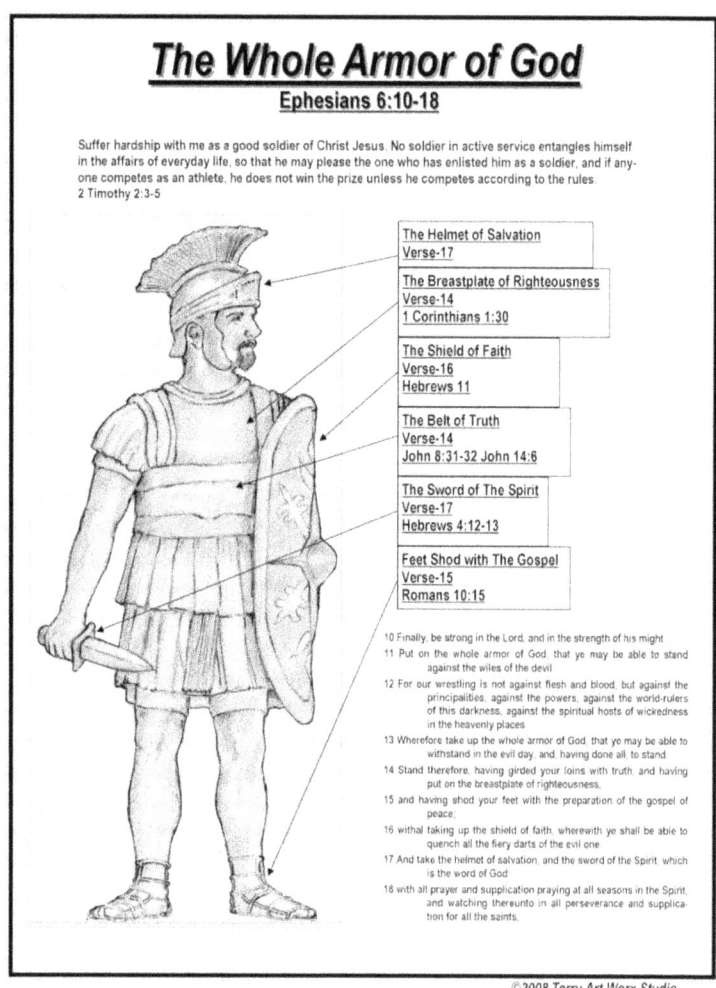

The hardest thing in some marriages is for people to let go of the single mentality. The idea of being an adult and have to answer to another, submit to them, or consider them at all can be a problem for some people.

It is imperative as you embark on the task of creating or recreating the foundation of your marriage and home that you are one with your spouse now and forever. It is so important that you settle this in your spirit because the enemy will always have a foothold in your marriage through your division. Consider the self-centered mindset as a crack in the foundation.

Unity, agreement in the Word of God and His way of doing things will be the most solid foundation your marriage can have. You need to be one as a couple and with God in order to fulfill your purpose because you are naturally and spiritually stronger together. Division in marriage is a situation whereby two people are going in different directions. There is only one way to go and that is the way of righteousness led by the husband.

It is imperative that the husband becomes strong in faith and the Word because he is the head and the savior/protector of the wife. The husband is the one to establish how the foundation is to be laid and the wife must become one with those decisions.

The enemy will always attack the husband first, directly or indirectly through his wife, job, finances, and family. He's the strongman of the house, so in order for the enemy to take over your house, he must bind up the strongman first.

That's why in Luke 11:24, the scripture says that the strongman that keepeth his palace, goods and peace is armed. In other words, you must guard your home, wife, goods and your peace! You must protect it before, during, and after you lay the foundation. Stay armed with the Word by putting on the whole armor of God.

Husbands, your spiritual foundation must be sure. Solid enough to endure major pressures like financial changes, health crisis, even death of a loved one. You do not possess the strength to endure life without God. He must be your rock, strength, and refuge. Remember, everyone is watching you because you are the leader.

Your wife is looking up to you to know what her assignment is because she is there to help you.

The enemy loves to attack finances and jobs because he knows that most men find their identity through their work. It's one of the easiest causes of division because for women, we need a sense of security and stability. Loss of income is often a direct attack of the enemy on the home front. However, sometimes, God uses apparent loss to get your attention and redirect you to where you and your spouse should be. Perhaps he doesn't want you working a job. Maybe he has a business in mind for you. Or maybe he is ready for you to go into full time ministry. Not all disappointments are losses. If you understand God is your source, you will have the faith to lean with the curves of life. Your spouse is not your enemy. Don't fight your wife because you are not where you want to be. Frustration or peace will come from whatever you decide, and the choice is yours…choose wisely. You are the king of your home.

> **Esther 1:22**
>
> *For he sent letters into all the king's provinces, into every province according to the writing thereof, and to every people after their language, that every man should bear rule in his own house, and that it should be published according to the language of every people.*

The wife, on the other hand, should support him with agreement. Stay on task by helping him naturally and spiritually when it comes to the direction, leadership, and vision for your home. Make sure you do all that the Word of God instructs wives to do regardless of how you feel. You don't stay one—in unity—through control and manipulation, you stay unified through love, prayer and obedience. Your husband covers you in the natural and the spiritual, and you must do the same. If the enemy binds up your husband, he is going to try to take over your entire house.

Clean & Organize (everything, the house, children, finances, hierarchy)

When things are clean and organized, there is a flow. Once everything is in its rightful place, your senses work in tandem with your spirit. If you have dirty windows, subconsciously it clouds your vision. Unbeknownst to you, you've gotten so used to the windows not being clean (even though you can still see through it), it's hard to see the negative impact it has had on your perception of what you're looking at and life overall. That is, until you finally clean it! Instantly, things feel brighter, lighter, and more optimistic.

A dirty house and clutter *does* affect your mood. When your children are out of order and are not disciplined or corrected and they continue day to day in that habit, it's the same effect as having dirty windows. Poverty, lack, hatred, dissention, contention, abuse is the manifestation of a dirty spiritual and literal house. It upsets the flow of blessings because you're not seeing things clearly.

When the man doesn't take his rightful place as the head of the house, it completely disturbs the equilibrium of the home because deep inside each one of us, consciously or unconsciously, we know when things are not right. A man that doesn't lead his home will set off a ripple effect of disrespect which ultimately kills everybody's spirit. Conversely, when the wife takes the role as the head of the house through manipulation, control or however she does so, no matter how subtle it may be, it disturbs the flow of blessings as well. As we discussed in the Order Chapter, God honors position.

Other times, you may have outside influence governing the inside of your home. It could be family, friends, and even clergy. This is out of order because the husband is the head, priest, and prophet of the home. The wife helps and meets with her husband and he has the final say.

Organize your home where everything can be reached and dealt with. It doesn't matter how much debt you have, in order to figure out how to get out of, first know how much debt exists. In order to continue to grow your money, you must manage it by knowing where every dollar is going and why it is going there. When you both can see those things and address each thing, you can overcome it and build your financial base. Remember, when things are visibly clear, you can instantly become more optimistic.

Note: finances are a major cause of divorce today. Please understand that when you are committed to the covenant, God gives you the wisdom and resources to do all that you need to do. Sometimes, He allows us to face certain challenges not to destroy us; rather, He uses the tool of discomfort and pain to draw you and your spouse closer to each other and to Him. He also uses this type of situation to purge things; wrong ideals, habits and people that don't belong in your life.

Clean up

Cleanliness is next to godliness. Believe it or not, a filthy house provokes an atmosphere of hostility, depression, confusion, discord, debauchery, and perversion. It doesn't matter if you have a mansion or a tiny one-room flat, you must keep it clean. Filth, on the onset may not appear to be a problem for you if you're used to being in it. However, it IS affecting your mood, outlook and atmosphere, and attitude, unconsciously.

Psychologists say that your environment is a reflection of what's going on inside of you. If your house is full of clutter and filth, examine yourself. Think about it, if you were healthy inside, you wouldn't want to come home every day to find dirty dishes that have been sitting there for days, unmade beds, dirty laundry, dirty car, etc. How can you facilitate romance and love in your home with your spouse like that? What about your children? If you are filthy, you're sending out a message that you don't care, which makes your spouse and children not care, too.

An unclean house also attracts unclean people. Only people who have the same spirit will be okay in that environment. In other words, uncleanliness in your home affects every relationship you have or could have had. Are you missing out on great friendships because you are ashamed of your home?

Dirt, filth, clutter comes from an unclean spirit. As you're laying the foundation of your home, you must clean it, physically and spiritually. The first step is to come into agreement with your spouse and with the Word of God and cast out every unclean, evil, wicked spirit out of the house you live in and out of your body. Prayer and fasting in this situation is best because you are claiming territory where there may be strong opposition. If possible, have your pastor and prayer warriors come over and pray over you and with you.

After you have dealt with spiritual things, then go onto the natural. Clean your house completely. Develop a system to maintain cleanliness. You may have to create a budget for a housekeeper to come every so often if you don't have the time. How you start laying your foundation will be how you finish. If you make cleanliness a priority, it will become part of your foundation and culture. The enemy hides and lurks in dirty, dark places.

Spiritual cleansing also includes removing any pagan/worldly ideologies, philosophies, artifacts and images. Go through all of your music, DVD's, etc., and if any of them is not good, clean material, get rid of it!

It's important to watch what you feed your spirit and atmosphere. Actually listen to the lyrics in the songs of your favorite artist. If what they are saying goes against the Word of God, His will and His way, get rid of it. It is through unconscious repetition of words that demonic influences are imparted.

Scary movies can also release demonic forces into your home unaware. Pay attention to what you and your children watch. The enemy is constantly subtly planting demonic ideas and imagery to seduce families into sin.

I've noticed in many childrens programs that the order of the home is completely distorted. Children on many of these shows are disrespectful to their parents, talking back to them, being disobedient. Some of these programs have it where the father looks and sounds like an idiot that doesn't know what to do, the wife is fearful and incompetent and they both end up consulting with the child who somehow has all the answers. Then parents wonder where their sweet innocent child learned such disrespectful behavior. Unbeknownst to you, on a daily bases, these children's programs are teaching your children how to be out of order.

Beware of video games as well, as they can be hypnotic and very demonic. For hours, a person can sit there having gaming fun with images of people, places and things. Then when it's over, their attitude becomes more aggressive or short. Why? Because they have been demonically influenced.

Your eyes and ears are gateways. It's imperative that you monitor what comes and goes into your home and as a couple. If you don't agree with this kind of purging, ask yourself, why do you think you need what you're holding onto?

Resistance to letting go of an unrighteous thing suggests a stronghold of some kind. If you find you and your spouse are at a standstill as far as letting something go, don't fight over it. Fight *for* each other in the Spirit through prayer.

Once your home is spiritually and naturally clean, keep it clean. Here's why:

> Luke 11:24-26
>
> *When the unclean spirit is gone out of a man, he walketh through dry places, seeking rest; and finding none, he saith, I will return unto my house whence I came out. And when he cometh, he findeth it swept and garnished. Then goeth he, and taketh to him seven other spirits more wicked than himself; and they enter in, and dwell there: and the last state of that man is worse than the first.*

Pray

> Jeremiah 1:12
>
> *Then said the LORD unto me, Thou hast well seen: for I will hasten my word to perform it.*

Since God is in you, when you pray and speak the word, God HASTENS to perform it! The caveat is we're not just talking about one person, we are talking about 2 people who have become one with God. Now your impact in prayer has increased significantly!

> Matthew 18:19
>
> *Again I say unto you, That if two of you shall agree on earth as touching anything that they shall ask, it shall be done for them of my Father which is in heaven. For where two or three are gathered together in my name, there am I in the midst of them.*

Agreement in prayer can help you overcome the various challenges you will face in your marriage and family. Building a house and home will inevitably have surprise twist and turns that you may not be prepared for at one time or another. However, through the power of prayer, you're not alone. You are enlisting the help of the Lord and all of His resources. Even if He doesn't change your situation, He can change how you feel about it. Matter of fact, some things can ONLY be dealt with through prayer!

> Mark 9:28, 29
> *And when he was come into the house, his disciples asked him privately, Why could not we cast him out? And he said unto them, This kind can come forth by nothing, but by prayer and fasting.*

Tithe

When you talk about order, there is always something that goes first. Within your family order, the husband comes first. However, God comes before the husband. Therefore, when prioritizing and organizing your life, Gods word, will and way should always come first. It doesn't benefit you and your family much to have everything in order and still live under a curse. Tithing, is where you give God 10 percent of your income first. Some may think that tithing is all about money. Howbeit, it is one of the many ways that God teaches us discipline and order. Giving God His portion *first*, signifies that he is Lord over you, your family, home, property, endeavors and finances.

As long as people continue to look at marriage in the natural sense, they will miss the mark and will be terribly confused when certain problems arise. Disobedience regarding the tithe opens spiritual doors that bring about a curse in the home. Since you and your spouse are one, you should be on one accord spiritually. If not, you can cast out the strongman and your spouse will invite them right back in. In other words, you cannot have one person tithing and the other not. Just as you need insurance for your tangible house, you need insurance for your spiritual house.

I believe people have a problem with tithing because they don't understand why they have to give 10 percent of their hard-earned money to their local church. It's hard (especially for men) to understand why they should hand over 10 percent to some pastor who is driving luxury cars and living in luxury houses, while he's struggling to keep a roof over his head?! "God doesn't need my money," I've heard plenty of people say that. I get it. However, please allow me to share with you why it's so important that you tithe.

Remember, I mentioned earlier that there are laws between dimensions. God is a Spirit so He gives spiritual things (i.e., blessings, health, wealth, etc.). On earth, when Adam sinned, God did not curse Adam, He cursed *the ground* because of Adam's sin.

> Genesis 3:17
> *Then to Adam He said, "Because you have listened to the voice of your wife, and have eaten from the tree about which I commanded you, saying, 'You shall not eat from it'; Cursed is the ground because of you; In toil you will eat of it All the days of your life.*

As long as you operate in the world system, you're working from a cursed ground. You will toil and work hard just to eat of it. In order for your production not to be cursed, you need to tithe. When you give God 10 percent of your income first, you are making a spiritual exchange. The reason why you give Him first is so that everything will be blessed henceforth. God blesses and multiplies what you have. Tithing activates your financial faith. Faith is the *substance* of things hoped for. You need money so you must sow money by faith. God doesn't just bless your money when you tithe. You release the blessings mentioned in Malachi 3 and Deuteronomy 28 for those who obey Him.

> ### Malachi 3
> *Bring ye all the tithes into the storehouse, that there may be meat in mine house, and prove me now herewith, saith the LORD of hosts, if I will not open you the windows of heaven, and pour you out a blessing, that [there shall] not [be room] enough [to receive it]. And I will rebuke the devourer for your sakes, and he shall not destroy the fruits of your ground; neither shall your vine cast her fruit before the time in the field, saith the LORD of hosts. And all nations shall call you blessed: for ye shall be a delightsome land, saith the LORD of hosts.*

Your marriage cannot survive without the help of the Lord! Malachi 3 is the only chapter in the Bible where God tells us to prove Him! He's saying if you do this, He will do what He said He will do. There are some awesome benefits here. For one, God says *He will* rebuke the devourer for your sakes. Have you ever felt like even when you have a lot of money, somehow it dwindles so fast, and you can't seem to figure out where it went? Or if you didn't pay your tithes because you felt you couldn't afford to, then your car broke down? That's because you are operating under a curse. But when you tithe, you may have a little bit of money but it goes a long way. You may find a ridiculous sale or people just start giving you stuff. Sometimes, He will simply extend the life of the things you already have. The concept of tithing ultimately is not about the money, it's about your relationship with God and His culture. It's the kingdom way of doing business.

Malachi also mentions how your vine shall not cast her fruit before the time. God is going to make sure that your production has perfect timing! The scripture also says that the enemy cannot destroy the fruit of your ground. How this all possible if the ground is cursed?

Because when you tithe, you no longer are using the world's currency, you're using spiritual currency. Money is just a piece of paper or coin but the currency is spiritual (perceived value).

Initially, what I'm saying may seem way off because most ideas of marriage is about how you *feel*. What does all this spiritual stuff have to do with anything? When you really think about it, everything is spiritual, lived out in a body. Therefore, as you're building your home, family and finances, understanding spiritual principles and concepts from the Word of God is a sure foundation. There may be times that you might not have enough money to survive or to take care of your family and you'll have to do something. God will show you what to do instead of you aborting your family and purpose. On the other extreme, you may have billions but you're dealing with the devourer in other areas of your life. There are some things money can't buy.

- Give thanks (be grateful).
- Count the cost.
- Come out from your relatives and go where God tells you (Abraham/Father/Husband).
- Build according to pattern.
- Wisdom builds a house.
- Houses come from the father.
- Whoever does what the Word says builds a sure foundation on a rock.
- A foolish woman plucks down her house with her own hands.

CHAPTER 9

Your Seed

> Genesis 3:15
>
> *And I will put enmity between thee and the woman and between thy seed and her seed; it shall bruise thy head and though shalt bruise his heel.*

> Genesis 22:18
>
> *And IN thy seed shall all the nations of the earth be blessed; because thou hast obeyed my voice.*

GOD IS VERY specific with His intentions regarding marriage. His desire is to produce godly offspring so that He can have one big happy family here on earth. Herein lies one of the most important assignments of your life. Your children are the birth of a nation—not just any nation, but a Holy Nation…the express image of Jesus Christ in the flesh.

Satan's worst fear is for your seed to multiply and increase because your children will possess the power and authority to dismantle the world system (his system of rebellion). It's not enough for you as an adult alone to be fruitful, multiply and subdue. More so, your children were also created to continue to crush the enemy by taking dominion and putting the enemy under their feet long after you're gone and so on and so on. If the enemy could kill your seed, he would stop production.

Therefore, your children must be instructed and taught the way of righteousness. Eventually, they will grow and expand the kingdom, passing on His legacy to their children. When I speak of offspring, I'm referring to natural or spiritual children. Along with land and domain, children are considered territory God assigned to you. You and your spouse are adults, stronger, wiser, and more mature (obviously), so you must be aware that the enemy may choose at times to attack your home/marriage through your children.

Let me segue for a minute. We all understand families do not always come in one seamless package where all of the children are from the same parents. There are blended families with stepchildren or adopted children that require special care and skillful attention. Whichever way you, your marriage makes you one. All of the children are *your children* regardless of the circumstances. Granted, there could be cases where a child may live with the other parent but they are still your children. I'm clarifying here because we must be aware of the trick of the enemy to cause strife and division by using these situations as a means to open the door to generational curses.

Women are notorious for being intercessors for the family. Husbands, as protector and king, should not only join spiritual forces with his wife in intercessory prayer to cover the family, he should initiate it. Between the two of you, the Holy Spirit will give you discernment regarding what's going on with your children and how to deal with whatever situation is at hand. There will be challenges but you're chosen, anointed, and endued with power for the task. That's why God put you two together. The assignment of raising children was not meant to be accomplished by any one person, it is a collective effort. Remember, God has already given you a nation, territory and land but there is an illegal occupant that you must destroy in order to have dominion.

That's what this is all about. God is using marriage to not only formulate a hostile takeover but to restore unto us our birthright. You shouldn't have to struggle so hard. Through prayer, fasting, wisdom, knowledge and understanding, you can prepare your children for the future. Not only that, if you're having problems with them, God can give you discernment as to what is going on, what to do and the power and authority to do it. What we're witnessing is a generation that was raised in broken homes. That's why many of them have no love and empathy, and they are self-destructive and lost. Nobody instructed them about who they are and *the way* they should take, in a safe, loving environment. This is why you must fight for the survival of your marriage and family.

Life & Death are in the power of the tongue

As you may have noticed, the reoccurring theme or message is about the importance of order, God's way of doing things. Man is created in the image and likeness of God. When God created the heavens and the earth, (aside from man whom he formed) God spoke everything into existence. Then the very first job God gave Adam was to name the animals. It was through that assignment, God was teaching man to be like him by decreeing and declaring a thing. Whatever Adam named the animal, it became that.

And out of the ground the Lord God formed every beast of the field, and every fowl of the air and brought them unto Adam to see what he would call them: and *whatsoever Adam called* every living creature, *that was the name thereof.* ~Genesis 2:19

Names and words are used to identify and describe people places and things. When words are spoken and heard, our brains conjure up images and whatever we believe and perceive becomes our reality. That is very powerful! Understanding of the power of naming someone or something and speaking life to it is not only a divine right but an instruction from God. It is part of your purpose. However, when it comes to divine order, it is the father that should be the one who is the one do have the final say and declaration because he is the head.

> Job 22:28
> *Thou shalt decree a thing and it shall be established unto thee: and the light shall shine upon thy ways.*

> Proverbs 18:21
> *Death and life are in the power of the tongue and those who love it will eat its fruit.*

The words that you speak over your children should be so carefully crafted that you may need to pause almost every time you are about to say anything to them. Fathers, it is scientifically proven that the words you speak to your children, contributes to how they think, perceive the world and themselves. If you have an unruly, disrespectful, mischievous children, you cannot speak according to what you see in the natural. You and your wife must stand in agreement in prayer and use discernment. Speak what you want to see in the spirit. Speak the good that you know is within them until it manifests.

When God created the heavens and the earth, He spoke His desire and things started moving. However, that whole creation took time to come to full manifestation. That's the same level of understanding parents you should have. You're in this for the long haul. Seeing your children transform into which you decreed and declared them to be is a process. Give them time and patience.

Fathers, you are not just a husband or a man, you are the king! When the king speaks and declares a thing it is so. That is why what YOU say is so powerful and important! Women tend to be more emotional than men. As a result, when women are in an emotional state, they may speak something over the children they didn't mean but nevertheless, it still has power. However, you as the head, husband, priest, prophet and king, you can overrule and override her words. We saw this concept at work with Jacob and Rachel.

Rachel was about to give birth to her second child and he labor was painful and intense. As a result of *her struggle*, when she gave birth to her son she named him according to how she was *feeling*. But his father, through discernment, came and renamed him. He was not going to allow his wife to decree a curse over his son because of her negative emotional state. He took the authority of the Father, priest, prophet, and king and overruled her decree over their son. That's exactly what God wants husbands and fathers to do today!

> Genesis 35:18
>
> *And it came to pass, as her soul was in departing (for she died) that she called his name Benoni: but his father called him Benjamin.*

NOTE Benoni means son of my sorrows and Benjamin means "son of the right hand". You will notice in the Bible that in most cases when they mentioned someone's name they described what it meant and whose lineage they are connected to.

Your name is your identity, showing you who you are and the family lineage you're connected to. Everyone has this innate desire to be a part of a family. If a family doesn't is broken and disfunctional, you will often see the children drift off and find their clan in the streets in the form of a gang. On a more positive, you can see the youth cling to a sports team have that sense of belonging.

Unfortunately, because children have little to no authority, it is so easy to forget how powerful the need to feel loved, accepted, heard and safe. When you have a parent you can trust to discipline and guide you, a sense of stability develops along with self esteem, with is so important in a child's development. They need more than just discipline, they need to feel valued and accepted. If all you are concerned about is keeping a roof over their head, feeding and clothing them, then chances are, your children feel neglected, which will cause them to rebel and act out, runaway, turn to drugs or seek affection through promiscuity (heterosexually or homosexually). Provisions can also be found in jail. What's the difference? Love and attention is the difference. Knowing your children and what's going on with them is the difference. Sometimes people get so caught up with provisions that they forget to parent. Children love things but nothing can replace relationship.

Children are unsure of who they are because they don't know who they are. Nobody told them. In most cases, they don't even realize that they don't know that they don't know. It is the job of the father, to name them. In other words, the father has to give them the reassurance of their identity and place in this world. They get this information through your actions with self, your spouse, other people and lastly with them directly through conversation and behavior. When you speak life into them, they will receive it faster from you then through the mother. God himself has given you this power and authority!

Wives, if your husband has a problem in this area, pray God give him wisdom. Intercede on behave of your husband and children. But never usurp his authority in front of the children. Even though he may be wrong, if you do so, you're equally guilty because you are out of order and inadvertently promoting further disrespect.

There are some situations you may go through and observe through your children that's contrary to the way that you want them to go or what you believe in. There are generational curses, DNA strains from family lines that you have no idea about working against you. Outside influences from kids in school, music, video games etc., are all out there trying to dictate to your child who they should be and what they should do. Some of these principalities and demons are very strong but they are no match for our God and God is working with and through you! You must speak to the mountain and command it to be removed! Start rebuking the demonic forces that are trying to influence your children!

> Mark 11:23
>
> *For verily I say into you, that whosoever shall say unto this mountain, Be thou removed and be thou cast into the sea; and shall not doubt in his heart but shall believe that those things which he saith shall come to pass; he shall have whatsoever he saith.*

Word of caution; before you speak to your children, examine your heart. If you don't like your child, if you don't believe in them, or have any negative feelings against them, deal with that first. For out of the abundance of the heart the mouth speaks. It is unfortunate, that parents allow themselves to reach a point of frustration that they forget their role as governors. Your children are part of the nation God assigned for you to manage. You cannot allow emotions to govern your children. The main reason you have allowed your children to frustrate you is because you decided to focus on the negative and whatever you focus on will expand.

Instead of focusing on all the things you don't like or are tired of, focus on what you expect to them to be and what you want to see so that would expand. Allow God to change your heart regarding your children. Sometimes, when you have stepchildren or adopted children, there could be a greater disconnect because as a married couple you haven't gone though the bonding that's formed during the pregnancy process. You may also be dealing with traits of DNA that's not the same as yours and it's so different that you have no idea how to handle it and it frustrates you.

It's only through love, truth, prayer and fasting that you can overcome this great challenge. You have to first admit to God that you are frustrated and you're not pleased with your child/children. Begin working on becoming the embodiment of love. It is through that Agape love that you burn through the wall of hatred and anger. Once you get your heart right, your prayers will be authentic, righteous and effective. But you cannot deliver someone you hate and dislike. Remember they are children and no matter how mature they may act or think they are, they don't really know what they don't know.

You're not perfect

Another common issue today stems from both parents working at the same time. Sometimes, as a result of not being able to be as present with your children as you think you should be, parents begin to feel a sense of guilt and will manage their children from that standpoint. You don't have to feel guilty for taking care of your children because you're doing it out of love. One of the greatest lessons you're teaching your children is about accountability, responsibility, love and the fact that nobody and no situation is perfect. Parents will simply do what's best for their children as much as they know how.

Are you doing what you think is best for them or are you pacifying them out of guilt? If you're raising your kids according to guilt, you're doing them a great disservice. Teach them in the way of the Lord. That is to obey your parents. If they are wrong, the parent is to discipline them with the rod of correction.

For the record, when I say rod, that doesn't necessarily mean corporal punishment. It means stern correction or punishment. Every situation doesn't require stern punishment but *every situation* requires love and patience. When you show them patience, you're showing them love. God teaches us this concept in the way he loves us.

> ### Hebrews 12:6
> *For whom the Lord loveth he chasteneth and scourgeth every son whom he receiveth. For whom the Lord loveth he correcteth; even as a father the son in whom he delighteth.*

As a parent, the most important thing you will need is a relationship with the Holy Spirit. He is the one that will give you the discernment for the direction to take the children, how to correct them and discipline them. Here some scriptures the Bible gives us on how and why you need to correct your children and don't spare them because of their tears.

> ### Proverbs 13:24
> *He that spareth his rod hateth his son: but he that loveth him chasteneth him betimes.*

When you don't discipline your children they become spoiled and tyrannical. After a while, not only will no one like them (other children, family, nannies, etc), you won't either. These are the children that will end up wanting to fight you, disrespect you and make your life a living hell. God's system of discipline and correction drives out foolishness and rebellion. Many people refuse to discipline their children because they didn't like it as a child and vowed not to do it to their children. Or, they love their children so much that they hate to see them cry. People, who withhold punishment, often encounter (much to their surprise) a hateful, angry child that feels unloved.

> Proverbs 22:15
>
> *Foolishness is bound in the heart of a child but the rod of correction shall drive it*
> *far from him.*

> Proverbs 19:18
>
> *Chasten thy son while there is hope, and let not they soul spare for his crying.*

> Proverbs 23:13
>
> *Withhold not correction from the child: for if thou beatest him with the rod,*
> *he shall not die.*

Know your History: The Family Tree

When people want to learn about their family lineage, they often do so by formulating a family tree. If you were to make a family tree, the diagram would begin with you and your immediate family. We are *like* trees. As your tree grows, you will see a collection of families that are all attached to this one tree.

> ### Mark 8
> *And he cometh to Bethsaida; and they bring a blind man unto him, and besought him to touch him. And he took the blind man by the hand, and led him out of the town; and when he had spit on his eyes, and put his hands upon him, he asked him if he saw ought. And he looked up, and said, I see men as trees, walking. After that he put his hands again upon his eyes, and made him look up: and he was restored, and saw every man clearly.*

> ### Psalm 1:1
> *Blessed is the man that walketh not in the counsel of the ungodly, nor standeth in the way of sinners, nor sitteth in the seat of the scornful. But his delight is in the law of the LORD; and in his law doth he meditate day and night. nd he shall be like a tree planted by the rivers of water, that bringeth forth his fruit in his season; his leaf also shall not wither; and whatsoever he doeth shall prosper.*

According to Genesis, there were two different central trees. One being the tree of life, the other was the tree of the knowledge of good and evil. Before Adam and Eve ate of that tree, the only thing they had inside of them was the breath of life. Together, they possessed the ability to reproduce godly offspring because Adam possessed the seed of righteousness.

Adam himself was a living seed. When they ate of the tree of the knowledge of good and evil, they did not create a new seed. They contaminated *the vessel* and lost connection to the tree of life. If you notice, the scripture says:

> **Genesis 1:9**
>
> *And God said, Behold, I have given you every herb bearing seed, which is upon the face of all the earth, and every tree, in the which is the fruit of a tree yielding seed; to you it shall be for meat.*

> **Genesis 2:9**
>
> *And out of the ground made the LORD God to grow every tree that is pleasant to the sight, and good for food; the tree of life also in the midst of the garden, and the tree of knowledge of good and evil.*

God told Adam that He gave them herb and fruit of a tree-yielding seed to eat from. He also told them that they could eat of whatever tree they wanted except for the tree of the knowledge of good and evil. Apparently, that tree was the only one that *did not have seed in it*. It was not fruitful, therefore it had no ability to reproduce and multiply. Knowledge of good and evil gave them a choice between doing right or wrong. The tree of life offered eternal life. Evil did not exist in it at all.

I brought up the tree of life and the tree of the knowledge of good and evil to emphasis how we are part of a family tree. You and your wife are branches stemming from Jesus, the tree of life. Your seed, natural or spiritual, has life in it. But before we go more in depth about the seed, it's important to understand the tree.

If you're familiar with the story of Jacob and Esau, Esau sold his birthright for a small bite to eat. As the first-born, he was supposed to get the promised inheritance and blessing of the father which was the best portion. Esau, after realizing the magnitude of his decision, sought his father to overturn things, with many tears but it was too late. We, like Esau, had lost our birthright until Jesus came. Through Him, our birthrights are restored. When you were born again and accepted Christ as your Lord and Savior, you became part of the tree of life, the body of Christ and the royal priesthood. This transaction legally restores you to a new birthright and inheritance.

In your family, you may have been experiencing challenges financially, spiritually, emotionally, health wise, etc., because you haven't come to the fullness of who you are and your purpose as a spouse and a parent. It's imperative that you understand the lineage you are connected to and what your rights are because that is how you are going to be able to protect and teach your seed. Before giving our lives to Christ, we were of the seed of Adam who *lost his birthright*.

After Adam's expulsion from the Garden of Eden, he was sentenced to work to the sweat of his brow, toiling to produce. His ground was cursed. That's exactly where the enemy wants to keep you, on ground zero. He wants you to feel like there is nothing you can do to change your circumstances and you and your children will only go so far. Believe it or not, the devil is right about that as long as you're not saved but if you are born again, the curse no longer applies to you because you're not of this world.

Knowledge of this transaction is so important because as a child of the king, you now have the same power and authority that Jesus had and more! It is not through power alone that demons, principalities and the enemy are defeated but through authority. In other words, you are endowed with power and authority by the name of Jesus.

Your children, whether you're godly or ungodly, will be created in your image and likeness. Whatever status or affluence your family name carries, it will be passed on to your children. It is your job then to make sure that your children learn about their family tree and heritage. The father is to instruct the children on the Way of the Lord and the mother is to teach the children.

> **Proverbs 1:8**
> *My son, hear the instruction of thy father, and forsake not the law of thy mother.*

> **Proverbs 6:20**
> *My son, observe the commandment of your father And do not forsake the teaching of your mother.*

> **Proverbs 4:1**
> *Hear, O sons, the instruction of a father, And give attention that you may gain understanding.*

Managing your seed/generation

> **Psalm 145:4**
> *One generation shall praise thy works to another, and shall declare thy mighty acts.*

> **Psalm 22:31**
> *They will come and will declare His righteousness To a people who will be born, that He has performed it.*

> **Joel 1:3**
> *Tell ye your children of it, and let your children tell their children, and their children another generation.*

> **Psalm 78:4**
> *We will not conceal them from their children, But tell to the generation to come the praises of the LORD, And His strength and His wondrous works that He has done.*

Sometimes, God will allow the enemy a season to oppress you in order for Him to show your children through you, how He defeats His enemies and that He truly is the Almighty, living God.

> **Exodus 10:1,2**
> *And the LORD said unto Moses, Go in unto Pharaoh: for I have hardened his heart, and the heart of his servants, that I might shew these my signs before him: And that thou mayest tell in the ears of thy son, and of thy son's son, what things I have wrought in Egypt, and my signs which I have done among them; that ye may know how that I am the LORD.*

Praying for Your Children
From Head to Toe

❶ Pray for Their Mind:
Pray that your children would earnestly seek wisdom and understanding; that they would value knowledge and discernment; and that their thoughts would stay centered on the truth of God's Word. (Proverbs 2:1-6; Proverbs 3:21; James 1:5; Psalm 119:97)

❷ Pray for Their Eyes:
Ask God to guard your children's eyes and protect their innocence. Pray that they would focus their attention on doing what is right. (Romans 16:19; Proverbs 4:25)

❸ Pray for Their Ears:
Pray that your children would be quick to hear and that they would incline their ears to listen to instruction. (James 1:19; Isaiah 55:3; Proverbs 8:32-34)

❹ Pray for Their Mouth:
Ask God to keep their tongues from evil and their lips from speaking lies. Pray that all their words would be pleasing to Him and edifying to others. (Psalm 34:13; 19:14)

❺ Pray for Their Heart:
Ask God to give your children a happy, cheerful heart. Pray that they'd come to faith early and would trust easily and completely in Him. (Proverbs 15:13; Psalm 28:7)

❻ Pray for Their Hands:
Pray that they would be diligent in their work and that their hands would not be idle, but that God would bless, confirm, and establish the work of their hands. (Ecclesiastes 9:10; Ecclesiastes 11:6; Proverbs 10:4-5)

❼ Pray for Their Legs:
Pray that your children would not walk in step with the wicked nor stand in the way of sinners, but that they'd find wise and godly companions along life's journey. (Psalm 1:1)

❽ Pray for Their Feet:
Ask God to direct their steps, to help them stand fast, and to protect them from stumbling. (Psalm 17:5; Psalm 37:23-24; Psalm 121:3; Psalm 119:133)

CHAPTER 10

Become A Nation

AS WE CONTINUE to try to understand the purpose for marriage, God is very clear about one thing, He's going to have His kingdom on earth. That is where you and your wife come in. You are to birth a Holy Nation. Rarely are married people cognizant of this mandate. Becoming a nation is one of the fortifying factors of the institution in itself. This is the end game, the reason to stay together and produce. Married couples are ordained to be intimate, conceive, and birth a nation. Your children are not just cute little offspring that look like you. They are divine legacy...the next generation.

na·tion

> a large aggregate of people united by common descent, history, culture, or language, inhabiting a particular country or territory.

The way of the world is composed of systems that are governed by self, being outside of God and led by the devil. We see these demonic systems in countries, government, laws, education, communities, and the like. Any changes or challenges to these orders will inevitably be confronted by fiery backlash and consequences. So how does God's kingdom (system) come on earth? He takes families and turns them into nations. Within that nation, He creates new laws, cultures, doctrine, and lifestyle.

Nation is a social concept with no uncontroversial definition, but that is most commonly used to designate larger groups or collectives of people with common characteristics attributed to them—including language, traditions, customs (mores), habits (habitus), and ethnicity. A nation, by comparison, is more impersonal, abstract, and overtly political than an ethnic group. It is a cultural-political community that has become conscious of its autonomy, unity, and particular interests.
*Wikipedia

What are nations for?

Modern nation-states were created by nations to give people sharing a common language and cultural characteristics the right to govern themselves as they choose. Nations provide protection against external threats and can ask their citizens to perform tasks, such as military service, in return. The more powerful a nation's military and economic power, the more it can promote its own interests.

How do nations deal with other nations?

Nations interact on many levels. Trade agreements allow businesses from different nations to buy and sell their goods and services with each other. Formal agreements, signed by political leaders or their diplomatic representatives, reinforce friendly relations and allow cooperation in different areas, such as military technology. International agreements ensure that all member nations abide by the same rules.

Borders

A border is a line marking where the territory of one nation-state ends and another begins. Borders are clearly marked on maps, but those between friendly nations may often be unmarked on the ground. Borders under dispute are often heavily guarded and have strictly controlled border crossings.

Nations often contest their borders, because of the need for land and valuable raw materials, such as oil, which are important to a nation's wealth. Borders are often redrawn as a result of wars. Sometimes, people end up on the wrong side of the border, such as in the former Yugoslavia, and this can lead to conflict, too.

> ### Deuteronomy 4:6
> *Behold, I have taught you statutes and judgments, even as the LORD my God commanded me, that ye should do so in the land whither ye go to possess it. Keep therefore and do them; for this is your wisdom and your understanding in the sight of the nations, which shall hear all these statutes, and say, Surely this great nation is a wise and understanding people. For what nation is there so great, who hath God so nigh unto them, as the LORD our God is in all things that we call upon him for? And what nation is there so great, that hath statutes and judgments so righteous as all this law, which I set before you this day? Only take heed to thyself, and keep thy soul diligently, lest thou forget the things which thine eyes have seen, and lest they depart from thy heart all the days of thy life: but teach them thy sons, and thy sons' sons.*

> ### Genesis 1:28
> *God blessed them; and God said to them, "Be fruitful and multiply, and fill the earth, and subdue it.*

> **Genesis 18:19**
>
> *For I know him, that he will command his children and his household after him, and they shall keep the way of the LORD, to do justice and judgment; that the LORD may bring upon Abraham that which he hath spoken of him.*

When you and your spouse came together in marriage, you were not joining two worlds together. On the contrary, you are beginning a new one. The purpose is found in the definition of nation: a large **body of people**, associated with a **particular territory**, that is **sufficiently conscious of its unity to seek or to possess a government peculiarly its own.** Abraham, the father of faith was promised nations of people. As a believer, you have inherited that promise. The idea for you and your spouse is to consciously be unified in seeking to possess a government and territory that God has promised. That territory is natural and spiritual.

In addition, it is imperative that both you and your wife speak the same language*. I'm not speaking of language in the natural, rather spiritual, commanding things that be, not as though they were by the Word of God, standing in agreement. And this brings you to the first necessity and that is to obtain power.

> **2 Timothy 1:7**
>
> *For God hath not given us the spirit of fear; but of power, and of love, and of a sound mind.*

> **Luke 10:19**
>
> *Behold, I give unto you power to tread on serpents and scorpions, and over all the power of the enemy: and nothing shall by any means hurt you.*

It's through families that God changes the world system and societies. This is why society today continues to empower women and devalue men in order to break up and undermine the patriarchal order God has ordained and established. The object of this feminist movement is to dethrone the king through division and insubordination, which is why the Word instructs us to be sober (aware/conscious) of what's going on and obedient to God's commands on a unified front. The enemy understands that once you and your wife are on one accord with the Word and with each other, your nation will take over and occupy the territory the enemy once enjoyed.

Territory is not limited to land; it also includes your home, legacy, and family name. Perhaps your family name was synonymous with people who were plagued with poverty or drugs. That generational stronghold may have been in effect for many, many years but through the blood of Jesus, your faith in God's promises, His Word and faith, you can break through that barrier and begin a new family legacy of wealthy, healthy, successful individuals. When you do that, you have just taken oven over your territory. The spiritual domains that dominated *your house* are territories the devil stole that belong to you. God has endowed you with the power and authority to evict the enemy and occupy while here on earth.

Understand that the person you are (thoughts, behavior, and deeds) will be reproduced through your children naturally and spiritually. Once they grow up, they will have the proclivity to continue the same patterns, thoughts, and behaviors, passing them down to their children and so on and so on. It is imperative for both spouses to be born again and Holy (dedicated or consecrated to God or a religious purpose; sacred) so that you can become a Holy Nation. Equally vital is the importance of the family being in alignment with the patriarchal order.

> Peter 2:9
>
> *But ye are a chosen generation, a royal priesthood, an holy nation, a peculiar people; that ye should shew forth the praises of him who hath called you out of darkness into his marvelous light: Which in time past were not a people, but are now the people of God: which had not obtained mercy, but now have obtained mercy.*

The word generation is usually taken out of context when it's spoken as one word. However, the trick is to understand that the word is of two parts—gene-*ration*. Every 20-years or so, a new gene-*ration* is produced. We've seen it in society, in the sixties, flower children with the free love and drugs movement; seventies, we saw rebellion in women (women's lib); in the eighties, there was a generation of crack addicts; in this generation, we see the explosion of lesbianism and homosexuality and so on and so. We even find Jesus referring to groups of people as a generation of vipers, wicked and adulterous generation and so on.

Today, we have the Holy Spirit who has the power to re-gene-rate us. When we get born again and converted, *re-gene-ration* occurs. God's goal is to 're-gene-ration' families all over the world until we all become like Him…a Holy nation, and His kingdom comes.

Within your marriage, you have to resolve within yourselves that you're committed to each other and God's way for life…PERIOD. Beyond being joined to each other, you and your spouse are heirs to the kingdom of God. Within that kingdom, God expects you to *birth* a nation.

Notice that I used the word *birth*. In other words, husbands have to **know** their wives and become *intimate* with them in order to conceive, not just sexually but spiritually. As a priest, prophet, and king, the husband has to hear from God the instructions for the kingdom (priest), convey it to his wife (as a prophet) as to their assignment so that she can come into agreement (conception). Together, you and your spouse will birth a nation.

Ecclesiastes speaks about a time and a place for everything. Marriage is a solution to a problem. Adam lost his authority when he ate from the fruit that he was instructed not to. It was through the disorder of their family that the enemy was able to infiltrate their home because Adam failed to correct or prevent Eve from disobeying God. He should not have been influenced by her, which was the disorder. As a result, they lost their *place*.

Since God is eternal and we are not, we have to have a place for him to come and meet with us. Satan understands this mystery, thus the war or conflict is over territory. God uses family and marriage to regain and restore territory for the Kingdom of God.

Most married people don't give their marriage this kind of consideration because they are consumed with their own wants and desires. Although the choice is yours, if do as you please, you miss out on the purpose and glory of God that He has promised you when you don't operate in purpose. Lack of purpose and direction is the cause of boredom, infidelity, poverty, poor health, and ultimately divorce. Children mimic that same pattern of selfish ambition without purpose. In other words, they will not know real love in a relationship because they have only witnessed *Eros* love without responsibility. Real love *cuts* covenant and *gives* beyond itself for a greater purpose.

PURPOSE PRINCIPLE

Common Law marriage is a contract that requires no sacrifice or promise. Marriage is a covenant sealed by an oath and blood. Real love cuts covenant voluntarily, not forced by law.

Your assignment, as a one impenetrable unit, is to be fruitful, multiply, replenish, and subdue. It's not enough to just conceive, birth and multiply, that's the easier part of the process. Where it gets bloody and violent is the subdue part. The word subdue means a *hostile* takeover. That means there is an illegal occupant residing in the territory God has promised you and does not want to leave. We're talking about generational curses and demonic forces that are trying to prevent the growth and prosperity of your family from now to generations to come.

Every powerful major person known to man had to come through someone's bloodline. How do you know if the next president, pastor, surgeon, or prominent person is not on their way through your bloodline? Could it be that the purpose of your marriage was just to birth this child? Or perhaps they will be your grandchildren or great, great grandchild!? We may never know but God does. We cannot forget that we are here to do His will. Our relationships go far beyond ourselves whether we accept it or not.

> Deuteronomy 7:9
>
> *Know therefore that the LORD thy God, he is God, the faithful God, which keepeth covenant and mercy with them that love him and keep his commandments to a thousand generations.*

Subduing is a commandment extremely vital to the purpose. There's an enemy sitting on your promised land very comfortably for generations in different forms. You can bet your bottom dollar that he has NO intentions on leaving. As one (you, wife and God/The Word), you will take over the world.

> 1 Corinthians 7:33
>
> *But he that is married careth for the things that are of the world, how he may please his wife.*

> John 10:14
>
> *I am the good shepherd, and know my sheep, and am known of mine. As the Father knoweth me, even so know I the Father: and I lay down my life for the sheep. And other sheep I have, which are not of this fold: them also I must bring, and they shall hear my voice; and there shall be one fold, and one shepherd. Therefore doth my Father love me, because I lay down my life, that I might take it again. No man taketh it from me, but I lay it down of myself. I have power to lay it down, and I have power to take it again. This commandment have I received of my Father.*

Blessings are already promised to you. That dream job, house, cars, health, wealth, obedient children, peace in your home, all these things and many more are already yours. Demonic forces are not going to release them without a fight. You'll be able to secure what's yours through **power and authority**. Satan's kingdom is organized by ranks and territory. However, God has given YOU power over ALL your enemies. The problem is, most of the time we don't know *who the enemy is*. So we fight each other instead of dealing with the evil spirit. In order to defeat the enemy, you must know who the enemy is.

PURPOSE PRINCIPLE

In order to defeat your enemy, you must know who it is.

The enemy knows that he's already been defeated on Calvary but he doesn't want *you* to *realize it*. He doesn't want you to pursue your inheritance. Did you know if you are dealing with confusion you can cast it out? If your child is disobedient, God gives you instructions on how to deal with that. If you or your spouse is sick, he has prescribed a word for it. You are not powerless! You probably just don't know how to fight. The enemy knows you though…he's banking on your ignorance so that you don't put him out. If he can convince you that your spouse or children, people are the problem, you will always fight *them*. So he tries to cause division within your household because he understands the Word, authority and unity. Being one with God and your spouse will make you unstoppable! Why…because you are the rightful heirs. You cannot stand against the enemy with your house divided.

> **Joshua 23:10**
> *One man of you shall chase a thousand: for the LORD your God, he it is that fighteth for you, as he hath promised you.*

> **Genesis 11:6**
> *And the LORD said, Behold, the people is one, and they have all one language; and this they begin to do: and now nothing will be restrained from them, which they have imagined to do.*

Let's examine how God established His nation. Every time God established and expanded His kingdom, He did it through a man. First, through Abraham (by faith), God made him the father of many nations. God continued building through the son of promise, Isaac, who is the manifestation of Abraham's faith. Then through Issac's son, Jacob who served Laban 14 years for his wife Rebecca and Leah, continuing on to have 12 sons. Jacob then had to face his past and wrestle with God (which was his right of passage). After successfully grappling with his past (which every man must do), God rewarded him with a name, Israel. It is through that name and family that a nation was born.

The first step was establishing the nation by faith. The next step in God's purpose was to make a royal lineage. Fast forward to David, we could see where God made him a king through *marriage* to king Saul's daughter Mical. He did this to make a royal bloodline. And finally, the priesthood came through the birth of Jesus Christ.

Your marriage is no different. By faith, you've said your "I do's," coming together as one; and through the vehicle of covenant to Jesus and your spouse, you are now a Holy nation. Husbands, before they were married, were sons of God that served the kingdom. By faith, you left singlehood and went to a land called marriage, a land you did not know (like Abram). That land, territory, and domain is your wife. You went into covenant with her and God, (like Abram).

God promised you blessings and multiplication, that He would never leave you or forsake you if you keep His commands. When you accepted this agreement, you went into covenant with God and just like when you get married, your name changed. Now, everything you do is in the name of Jesus. His name gives you the legal right to take over the land and to put out all enemies. As a king, after you put out your enemies, you can decree and declare blessing, health, wealth, and prosperity over you and your nation.

Here are the rules of engagement. You and your spouse must:

- Choose whom you are going to serve, then make the decree as in Joshua 24:14-15:

> *Now therefore fear the* LORD, *and serve him in sincerity and in truth: and put away the gods which your fathers served on the other side of the flood, and in Egypt; and serve ye the* LORD. *And if it seem evil unto you to serve the* LORD, *choose you this day whom ye will serve; whether the gods which your fathers served that were on the other side of the flood, or the gods of the Amorites, in whose land ye dwell: but as for me and my house, we will serve the* LORD.

- Have faith in God
- Operate in Power & Authority
- Be in Unity
- Fear God
- Be righteous
- Be clean
- Be obedient

Ultimately, your nation is going to be the change that this world needs. It starts with you and your spouse. Your home/family is a government within a government.

CHAPTER 11

Occupy: Possess The Land

GOD DESIRES FOR you to be an owner not a renter. He is literally guaranteeing you success if you listen to His Word/commandments. This word of knowledge is pivotal in your marriage as you grow and move into your promised land. If you haven't arrived at ownership yet, set your face in that direction. God has already promised you to be the head if you follow His instructions.

> Deuteronomy 28:13
>
> *And the Lord shall make thee the head and not the tail; and though shalt be above only and thou shalt not be beneath; if that thou hearken unto the commandments of the Lord thy God, which I command thee this day, to observe and to do them.*

Every nation needs a place/land to occupy. This new place will also have to have a governing body, laws, rules and regulations. Having a nation with a sound government is a form of civilization and order. Everyone should be clear about what goes on in this nation. As we know, what makes a nation is common interest, culture, and language. Your common interest, culture, and language are the Word of God, the culture is within the Kingdom of God, and the language is Love.

Now that you and your family have decided to fulfill your purpose and have made the decree and declaration that you and your house will serve the Lord, you must prepare for the next step. Preparation for possessing the land and territory that God has given you. The reason why I say land and territory is that you are fighting to reclaim actual physical property but also subduing spiritual territory. Both are intrinsically connected, so both have to be dealt with in order to have success.

One of the original mandates that God gave married people is to be fruitful, multiply, replenish, and subdue. To subdue means, a hostile takeover. When you go to occupy the land, if you have to subdue it, then that means there is someone or something already residing there that doesn't want to leave. You will experience some kind of resistance where you will have to fight in order to occupy.

Don't think for one minute that enemy who has enjoyed wreaking havoc throughout your family for generations is going to just let you evict him without confrontation. You must understand that God has already given you victory before you even threw your first punch but you still have to show up for the fight. Occupancy can only occur if you make your move to take over.

In order to assure yourself of victory you must have faith and the only fear you should have is the FEAR OF THE LORD, YOUR GOD! Observance of the fear of the Lord will CHANGE EVERYTHING!

Most of our worst sins, iniquities, transgressions and decisions whether financial, relational, you name it, were more than likely because we did not fear the Lord by adhering to His way of doing things. If you really feared the Lord, there are some things that you just would not do. We are led and governed by our thoughts; that's why the war is for the mind. Who are you going to listen to? The enemy will paint pictures of desperation, lust, anxiety, sin etc. while God will show you a righteous picture. Both have consequences but the question is, whom do you choose to believe and listen to? Whomever you choose to listen to is your God because thoughts control your actions.

PURPOSE PRINCIPLE

Whomever you choose to obey is your God because your thoughts control your actions.

There's a war going on in the mind. The enemy wants to gain control of your thoughts. God has already instructed us on how to think:

> **Philippians 4:8**
> *Finally, brethren, whatsoever things are true, whatsoever things are honest, whatsoever things are just, whatsoever things are pure, whatsoever things are lovely, whatsoever things are of good report; if there be any virtue, and if there be any praise, think on these things.*

Think on whatsoever is true, honest. The enemy always creeps in with a negative thought. For example, your wife may ask you a question regarding your plan of action, instead of simply answering the question, your mind produces a negative thought with something like, "*She thinks* that I don't know what I'm doing." That negative thought about what you think she is thinking, provoked you to embrace and embody the negative emotion without facts. The truth is you will NEVER truly know what she is thinking because we are not mind readers. Since we don't have the power to read minds, we have to assess situations and decide what thoughts we are going to believe and deem to be true. Either way, you are going to have to choose to believe, silence, or replace a thought. Think on what is actually true, honest, just, pure, and of good report that has any virtue or praise, dwell on that thought. Don't assume the worst, ALWAYS assume the best! Believe it or not, positive thinking is a military strategy.

In the midst of conquering territory on earth, one of the greatest conquest you will have is conquering your own self/flesh. Master your own mind first with the Word of God and everything else will fall into place. Sometimes, the loneliest place to be is with someone who doesn't believe in you or doesn't see or support you. During those seasons, you must learn to strengthen yourself and be courageous. Whatever you do influences the entire body to follow!

Entering into a new territory to occupy it can be very scary. Some people when they get scared become paralyzed. That's why we see so many unproductive marriages. People are afraid to take risks. Fear is natural when you are doing something new and big. Although you are afraid, move forward anyway. If your spouse is paralyzed by fear, you can have greater faith FOR THEM!

Four men carried their paralyzed friend on mat to Jesus. The house where Jesus ministered was so crowded that these four men had to climb to the roof, cut a hole in it, and let the paralyzed man down so that Jesus could heal him. The Bible said when Jesus saw *their faith*; He said to the paralyzed man, "Son, your sins are forgiven." Sometimes, you may have to go the extra mile and fight the good fight of faith for your spouse when they are stricken with fear.

Even though the scripture doesn't specify it, but I guess one of the sins that Jesus was referring to was *fear*. God has *not* given us the *spirit of fear* but of power, love and a sound mind.

It's the fear that lets you know that you are about to occupy and the enemy is waiting to confront you. Remember David and Goliath. Goliath was a giant, towering over David and the children of Israel, threatening complete annihilation. That is what our struggles do to us. It threatens to kill our bank accounts, marriage, peace of mind, children, etc. David was considerably smaller but he did not go to war in his own strength. Listen to what he said while he was approaching Goliath:

> 1 Samuel 17:45-47
>
> *Then said David to the Philistine, Thou comest to me with a sword, and with a spear, and with a shield: but I come to thee in the name of the LORD of hosts, the God of the armies of Israel, whom thou hast defied. This day will the LORD deliver thee into mine hand; and I will smite thee, and take thine head from thee; and I will give the carcases of the host of the Philistines this day unto the fowls of the air, and to the wild beasts of the earth; that all the earth may know that there is a God in Israel. And all this assembly shall know that the LORD saveth not with sword and spear: for the battle is the LORD'S, and he will give you into our hands.*

God is saying to us, just show up for the fight and I will deliver victory into your hands. If you never show up, then God doesn't have anyone to work with. If you won't confront your past, confront your finances, confront your issues, how can God fight a battle for you that you won't engage in?

That's why you have to have the courage to be vulnerable and transparent to your wife and courage to face life's challenges together. Every couple should know and read this scripture together. Put your name into it to make it personal to you:

> ### Joshua 1
>
> *[insert your name] Every place that the sole of your foot shall tread upon, that have I given unto you, as I said unto Moses. From the wilderness and this Lebanon even unto the great river, the river Euphrates, all the land of the Hittites, and unto the great sea toward the going down of the sun, shall be your coast. There shall not any man be able to stand before thee all the days of thy life: as I was with Moses, so I will be with thee: I will not fail thee, nor forsake thee. Be strong and of a good courage: for unto this people shalt thou divide for an inheritance the land, which I sware unto their fathers to give them. <u>Only</u> be thou strong and very courageous, that thou mayest observe to do according to all the law, which Moses my servant commanded thee: turn not from it to the right hand or to the left, that thou mayest prosper whithersoever thou goest. This book of the law shall not depart out of thy mouth; but thou shalt meditate therein day and night, that thou mayest observe to do according to all that is written therein: for then thou shalt make thy way prosperous, and then thou shalt have good success. <u>Have not I commanded thee</u>? Be strong and of a good courage; be not afraid, neither be thou dismayed: for the LORD thy God is with thee whithersoever thou <u>goest.</u>*

> ### Joshua 24:14
>
> *Now therefore fear the LORD, and serve him in sincerity and in truth: and put away the gods which your fathers served on the other side of the flood, and in Egypt; and serve ye the LORD.*

Jesus is the King of kings and your husband is a lesser king who has been entrusted with the assignment of governing your nation on His behalf. All of your power and authority comes from *Him (Jesus)*. He's not only King of kings, He's Lord of lords. When the husband and wife make decisions for the family, *God's will and way* should always be reverentially considered. This is a form of *government*. Therefore, the laws and statues of your government are already written:

> ### Deuteronomy 6:1-9
>
> *Now these are the commandments, the statutes, and the judgments, which the LORD your God commanded to teach you, that ye might do them in the land whither ye go to possess it: That thou mightest fear the LORD thy God, to keep all his statutes and his commandments, which I command thee, thou, and thy son, and thy son's son, all the days of thy life; and that thy days may be prolonged. Hear therefore, O Israel, and observe to do it; that it may be well with thee, and that ye may increase mightily, as the LORD God of thy fathers hath promised thee, in the land that floweth with milk and honey.*
>
> *Hear, O Israel: The LORD our God is one LORD: And thou shalt love the LORD thy God with all thine heart, and with all thy soul, and with all thy might. And these words, which I command thee this day, shall be in thine heart: And thou shalt teach them diligently unto thy children, and shalt talk of them when thou sittest in thine house, and when thou walkest by the way, and when thou liest down, and when thou risest up. And thou shalt bind them for a sign upon thine hand, and they shall be as frontlets between thine eyes. And thou shalt write them upon the posts of thy house, and on thy gates.*

Territory defined:

The extent of land belonging to, or under the dominion of, a prince, state, or **other form of government**; often, a tract of land lying at *a distance from the parent country* or from the seat of government; **as, the territory of a State**

Hebrew translation of Territory:

> gebul — border, boundary, territory.

We must understand that God is eternal and He is all knowing. Whatever God has done is already done. In other words, He created this world for Himself and made us joint heirs through Christ. Therefore, God has ALREADY given you power, authority, and territory. The object then is to claim your rights. He tells us to be strong and of good courage because we are going to have to fight in order to subdue.

Before you subdue, you must first identify the enemy and learn how to defeat them. What is their weakness? What is your weakness? You must understand that the enemy has studied you too. In essence, the enemy we are fighting is spiritual. However, just as God uses us to do His will, the enemy uses people to execute His will because He is a spirit too. The reason why this is important to understand is that the enemy wants you to fight and attack *people* instead of fighting and attacking him and his demons. Or, who knows, maybe *you* are your worst enemy. Disobedience, sin, and fear are gateways to destruction.

> Ephesians 6:12
>
> *For we wrestle not against flesh and blood, but against principalities, against powers, against the rulers of the darkness of this world, against spiritual wickedness in high places.*

Ephesians 6:12 is interesting to me because the Word is not only telling us *who* we are fighting but *where* we are fighting. The scripture says we're coming against spiritual wickedness in high places. A **place** is part of a **territory**. This is the part many married people miss. When all hell is breaking loose in your home, spouse, children, finances, and health, we oftentimes don't acknowledge or address the fact that you are under *spiritual* attack. So we deal with the land (people), remember we were created from the dust (land) while neglecting the true culprits—principalities, powers, rulers of darkness of this world, and spiritual wickedness.

You cannot defeat the enemy in the flesh. Matter of fact, operating in the flesh opens the door to the enemy. You must deal with the enemy on both levels by closing the door to sin and walking in power and authority. The way to walking in the power and authority of God is first to love and fear HIM. Learn His laws and statutes (His word) because HE is His Word. The enemy responds to His Word, not yours. You must also understand the enemy and learn how to identify them because there are different ways to war against them. Here is a brief overview of spiritual warfare:

***Our Spiritual Warfare is Against "Principalities"*

The concept of principalities is understood by the Greek word *arche* meaning chief or ruler. These principalities are ruling devil spirits possessing executive authority or governmental rule in the world. As we will see, this ruling power usually involves a particular nation, people or race. There are evil angels ruling the kingdoms of the world that oppose the truth of God, and of which Satan is the chief prince or ruler of both the world system and its organization of demons, as noted in the gospel of Matthew.

In Matthew 12:24, the devil is called "Beelzebub" meaning lord of the dwelling, in which these wicked spirits are subject to and operate under Satan's dominion. They, like their chief prince, direct, control, rule and carry out the present darkness of this world.

The *American Heritage Dictionary* defines principalities as:

1. A territory ruled by a prince or from which a prince derives his title.
2. The position, authority, or jurisdiction of a prince; sovereignty.

The idea of prince devil spirits ruling or controlling a region is supported in the Old Testament book of Daniel, chapter 10. Daniel was visited by an angel in response to his prayer to God. This angel, who was sent by God to answer Daniel's prayer, was delayed for 21 days because of a battle that took place between God's angel and "a prince of the kingdom of Persia." Daniel reveals the angel's message in the following verses:

> ### Daniel 10:12-13
> *"Then said he [the angel] unto me, Fear not, Daniel: for from the first day that thou didst set thine heart to understand, and to chasten [humble] thyself before thy God, thy words were heard, and I am come for thy words. But the prince of the kingdom of Persia withstood me one and twenty days: but, lo, Michael, one of the chief princes, came to help me; and I remained there with the kings of Persia."*

The spiritual battle, for this angel, was of such magnitude that Michael, the archangel of God and designated prince of Israel, came down to assist the angel in battle. Another enemy of God, the prince of Greece, is also mentioned in the verses below.

> ### Daniel 10:20-21
> *"Then said he [the angel], Knowest thou wherefore I come unto thee? and now will I return to fight with the prince of Persia: and when I am gone forth, lo, the prince of Grecia shall come. But I will shew thee that which is noted in the scripture of truth: and there is none that holdeth with me in these things, but Michael your prince."*

The book of Daniel gives us an excellent example of how these unseen spiritual entities fight to increase and maintain their realms of influence and control in order to hinder God's purposes. In addition, as previously stated, these princes are named after the nations or rather their principalities in which they rule. It is Satan's purpose to **deceive these nations** and to keep them from obtaining knowledge of God's truth and salvation through His Son Jesus Christ.

In the book of Revelation, chapter 20, Satan is depicted as a deceiver of *nations*. The Greek word for deceive is *planaho*, and according to Strong's Greek Dictionary, this word means to "cause to roam from safety, truth or virtue, go astray, seduce, wander, and to be out of the way."

Satan's major success in deceiving a nation (your marriage and family) is due to a lack of discernment on the part of both spouses. They're blind to the invisible forces of supernatural evil that are operating and influencing their visible human agents of political, social, religious and philosophical programs.

Satan's greatest victory would be to convince the world that he just doesn't exist. However, God signifies the devil as the author of sin, sickness, and death, and warns us to be alert and vigilant because the devil, as a roaring lion, roams about seeking whom he may devour (1 Peter 5:8).

The devil controls the kingdoms of the world and we are not to underestimate his influence and power, nor believe that this is the will of God. God is telling us to "stand" against these evil forces by equipping ourselves with the power of God, and looking unto Christ as our example. He usually attacks through lust of the eyes, lust of the flesh, and the pride of life. Oftentimes the *manifestation* of that fact comes as an extramarital affair, selfishness, foolish spending, superficial relationships, materialistic attitudes, and so on.
His tactical prey on you is to make you unsatisfied and discontented with what you have.

> ### Luke 4:5-7
> *And the devil, taking him (Jesus) up into an high mountain, shewed unto him all the kingdoms of the world in a moment of time. And the devil said unto him, All this power will I give thee, and the glory of them: for that is delivered (to surrender or yield up) unto me; and to whomsoever I will I give it. If thou therefore wilt worship me, all shall be thine.*

You see, the devil is trying to tempt Jesus with material things. All the devil is asking Jesus to do is bow down and worship him and he'll give Him power, wealth and prosperity. Jesus understood who He was and His purpose. Pleasing His father by doing His will was His power, wealth and prosperity, not material things. Jesus wasn't seduced because He already had everything He needed. Your strength is in God. Satisfaction, faith, and trust in God's word is a spiritual military stance. It is in His word that you stand. It's impossible to seduce a satisfied person.

> ### Ephesians 6:10-17
> *Finally, my brethren, be strong in the Lord, and in the power of his might. Put on the whole armour of God, that ye may be able to stand against the wiles of the devil. For we wrestle not against flesh and blood, but against principalities, against powers, against the rulers of the darkness of this world, against spiritual wickedness in high places. Wherefore take unto you the whole armour of God, that ye may be able to withstand in the evil day, and having done all, to stand. Stand therefore, having your loins girt about with truth, and having on the breastplate of righteousness; And your feet shod with the preparation of the gospel of peace; Above all, taking the shield of faith, wherewith ye shall be able to quench all the fiery darts of the wicked. And take the helmet of salvation, and the sword of the Spirit, which is the word of God:*
>
> *cont/d...*

> PRAY CONTINUALLY
> *Praying always with all prayer and supplication in the Spirit, and watching thereunto with all perseverance and supplication for all saints.*

You stand against the enemy with truth, righteousness, peace, and faith. Sounds simple enough, right? But the fact of the matter is the enemy gains access and legal authority to your territory when you are a liar or live a lie and are unrighteous with no faith. These are keys to the kingdom. Access to you, your spouse, family, finances, and other areas will be given to the enemy through disobedience or taken through that same door.

Our Spiritual Warfare is Against "Powers and World Rulers of Darkness."

The Greek word for "powers" is *exousia* which means derived or conferred authority, the warrant or right to do something, or delegated influences of control. Although the word "powers" is left unclear as to Paul's precise meaning in the verse, this expression is used elsewhere in Scripture to infer the powers that be in authority. In keeping with the context of this verse, this would include all high-ranking, evil supernatural powers and the power of sin and evil in operation in the world. The fruits of this type of evil can probably be seen in drug cartels, gross poverty, plagues, terrorism, and other heinous crimes against humanity, even toward the animal kingdom.

Our Spiritual Warfare is Against "Spiritual Wickedness in Heavenly Places."

The Greek word for wickedness is **ponēria** and means depravity and particularly in the sense of malice and mischief, plots, sins, and iniquity (Strong's Gk. Dict.).

Malice [A. H. Dict.] is defined as:

1. A desire to harm others or to see others suffer; extreme ill will or spite.
2. Law — The intent, without just cause or reason, to commit a wrongful act that will result in harm to another.

Since Satan is the prince of the power of the air, these wicked spirits, in high places, are often understood to be the collective organization of all of Satan's devil spirits. These malevolent spirits work evil and mischief and operate in our atmosphere. They operate as close to the very air we breathe, and reach to realms beyond. All kinds of spiritual filth are propagated, in these realms, for the purpose of humanity's deception and subsequent destruction. Prior to becoming a Christian, we too walked according to the prince of the power of the air.

> Ephesians 2:2-3
>
> *Wherein in time past ye walked according to the course of this world, according to the prince of the power of the air, the spirit that now worketh in the children of disobedience: Among whom also we all had our conversation in times past in the lusts of our flesh, fulfilling the desires of the flesh and of the mind; and were by nature the children of wrath, even as others.*
>
> *For all that is in the world, the lust of the flesh, and the lust of the eyes, and the pride of life, is not of the Father, but is of the world.*

The details of God's plan, His provision of escape from Satan's kingdom of darkness through faith in Christ, were kept a mystery from the beginning of time. It wasn't until the revelation of the Son of God on earth, and His complete victory in His death and resurrection for the salvation of humanity, that the mystery of salvation through Christ is revealed to us. The Apostle Paul states,

> **1 Corinthians 2:7-10**
>
> *"But we speak the wisdom of God in a mystery, even the hidden wisdom, which God ordained before the world unto our glory. Which none of the princes of this world knew: for had they known it, they would not have crucified the Lord of glory. But as it is written, Eye hath not seen, nor ear heard, neither have entered into the heart of man, the things which God hath prepared for them that love him. But God hath revealed them unto us by his Spirit: for the Spirit searcheth all things, yea, the deep things of God."*

In other words, if God's enemies knew that the Lord's death would bring the Kingdom of God and His power into the hearts of every believer, with His gift of Holy Spirit, and thus bring God's light into the world, they would not have crucified Him. That is the same thing for your marriage. When each spouse crucifies their flesh by sacrificing their will for the will of God, they unleash the undefeatable power of God in their life and nation. The enemy does not expect us to lay down our lives for another. He's banking on you being selfish, self-centered and carnal which is very predictable.

PURPOSE PRINCIPLE

When each spouse crucifies their flesh by sacrificing their will for the will of God, they unleash the undefeatable power of God in their life and nation.

The Mystery Revealed—Colossians 1: 26-27

The mystery revealed is stated in Scripture as, "...Christ in you, the hope of glory." Jesus Christ came as a light in the world, a light that the kingdom of darkness tried to extinguish. But through the sacrifice of Christ, the Son of God, God's gift of Holy Spirit is given to every believer in Christ (Christ in you), in which through the manifold wisdom of God, one Lord and Light continues to sow a vast Kingdom of Light.**Magdeline, battleinchrist.com

So how do you fight?

1. Fight the good fight of faith. You are going into the realm of your promised land and you have to believe that God has given you the victory. Example: If your family has suffered from a generational curse of cancer, you have to have faith that as you appropriate the promises of God for you and your family, the curse is broken. Just because *that* demonic force has run rampant through your family, it doesn't automatically give it authority to exist forever. Focus on what is true, all God says in His Word regarding your authority. Speak and believe the scriptures that declare healing. Regardless of the challenge your family has faced, this war strategy applies to you. Fight the good fight of faith by believing you will be victorious.
2. Pray and Fast. This is probably one of the most effective warfare tools in the chest. When you pray, you are inviting God Himself and His angels to operate on your behalf. The scriptures tell us to make our request made known unto God. But when you pray and fast, you become much more powerful; the reason being that when you deny the flesh, the spirit is magnified. You hear and see what the Lord is telling you quicker and clearer. You are also less susceptible to the enemy because he cannot seduce you as you have denied your flesh. It is not through your own strength but through the power of God.

> **2 Corinthians 10:4**
>
> *For the weapons of our warfare are not carnal, but mighty through God for to the pulling down of strongholds.*

3. Cast down imaginations. Crazy, demonic, hateful thoughts plague our minds sometimes to the point that the devil doesn't actually have to do anything but make suggestions. He gives people wicked ideas, causing illusions and delusion—nothing real, just images of what might be going on. The Bible tells us to think on whatsoever is lovely and of good report. Especially in marriages, the enemy will bring up your history with ex-es, or perhaps you cheated in the past. Now all the enemy has to do is make a suggestion. In order to conquer this demonic deploy of the enemy, love your spouse and always think the best. Cast down any fearful idea, past images that hurt your heart; don't entertain them. Plead the blood of Jesus over your mind and govern your thoughts with love. After a while, you will realize that your spouse is (in most cases) innocent.

> 2 Corinthians 10:5
>
> *Casting down imaginations, and every high thing that exalteth itself against the knowledge of God, and bringing into captivity every thought to the obedience of Christ.*

4. Speak the Word to your situation.
5. Love your spouse. Love your neighbor. Love conquers *all*.
6. Be righteous. This is the most simplest strategy of all. Simply do the right thing. The enemy will no doubt come for you but he will have no authority to stay or defeat you if you are living right. No ex can threaten your marriage if you honestly don't secretly interact with them. You can't abuse drugs and think there won't be any damages. The enemy gains access to your territory through sin. You shut the door on sin through righteousness.
7. Study and KNOW THE WORD.

It may seem off topic, preachy even, to go into all this detail about the enemy. However, you cannot subdue your land without this knowledge. The enemy is skilled, prepared, filled with hate towards you and everything you stand for. Regardless if it's the devil or an angel or whatever, there is spiritual protocol. Before you occupy the land and territory that God has *given you*, there are certain legal stipulations you must abide by. Violation of these laws comes with dire circumstances. Not because God is going to punish you, the punishment is built in. When you sin, you separate yourself from God/love. When you don't tithe, you are living under a curse. If you disobey God, you will live under a curse. Reason being, you no longer have protection from the enemy. It is only through the power of God that you are able to stand against the enemy. When you move out of the position of obedience and righteousness, the enemy will come for you even more ferocious than the first time. That's why God's first command is to love Him with all your heart, soul, might and to fear *Him*. Those things will protect you, your marriage, and your family as you subdue and occupy the land.

According to the order of the family, the husband is the priest, prophet, and king. He is the one who is an ambassador for Christ. Your wife is your helpmeet. Together, it's your job to wage war on the enemy and reclaim your territory. The way he does it is by decreeing and declaring his legal right according to the Word over his nation (family) and kingdom. In the spirit realm, there is order, rank, and laws. God reigns supreme over them all! It is up to you to walk in that authority!

The scriptures go further to tell us before you try to occupy the land, get rid of all your *strange gods*. Many of us can get rid of strange gods for a season but then we forget and bring them right back in. God strictly forewarns us that when we finally obtain the land that God has given us, we should not forget how he has delivered us from trials and tribulation. Nor should we forget all that He has done for us once we are satisfied.

> ### Deuteronomy 6:10-15
> *And it shall be, when the LORD thy God shall have brought thee into the land which he sware unto thy fathers, to Abraham, to Isaac, and to Jacob, to give thee great and goodly cities, which thou buildedst not, And houses full of all good things, which thou filledst not, and wells digged, which thou diggedst not, vineyards and olive trees, which thou plantedst not; when thou shalt have eaten and be full; Then beware lest thou forget the LORD, which brought thee forth out of the land of Egypt, from the house of bondage. Thou shalt fear the LORD thy God, and serve him, and shalt swear by his name. Ye shall not go after other gods, of the gods of the people which are round about you; (For the LORD thy God is a jealous God among you) lest the anger of the LORD thy God be kindled against thee, and destroy thee from off the face of the earth.*

This is a common mistake we often see married couples experience. God blesses them with good work/income, a beautiful family, homes, cars, etc., then they forget who gave it to them. They begin to worship the gift instead of the Giver. Idolatry sets in and people begin to think too highly of themselves. When this happens in your marriage, strange things begin to happen. Love leaves the building and strange things appear.

It is at this juncture that men are often seduced with strange women. They lose sight of their purpose as a king and governor. A king doesn't get to retire from being king, nor can he abandon his post as a prophet or priest. Unfortunately, the husband is generally susceptible to strange things when they lose focus and purpose. When you lose those things, you can lose desire. Desire is the drive that God gives you. Lust is the vehicle used by the enemy to lure and deceive you.

When you and your spouse enter a spiritual and physical territory, there is already an occupant there. These people, spirits, entities are squatters, illegal residents. They're not part of your family. In other words, they are not part of the body of Christ, for they are of the world—a strange nation, with strange gods, practices, language and strange women. These people do not honor the Word of God and His way, which is why God does not want us to connect with them. If you operate in the flesh, you will be susceptible to their ways, which appeal to the senses. Riches, beauty, sensuality, sex, etc., everything that will make you feel good will try to make you leave your estate. When you indulge in these thoughts, that's when your spouse will no longer be appealing because the true beauty and value of your spouse is spiritual. It's the kind of love that lasts a lifetime.

Occupying territory is not limited to the process of you and your spouse becoming one. The husband assumes the position of a father and the wife, a mother. The enemy has no problem residing in the mind and attitudes of your children. Because we love our children so much, it is hard to conceive the idea of them being possessed or demonically influenced. Regardless of whether your child inherited a generational curse, or if they're disobedient and defiant, whatever it is, they are subject to your natural and spiritual authority. Order is the utmost important thing when dealing with children. Seek God first, then the husband and finally the wife.

Wives, avoid questioning or challenging your husband's decision or authority in front of the child. The husband is anointed and ordained to rule over his ENTIRE HOME. You are anointed to help him. When you two are one in raising your children, you will be unstoppable. It doesn't mean that there won't be a fight or resistance. However, you understand that we wrestle not against flesh and blood. Your children are not the enemy but they can be if you allow the enemy in. The enemy comes in through disorder and disobedience.

Husbands, it is important to remember that the scriptures says not to provoke your children to wrath. Although you're the head, you have a head as well. Abusing your authority actually gives the enemy legal right to attack you through your children. Wives, when you usurp your husband's authority, it's the same thing. You give the enemy access.

When you're up against strong generational curses in your household and through your children (children born to you or stepchildren), you can break the stronghold, but that kind of deliverance comes forth through prayer, fasting, power and authority. Pray in the Spirit, in righteousness, in order and authority in Jesus' name. Throughout the process, God will give you wisdom on what to do and will send you help if you need it. Trust the process and have faith in God til the end.

However, if you just have a disrespectful, disobedient, unruly child, the Bible says the rod of correction would drive it out. The word rod is defined as *punishment* or *discipline*. Do not spare the rod of correction when needed. God is telling you in His word that this is how you drive foolishness out of your children. This correction is not to destroy them but actually to save their lives and bring them to order.

> Proverbs 13:24
>
> *He that spareth his rod hateth his son: but he that loveth him chasteneth him betimes.*

> Proverbs 22:15
>
> *Foolishness is bound in the heart of a child; but the rod of correction shall drive it far from him.*

If you find yourself exhausted from fighting to take back what God has given you, check to see how and whom you are fighting. When you fight in the Spirit and in the Word, God will restore you. But you must stay focused on the purpose of marriage. Remember why you are fighting, whom you should be fighting, and when to wage war. Before you start cleaning up shop on the warfront, make sure you put away the strange gods because they represent a chink in your armor. Then stand in agreement in prayer and action with your spouse as to the strategy and plan to subdue the land. It's already yours.

SECTION THREE

It's getting real

CHAPTER 12

You Get Out What You Put In

> Matthew 13:24
>
> 24. *Another parable put he forth unto them, saying, The kingdom of heaven is likened unto a man which sowed good seed in his field.*

WE UNDERSTAND NOW that marital responsibility is a national one. God has given you power, dominion, and territory. The land that you subdued, (your spouse) that you obtained is fertile ground. The question then is what have you sown into your marriage? This rhetorical question is addressed to *each* spouse. Marriage is an institution, so when asked about what you have sown into your marriage, it's not just about how you treat your spouse. Remember, God is also a part of your covenant. In your marriage vows, you gave your word to your spouse in the sight God. Even if you tried to be savvy, neglecting to add verbiage like, "to honor and obey" or "for richer or for poorer" into your vows, *you still agreed* to it as a *believer*. So, have you sowed obedience or disobedience into your marriage?

When you got married, two became one and God holds each person accountable. In the principle of sowing and reaping, Jesus shows His *disciples* the mysteries of the kingdom and to *the other* in parables. He explains:

> Matthew 13:10-13
>
> *And the disciples came, and said unto him, Why speakest thou unto them in parables? He answered and said unto them, Because it is given unto you to know the mysteries of the kingdom of heaven, but to them it is not given. For whosoever hath, to him shall be given, and he shall have more abundance: but whosoever hath not, from him shall be taken away even that he hath. Therefore speak I to them in parables: because they seeing see not; and hearing they hear not, neither do they understand.*

When Jesus says, *for whosoever hath, to him shall be given and he shall have more abundance*, what does He mean? Have more of what? The answer is more of Him (the Word). Faith comes by hearing and *hearing* by the Word of God. He also says it is given to YOU, to know the mysteries of the kingdom of heaven. The concept of sowing and reaping is spiritual. We are not privileged to witness the process until it's done but the mystery of the *system* is revealed to us who BELIEVE. Sometimes, YOU may be in a season of your marriage where you're the only one sowing. Therefore, it's incumbent on you to understand the principles as well as the opposition.

As much as we would like to think that the more topical solution to keeping a marriage at its best is the answer, truth is *it's not*. Simple realignment of our understanding of basic principles can change everything. For instance, every husband expects his wife and children to respect, honor and hold him in high esteem. In order for this to happen, the husband has to sow these same qualities *to God first*. He does so by loving his wife as Christ loves the Church...*first*. Obeying God's word on how to treat his wife, *he puts God first* by applying the correct principle of sowing and reaping. In doing so, he just honored, respected and held God in a higher esteem than himself. Whether he considered his wife worthy or deserving of that treatment is inconsequential. He will reap, in due time, the harvest of respect, honor and high esteem from his wife and children because it's a spiritual law.

Oftentimes, problems persist in marriages or fail to grow as a result of personality flaws, clashes, stress, dysfunction; the list goes on and on. However, some people are set in their ways. They may NEVER CHANGE. Sometimes God will allow this. The saving grace is that if God allows it, he can change your perception of *how you see them*, things and how you feel about it to the point it doesn't bother you anymore. Therefore, someone in the marriage has to take the initiative to change their stance from being a rhetorical *others* or non-believer, into a disciple, where God reveals to you the mystery of the kingdom. It's important to choose the later because your marriage is a lifelong covenant not a *voidable contract*. Since divorce is not an option, God desires to reveal to us the knowledge of how to not become the enemy or make your spouse the enemy.

Spiritual hierarchy must be adhered to, beginning with God. Doing so requires faith. The second first is the husband, then the wife in that order. When this order is disturbed, even if divine principles are applied, the blessings take longer if ever, to reach its ordained destination. Principles that are obeyed out of order are not acceptable.

> **Malachi 1:6-8**
>
> *A son honoureth his father, and a servant his master: if then I be a father, where is mine honour? and if I be a master, where is my fear? saith the LORD of hosts unto you, O priests, that despise my name. And ye say, Wherein have we despised thy name? Ye offer polluted bread upon mine altar; and ye say, Wherein have we polluted thee? In that ye say, The table of the LORD is contemptible. And if ye offer the blind for sacrifice, is it not evil? and if ye offer the lame and sick, is it not evil? offer it now unto thy governor; will he be pleased with thee, or accept thy person? saith the LORD of hosts.*

Notice, I put *due time*. When a farmer plants a seed, he doesn't get a harvest the same day it's planted. There's a process the seed goes through that the natural eye is not authorized to see until germination is complete. This germination period is a critical time that the enemy likes to use against us. It's that dark time of waiting, being faithful, sucking up your attitude, turning the other cheek, while people treat you like crap. You've done all God asked you to do, held your tongue and prayed. Yes, this is precisely when the enemy comes in for the attack. HE HAS TO MAKE YOU FEEL AS IF NOTHING IS WORKING! Did you hear what I just said?! Right here, at this juncture is where the warfare begins!

Don't forget God is in the marriage covenant with you! God is the secret ingredient to the success, health, wealth, prosperity, and protection of the family. His power is unleashed by obedience to the Word and activated by faith. You will not gain much traction if you constantly sow retaliation, unforgiveness, and strife into your spouse. The devil loves to use the divide and conquer strategy. We've all experienced frustrations and a multitude of emotions that we give credence to, whether good or bad. However, in order for God's purpose to emerge in your marriage, you cannot fight or stand on emotions (feelings always change). We are spirit, God is a Spirit, and God is also the Word.

> ### Ephesians 6:12
> *For our struggle is not against flesh and blood, but against the rulers, against the powers, against the world forces of this darkness, against the spiritual forces of wickedness in the heavenly places.*

If the husband doesn't put God first (who is His head, master, high priest and father), he dishonors God. Therefore, he sows and reaps the same dishonor from those beneath him. Likewise, with the wife, if she sows dishonor, disrespect, and rebellion into her husband, that's what she will reap from him and her children! This is what I call a death cycle.

> ### Malachi 1:6-8
> *A son honoureth his father, and a servant his master: if then I be a father, where is mine honour? and if I be a master, where is my fear? saith the LORD of hosts unto you, O priests, that despise my name. And ye say, Wherein have we despised thy name? Ye offer polluted bread upon mine altar; and ye say, Wherein have we polluted thee? In that ye say, The table of the LORD is contemptible. And if ye offer the blind for sacrifice, is it not evil? and if ye offer the lame and sick, is it not evil? offer it now unto thy governor; will he be pleased with thee, or accept thy person? saith the LORD of hosts.*

Where does the death cycle begin? Generally, this occurs when your wants and desires (governed by feelings) supersedes God's will and Word. How each spouse responds to offense is of utmost importance because the husband has the power to sanctify the wife and vice-versa. But if the couple sows into *emotions* instead, the cycle begins. Through God's system and divine order, it's the only way to get back to peace and remain on track.

Good Ground

Discouragement often comes when a person keeps giving and giving without any reciprocity. When a spouse gets to this point, it's the beginning of the end. Reading passages like what I just wrote about sowing and reaping goes into one ear and out of the other because you're just tired! You're spent and have nothing else to give at this point. If I looked at you from a carnal perspective, I would feel sorry for you and tell you to count your losses and move on. However, God has ordained for me to speak life into your marriage through the knowledge of His word.

If this is you, God wants you to know that it's nothing wrong with you or what you're giving. The problem is one or two things, the *soil* or the *enemy*. You may ask yourself, what is the soil? The soil is the heart of whom you are sowing into. Just because you sow doesn't mean that it's falling into *good ground*. People have issues, deep rooted, hidden, hurtful past that we're privy to and other times have no clue. Because we all communicate differently, you may have offended your spouse and don't even know it. As a result, you are just sowing your heart out but to no avail because the soil is hardened and difficult to breach. Jesus describes different circumstances as to what happens when a seed doesn't penetrate into good ground:

> Matthew 13:3-7
>
> *And he spake many things unto them in parables, saying, Behold, a sower went forth to sow; And when he sowed, some seeds fell by the way side, and the fowls came and devoured them up: Some fell upon stony places, where they had not much earth: and forthwith they sprung up, because they had no deepness of earth: And when the sun was up, they were scorched; and because they had no root, they withered away. And some fell among thorns; and the thorns sprung up, and choked them.*

CHAPTER 12 | YOU GET OUT WHAT YOU PUT IN

> *Matthew 13:18-23*
>
> *Hear ye therefore the parable of the sower. When any one heareth the word of the kingdom, and understandeth it not, then cometh the wicked one, and catcheth away that which was sown in his heart. This is he which received seed by the way side. But he that received the seed into stony places, the same is he that heareth the word, and anon with joy receiveth it; Yet hath he not root in himself, but dureth for a while: for when tribulation or persecution ariseth because of the word, by and by he is offended. He also that received seed among the thorns is he that heareth the word; and the care of this world, and the deceitfulness of riches, choke the word, and he becometh unfruitful. But he that received seed into the good ground is he that heareth the word, and understandeth it; which also beareth fruit, and bringeth forth, some an hundredfold, some sixty, some thirty.*

If you're not yielding a harvest from the seed that you have sown into them, the soil of their heart has been hardened. You may have hardened it through your action and inaction, or it could be extenuating circumstances of how they were raised or their own personal insecurity.

Trials and pressures of life or the cares of this world and the deceitfulness of riches have hardened the soil. Those are the things you are contending with, thus preventing clear communication and reciprocity.

Consequently, the heart also has an ear. It's not the natural ears on the side of our head but the SPIRITUAL ear of the heart. Now the question is, how do you break that ground? How do you soften the soil so that you're not just wasting time toiling over a bitter person that refuses to change?

The Bible says:

> **Romans 10:17**
> *So then faith cometh by hearing, and hearing by the word of God.*

In order to get the soil to become good ground, you have to apply Love and the Word *in action*. Now, here's where it gets tricky. For the wife, the Bible says that the husband is won over by SUBMISSION, *CHASTE* CONVERSATION and her BEHAVIOR! Right here is probably the hardest things for a woman to do, especially when she feels neglected and unloved. However, this is the most effective method because Matthew 13:23 says, *good ground* is he that *heareth* the Word and *understandeth* it. When the wife takes the pressure off herself and husband by sowing her faith into the Word of God, God changes the soil! The body of your husband belongs to you but his *heart is in the hand of God*:

> *Proverbs 21:1*
> *The king's heart is in the hand of the LORD, as the rivers of water: he turneth it whithersoever he will.*

Again, wife, I ask you, 'What have you sown into your marriage?' Have you cursed your marriage with your mouth and behavior? Although you may have sown good seeds, meaning, you have done some good things, have you sown into good ground according to understanding and order? Did you hear? Did you understand? The answer is in submission to your husband, because it is actually submission to God. It is also in your behavior. Have you violated with bad behavior, such as the silent treatment, denying sex, mishandling money, and not taking care of your husband, home, and children properly? Have you allowed family, friends, and children to disrespect your husband? Have you disrespected him? Good behavior is great but *godly behavior* of obeying His word regarding your husband is the actual *good ground*.

Realization of this simple change within self, changes the harvest in due season, which is why I envision that same proverbial frustrated, fruitless woman differently. She just needs to tap into the power of faith in the Word of God. Faith is definitely required because if you just look at the situation alone, you would feel defeated and leave. Remember, we walk by faith, not by sight!

The husband, on the other hand, softens the soil through love and death to self. The more he loves his wife like Christ loves the Church, God intervenes and begins to heal those parts of his wife that he cannot see, reach or perhaps doesn't even know about. Let me be clear about the Love characteristics that God is talking about:

> 1 Corintians 3:4-7
>
> *Charity suffereth long, and is kind; charity envieth not; charity vaunteth not itself, is not puffed up, Doth not behave itself unseemly, seeketh not her own, is not easily provoked, thinketh no evil; Rejoiceth not in iniquity, but rejoiceth in the truth; Beareth all things, believeth all things, hopeth all things, endureth all things.*

Both men and women have deep dark places and wounds within. Some we know about, others we may have forgotten or haven't even realized. Yet, these wounds (thoughts, memories, and feelings) are choking us, preventing us from getting to our maximum potential. This leads me to the other thing messing with our seed...the enemy. Outside influences, friends, family, co-workers, church members can become the enemy by influencing you with their opinions or interpretation of your marriage. Its wise to get godly counsel when you have problems. However, you must make sure whatever advice is suggested lines up with the word and the spirit of truth. There can be information that is true to an extent but not applicable to your marriage. No one will ever truly know the depth of your spouse except for you and God. Don't all the words of others to choke the seed of healing, love and progress in your marriage.

You can be sowing good seeds into your marriage but sometimes you are up against secret enemies that plants weeds into it. Not everyone who claims to be your friend or happy for you, actually are. Some people may like you as a friend but secretly desire what you have and will try to destroy your marriage out of jealousy. Therefore, you must be careful with your private information.

> Matthew 13:36-39
>
> *Then Jesus sent the multitude away, and went into the house: and his disciples came unto him, saying, Declare unto us the parable of the tares of the field. He answered and said unto them, He that soweth the good seed is the Son of man; The field is the world; the good seed are the children of the kingdom; but the tares are the children of the wicked one; The enemy that sowed them is the devil; the harvest is the end of the world; and the reapers are the angels.*

CHAPTER 13

Husbands, Prepare To Die

WHENEVER YOU SAY something is *like* something, its similarities are being compared to an original—not an exact replica, rather something close. With that being said, the idea of a man dying *like* Christ is not appealing at all. I mean, how do you get someone to sign up for that? Who in their right mind would want to be lied on, punched, slapped, spit on, whipped, stabbed, and crucified, for a bride? I don't know a single person on this planet that would sign up for that, no matter how much you love your wife.

God is not asking you to physically die on a cross for your wife like Jesus did per se, but He is instructing you to die *like* Him. The operative word is *like*. Jesus had no desire to go through the beatings and the crucifixion. Salvation and doing the will of the Father was His reason and desire. In that purpose, He was able to endure the *process* of accomplishing His mission. Jesus knew what He was doing and why, took the punishment, and rose up to the throne as God.

In your marriage, there's a process of development that you'll have to endure at one point or another as a "right of passage" for leadership. Becoming one with God and your wife requires a sacrifice. As the head of the wife, you are like Christ (the Anointed One) in the respect that you are the king, priest and prophet of your home. You are the savior of the body. It's your divine purpose to be fruitful, multiply, replenish, subdue, become a Holy Nation and a royal priesthood. Accomplishing that task requires you to lead, fight, and die, in order to live again on purpose.

> Matthew 10:39
>
> *He that findeth his life shall lose it and he who has lost his life for My sake will find it.*

What do I mean by that? You must die to self. Prior to marriage, you were free to do as you please without consulting with anyone. At least so you thought. You didn't realize how many people/places and things you've been consulting with and reporting to unconsciously. The reason why is because you simply chose who you wanted to talk to, when you talk to them, how, etc and if you didn't like them you would just stop talking. Everything was about you. The only thing you had to be responsible for is yourself and your interest. Everything was yours; time, money, resources, interest, etc. Then it got lonely. Real lonely. That's when you realized a helper, someone who could help hold you accountable, wouldn't be so bad.

Now that you have a wife, you must love her like Christ loves the church. This is not an easy task when you think about it because the church (the bride) did not recognize Jesus at first. They saw Him as a prophet but they did not see Him as a Savior. Sometimes, in your marriage, your wife may behave the same way. She may value what you have to say but will not recognize the God in you as having the power to save her (in so many ways and on so many levels). The world and the then *church* rejected Christ, beat him, lied on Him, and tried to kill Him. It's easy to love someone who is likeable but what about when they are not likeable? How do you endure the abuse of being an unappreciated, unrecognized genius?

Regardless of whether your wife sees your greatness or not, it doesn't take away the fact of who you are. You are the visionary for her and the family. Matter of fact, she will not see your fullest potential until you die to self! Like the church, they didn't see or understand who Jesus was and what He was doing. It took them a while to learn and understand His love for us. It wasn't until Jesus died that people truly realized and recognized Him for who He was…our Savior. Likewise, you wife will never really know and understand how much you love her until she sees you die for her because it is the greatest act of love you can make.

PURPOSE PRINCIPLE

Dying to self for your wife is the greatest act of love she can witness!

This spiritual death I'm referring to is not what you think. On the onset, it appears as if you are losing something but you're not. Remember, God is in this with you, governing, guiding, and protecting you. God made promises to you. Like Abraham, God promised him a son. That promise was fulfilled. Here's where things get dicey; after waiting all these years for a son with Sarah and finally getting it, God asked him to sacrifice this same son of promise! Seems crazy, right? What kind of head game is God playing? Why would God promise Abraham a son, give it to him, and then ask him to sacrifice him?

Why would God give you the woman of your dreams then turn around and tell you to spend the rest of your life pleasing her? What about you and what you want? There are things in your life that you value and treasure beyond all else, it could be yourself, money, time, animals, sports, friends (you fill in the blank). Trust and believe there will come a time, many times that life will require you to sacrifice what you love. As sadistic as it may seem, God is not playing a head game with you. He's transitioning you from sonship to kingship, from employee to boss. In that leadership position, there is no room for emotional decisions. It's your assignment to operate God's will through your marriage. In order for you to complete that task, like Jesus, you have to die to self for your wife.

When you do this, you are activating the spiritual law of sowing and reaping. Sacrificing self is death to the carnal flesh (your feeling/emotions/wants). It has to die in order to germinate the seed within which is love. That's what it took for you to die to self. The new self you'll be harvesting is the spiritual body of love that resides in you. That new *you* without self is your *wife*.

Consider this, God required Abraham to sacrifice Isaac, his most valued possession (Abraham was COMPLETELY WILLING to do so). It wasn't what he *wanted* to do but he was WILLING. Why? Because Abraham KNEW GOD. Consequently, many people overlook the fact that GOD KNEW ABRAHAM! He called him *friend*. God was looking at Abraham's heart, faith, and motives. Abraham was more concerned about doing God's will and being obedient. God counted *his actions as righteousness* and right before Abraham was about to kill what he loved, God told Abraham to stay his hand. In other words, God stopped Abraham from going all the way through with the sacrifice because he already did it in the spirit. Now the sacrifice still had to be made but instead of Abraham being responsible for a replacement offering GOD SUPPLIED it! Jesus died on the cross so you don't have to.

No matter how frustrated you may be about the sacrifices or challenges of marriage you may face, God will always provide for you if you are willing to lay down your life. God is your friend, not a harsh taskmaster hovering over you, waiting to take away every joy and blessing you have. He will give you the desires of your heart if you delight in Him.

The key then to being most effective as a husband, father, and leader is to KNOW GOD. That requires an intimate relationship with Him so that when He tells you to do something, you do it with confidence because you know *His character*. He has to be more to you than a cliché or a God that your grandma and mother have taught you. That's not enough to make you lay down your life.

God never intended for you to face your giants alone. He just needs you to show up for the fight, WILLING TO DIE. You're *like* Christ but you are not Him. He died on the cross so you don't have to. The only death that you have to suffer is death to self (your will) because you love God more than whatever it is you're wanting outside of His will. Your flesh (feelings, emotions) doesn't want to suffer or sacrifice for another unless it benefits itself. Guess what? That's not marriage, that's singlehood and contrary to the will of God. If the leader goes rogue, then guess what, you have just taught your wife and kids to go for self as well.

We understand that God requires you to love your wife as Christ loves the church. However, the Word does not tell the wife to love *you* like the church! Her mandate is to submit to your leadership and she has to so whether she likes it or not (out of her love for God). Wow! If you look closely at that dynamic, you'll observe the similarities between the husband and wife compared to Christ and the church. The church did not love Jesus first, He first loved us. It is through *His love that we are saved*. Therefore, Jesus' love was NOT contingent on the response or approval of the church but according to who He is and His purpose for being.

Your wife will learn how to love you through observation because you are the head and the leader. If you follow her, you will be lost in confusion because God didn't give her vision. Ultimately, in this case, your marriage will be led by myriads of emotions that change all the time. That is an unstable environment. Everyone is watching you, your wife, kids, people, everyone! When you die to self for the sake of your divine purpose, you are more like God than ever because when you stand down, He stands up! When you speak, everyone will listen. You will accomplish the impossible because you are one with God and that's all He does!

When your wife (and children) see you die to self, it's the most fearless thing she could witness you do and it satisfies her need for security and stability under your covering, which causes her to love you more (just like Christ).

Jesus didn't walk in fear and He didn't spend time battling demons. He knew who he was and His purpose, and he thus walked in full authority. Consequently, Satan and his demons knew who He was too. When the devil approached him, all the devil could do was try to seduce Him with lust of the flesh, lust of the eyes, and pride of life—all of which appeals to the senses. What Satan didn't realize is that before he approached Him, Jesus had already fasted. In other words, He already killed His flesh. When the enemy came, Jesus appeared weak (which was a good thing because the flesh represents emotions and feelings) but He wasn't weak at all. Domination of your own carnal ways is a divine military strategy God gives you that the devil will ALWAYS underestimate. The enemy did not anticipate Jesus' *spirit man* to be so strong.

> **1 Corinthians 12:10**
> *Therefore I take pleasure in infirmities in reproaches, in necessities, in persecutions, in distresses for Christ's sake: for when I am weak, then I am strong.*

PURPOSE PRINCIPLE

It is imperative that a wife witness her husband die to self.

Let me go deeper on that. When you are satisfied in your spirit, you don't want anything and you're not governed by lust. No one can seduce you into something you don't want because you don't want it. Discipline of the flesh is one of the most powerful things a husband can do. A man that is governed by his spirit and dead to the flesh is like God. No one can stop him. For this reason, God requires you to lay down your life for your wife because you are leading her to the path of victory. He doesn't want to make you weak by taking away the things you want. There is nothing that you *want* that you *need*. If you *need it*, God will supply it. Armed with that knowledge, you should ALWAYS be satisfied in spirit. The Lord is conditioning you to be so powerful that no one and nothing can distract, defeat, or destroy you. Remember, you are the one to beat. In order to take over a man's home, you must first bind up the strongman.

Satan knows he cannot defeat you. Satan is not the real enemy. If there were an enemy that needs to be defeated, that would be you. Think about it, Satan approached Jesus but could never touch Him until Jesus *laid down His life*. Although it looked like the enemy had the upper hand, Jesus was in control the entire time. He allowed the enemy a moment in time to appear victorious in order to destroy him forever.

PURPOSE PRINCIPLE

When you die to self, no one can kill your spirit.

Like Christ, you will do the same in your marriage. There may come a time where you sacrifice for her and it appears as if you are losing, she doesn't appreciate, understand, care or even love you. Don't pay attention to any of that! Understand that your discipline and power will set off a precedent in your marriage; whereas once you get through this, you will never have to die again! Everyone including your wife will respect you. Like God, you ought to know and understand your position as a husband, along with your purpose and relationship with God in His likeness. The only fear you should have is the fear of the Lord.

PURPOSE PRINCIPLE

If you're not willing to lay down your life for your wife, you cannot be her savior.

> **Revelation 1:18**
> *I am he that liveth, and was dead and behold, I am alive forevermore, Amen; and have the keys of hell and of death.*

CHAPTER 14

Wives That Win

WHENEVER GOD DECIDES to reveal His mysteries, it is absolutely astounding to know how far removed from the truth we were prior to the revelation. For instance, the idea of submission was one that I (and many women I know) had major issues with. I often wondered, how could God expect grown women, who've spent years learning, forming ideas and opinions, giving birth to children, and doing countless other things, to submit to a man just because he's your husband? What, are we supposed to just go dumb and play stupid?

> 1 Corinthians 9:25
>
> *Everyone who competes in the games goes into strict training. They do it to get a crown that will not last, but we do it to get a crown that will last forever.*

And there it was…the revelation. How can a wife win her husband over? In order to win anything you have to play the game. Yes, being a wife is a game of wits, endurance, and strategy. God expects us to play to win and He wants us to have fun while we do it! Maybe you're saying to yourself, "so I just have to lose myself and be a *yes* woman? Not trying to sound condescending but… yes! Wives who understand *the game* of submission have mastered the art of losing themselves to gain their desire—not to be confused with manipulation where you're *making* someone do what you want them to do against their own will. On the contrary, God through His infinite wisdom is teaching His daughters how to help their husbands fulfill their purpose as well as hers through influence, motivation, inspiration and surrender.

> **1 Peter 3:1**
> *Wives, in the same way submit yourselves to your own husbands so that, if any of them do not believe the word, they may be won over without words by the behavior of their wives.*

As I mentioned in previous chapters, God is in covenant with you and your husband so He expects to be the third cord in your marriage. He is what makes your relationship everlasting, impenetrable, and loving. Therefore, not only does He expect you to lose yourself, He expects you to get into character. Just like an actor in a movie who takes the overall scope and vision from the

LOVE
is patient
is kind
it does not envy
it does not boast
it is not proud
it is not rude
it is not self seeking
it is not easily angered
it keeps no record of wrongs
never fails

director (God is the director), learn their script (the Word of God), find their motivation and get into character. The character that you're playing is Love/God. Every day, you should wake up, read your script, pray for motivation, and then get into character. These are the characteristics of Love.

In order for your marriage to be successful, you must play your part. There will be times when your husband will lose focus or his way. You're the embodiment of who he *should be*. Everything about you should be a living breathing reminder of himself and God. The Bible says that out of the abundance of the heart, the mouth speaks. If you are filled with the Word/the Holy Spirit, whenever you speak, your conversation will be loaded with power and conviction because it is not you alone speaking to him but God Himself. That's why God said in 1 Peter 3:1 that He would behold your *chaste conversation* coupled with fear. Contrary to popular belief, it's not through nagging or what you may consider *rational* dialogue that he responds best to.

> **1 Peter 3:1**
>
> *Likewise, ye wives, be in subjection to your own husbands; that, if any obey not the word, they also may without the word be won by the conversation of the wives; While they behold your chaste conversation coupled with fear.*

It is not we that do the work of faith but God alone. Therefore, in order for God to meet your need and answer your prayer, you must be in the position to receive. The position or posture, if you will, is through the mind*set* of obedience to His Word. A woman cannot make a man, nor can she control him. That was never God's intention in the first place. His desire is a relationship with *them*. And because He created a man to be a ruler, priest and prophet, the man must always be the head.

PURPOSE PRINCIPLE

Wives: Do not try to CHANGE his mind, INSPIRE change with godly behavior and conversation.

The husband is the HEAD of the wife. The MOUTH is in the head. The body moves and executes the will of the mind but does not have the capacity to verbalize how it feels. From the neck down, the BODY can only speak through *body language*, gestures that form patterns of memorable language that men understand.

PURPOSE PRINCIPLE

When a spouse listens attentively without interruption, the other spouse will feel like they've been heard and in some cases understood.

When the wife listens without speaking, the husband feels like he has been heard (and in some cases understood). If he's being foolish, your silence will allow him to hear himself and possibly come to a more sound resolution. Remember, the wife is the helpmeet. When the husband meets with his wife, he expects to be reverentially heard. He is the king and has the final say. As glorious as that may sound, heavy is the crown. Every decision that he makes for his wife and family, affects everyone. If your husband has ever failed you, trust me, he never intended to and probably beats himself up inside. Wives, it's not easy to talk to you when so much is on the line. Some men really don't know what to do in order to provide so he comes up with *ideas* (smart, crazy, brilliant, absolutely absurd ones).

God said, "Commit thy way unto the Lord and he will establish your thoughts." Your loving character and behavior will convict him if he's wrong because he'll feel guilty. If YOU'RE wrong, you'll be convicted by His Words and will feel guilty. When we obey the voice of the Lord, He comes in doing miracles. Let your WORK SPEAK FOR YOU—not your "works" (how you did everything).

> Habakkuk 2:18
>
> *What profiteth the graven image that the maker thereof hath graven it; the molten image, and a teacher of lies, that the maker of his work trusteth therein, to make dumb idols?*

God created man. A woman cannot "MAKE" a man do anything. To *make* something, you put together a creation with materials that already exist. Thus inevitably, the *maker* is not authentically a creator. When a woman makes a man, she consequently turns him into HER OWN IMAGE AND LIKENESS (this is idolatry), thereby becoming like a *graven* image (a dead a man walking).

> Habakkuk 2:20
>
> *But the LORD is in his holy temple: let all the earth keep silence before him.*

When you get into character, God will perform His word *on your behalf*. Submission, patience, and chaste conversation are very powerful strategies. Women are generally susceptible to responding to verbal communication because that's how we normally express our feelings. Most men, on the other hand, have a different nature. They don't go around verbalizing and communicating all of their feelings because they communicate and respond better to action.

Look at the definition of the word *chaste*:
1. free from obscenity; decent.
2. undefiled or stainless.
3. pure in style; not excessively ornamented; simple.

Things to consider:
- Time
- Place
- Tone
- Body language
- Authority

Master the art of persuasion, not manipulation. You are the helpmeet. It is the job of the wife to help him accomplish the goals of the family. If your husband allows you to work, do business or whatever, great.

However, if any of those things get in the way of *his plans* for your marriage, YOU ARE THE ONE WHO HAS TO SUBMIT TO HIS VISION. YOU MUST GIVE UP WHATEVER YOU NEED TO, MOVE IF YOU HAVE TO. BE WILLNG TO LOSE, and you will gain in the end.

Many wives lose their husbands or destroy their marriage because they lack knowledge, wisdom, and understanding. It is virtually impossible to accomplish the will and purpose of God with good intentions alone. Even if your husband threatens to leave you or if you don't seem to like each other anymore, if you make these changes, more than likely you will see a positive turnaround in your favor!Most of the times, when you have strife, confusion or lack of growth, it is because one or both of you were out of order. Considering the scriptures and actually applying them is like a supernatural healing balm that cures just about anything. But you have to take the first step to learn how to play the game and win!

The playbook:

RESPECT HIM. Respect him above all others and treat him like a king. Be able to receive a commandment/instruction without offense. That means, your husband can tell you (not ask) to do something that you may not like but do it anyway (with a cheerful spirit). In those moments, you are consciously losing yourself and operating in character, not for him, but as service unto God. He will reward you for your obedience. This is wisdom. Unbeknownst to most women, this act of submission creates trust with their husband. Not only does your reaction to him make him better, more successful and more confident, it makes him feel more secure and loved, which in turn will make him love you more.

> Proverbs 10:8
>
> 8The wise in heart will receive commandments: but a prating fool shall fall.

1. DON'T TALK, SCREAM, FUSS, OR GOSSIP TOO MUCH.

> Proverbs 10:19
>
> In the multitude of words there wanteth not sin: but he that refraineth his lips is wise.

2. BEWARE OF A PRIDEFUL SPIRIT. I've seen pride arise in many wives who think they're so beautiful or special that they should be worshiped, make more money, or have more education than their spouses. Nothing wrong with making a lot of money or furthering your education. It's the pride/attitude/motive behind those ambitions that's the question. If you allow the demon of pride to take residence in your home, not only can you lose your husband, you can lose everything. When pride comes, destruction is imminent. No matter how educated or successful you are, it doesn't change the order that God has set. And we all know that

beauty fades. The Word suggests that wives that win are gracious. That is the character trait you must embody when tempted to be vain with pride.

> **Proverbs 11:2**
>
> *When pride cometh, then cometh shame: but with the lowly is wisdom.*

> **Proverbs 11:16**
>
> *A gracious woman retaineth honour: and strong men retain riches.*

> **Proverbs 12:4**
>
> *A virtuous woman is a crown to her husband: but she that maketh ashamed is as rottenness in his bones.*

PURPOSE PRINCIPLE

Mastery of the mouth creates a happy wife and happy life!

3. USE YOUR TONGUE/MOUTH FOR EDIFICATION. Build your husband up; don't tear him down with vicious words. You can literally bring healing to his spirit with kind, loving words because whether he says so or not, he does care what you say. Even if he is depressed, the right word at the right time spoken from you (because you have the Word of God in you) can make him glad again. Mastery of the mouth creates a happy wife and happy life!

> **Proverbs 12:18**
> *There is that speaketh like the piercings of a sword: but the tongue of the wise is health.*

> **Proverbs 12:25**
> *Heaviness in the heart of man maketh it stoop: but a good word maketh it glad.*

> **Proverbs 21:9**
> *It is better to dwell in a corner of the housetop, than with a brawling woman in a wide house.*

> **Proverbs 21:19**
> *It is better to dwell in the wilderness, than with a contentious and an angry woman.*

> **Proverbs 13:13**
> *Whoso despiseth the word shall be destroyed: but he that feareth the commandment shall be rewarded.*

4. USE WISDOM. Don't be foolish being governed by emotions, demonic thoughts, and outside influences. Don't even let your culture or bad habits rule because "It's just who I am." If you don't fear God and use wisdom in your marriage, you will be the co-conspirator of your own demise. Men are not designed to take orders, ridicule, or insult kindly from women. They are simply not wired that way because their nature is that of a king. Even if they don't say anything

and it seems like they may have just accepted your way, you will find that you're in that marriage alone with him physically there and spiritually gone. Or he may simply decide to leave you, all because of your *uncircumcised* mouth.

> **Proverbs 14:1**
> *Every wise woman buildeth her house: but the foolish plucketh it down with her hands.*

5. USE PRUDENCE. Who you are, whether you have matured to this nature yet or not, is a prudent wife. Part of your purpose is to become whom God called you to be. Consciously begin walking in to the character of God and you will see the prudent wife emerge. Then watch how your husband, children, and everyone around you begin to respect and love you more, not from you controlling them but from you controlling yourself, submitting to the Lord.

Initially, this may feel unnatural or fake to you. This is to be expected because your flesh is used to being in control. Prior to being married, you could say or do whatever you wanted without having to submit to any man besides your father (many women didn't even have a father around to submit to). You're used to doing things and having things your way. The key to fulfilling your purpose as a wife is simply learning how to do things God's way. Study the Word and ask God why, if you don't understand something. It's easier to do what He says when you understand why you're doing it. However, if you really love God and your husband, the Word says, *you will keep my commandments.*

> Proverbs 14:8
>
> *The wisdom of the prudent is to understand his way: but the folly of fools is deceit.*

> Proverbs 16:21
>
> *The wise in heart shall be called prudent: and the sweetness of the lips increaseth learning.*

> Proverbs 19:14
>
> *House and riches are the inheritance of fathers: and a prudent wife is from the LORD.*

> Proverbs 19:16
>
> *He that keepeth the commandment keepeth his own soul; but he that despiseth his ways shall die.*

6. GET WISDOM. Wisdom *is* the principal thing; *therefore* get wisdom: and with all thy getting get understanding (Proverbs 4:7). I love this quote by Steven A. Covey, "Seek first to understand then to be understood." Women are natural verbal communicators and we respond according to what we see and feel. Men are not necessarily like that. Although they may feel everything that you do, their response is generally internalized and will manifest through working a lot, substance abuse, avoidance (silent treatment, coming home late, long hours at the gym, traveling a lot for work) and even through sex (or the lack thereof). In most cases, they don't like to talk everything out. There are many reasons to this, which I am not a man so I personally cannot say. However, I've heard from men that they go silent or violent

because they do not feel heard or understood. In which cases, their wives are confused because they have verbalized their grievances, expressed their concerns, or even offered to help, yet the husband continues to block her out.

From my understanding and what I have heard from many husbands, they often feel like they are not understood because they don't feel like their wives heard them. Yet, the wife will say that she heard every word he said (she can quote it verbatim).

So where is the discrepancy? He doesn't feel heard because she won't STOP TALKING and won't submit (stop talking). She won't stop talking because she is trying to win the argument or convince him of something instead of just listening. When talking to the King, learn to hold your tongue, your peace, watch your body language, and listen to him completely. Whether you agree or not, pick your battles. Ask the Holy Spirit for discernment in your timing.

Learn to understand you husband's habits, likes and dislikes and behave accordingly. Let it be all about him and you will find that he will make things all about you. Keep in mind, your purpose is to help him first, not the other way around. He can and should help you, but if there's a faceoff between you two, start trying to understand and accommodate him. He needs your acceptance, it's *very* important to him. Your support could make or break his motivation for success.

> Proverbs 19:22
>
> *The desire of a man is his kindness: and a poor man is better than a liar.*

> **Proverbs 20:5**
> *Counsel in the heart of man is like deep water; but a man of understanding will draw it out.*

> **Proverbs 23:9**
> *Speak not in the ears of a fool: for he will despise the wisdom of thy words.*

> **Proverbs 24:26**
> *Every man shall kiss his lips that giveth a right answer.*

> ***Very important*** **Proverbs 25:5-7**
> *Take away the wicked from before the king, and his throne shall be established in righteousness.*

Wives that win have learned to master the art of timing and presentation. A wise wife never forgets that her husband is her king. She is not presumptuous and careless with her timing and she doesn't try to sit in his seat. In other words, she doesn't get all up in his face, yelling and screaming, confronting him, and challenging him in arguments or disagreements. Nor does she override his decisions with blatant disrespect and do what *she thinks* is best. The woman who does this errs against the Word of God and will find herself disappointed, alone (with her husband right there), or divorced.

> **Proverbs 25:6-7**
>
> *Put not forth <u>thyself</u> in the presence of the king, and stand not <u>in the place</u> of great men: For better it is that it be said unto thee, Come up hither; than that thou shouldest be put lower in the presence of the prince whom thine eyes have seen.*

7. **Love and Patience.** One thing you can count on is that God rewards the righteous and the diligent. This may feel like a poor consolation prize because you're being righteous while your spouse might not have been. If you want to persuade your husband to do the right thing, the key is to continue to Love him (remain in character) and learn to speak softly and sweetly to him. I don't care if he comes in everyday like a Tasmanian devil you continue to do what's right *unto God.* At times, you will have to be *long-suffering.* That too is one of your strategies. You're not speaking softly because you're a push over, settling, or stupid. It's a sign of meekness, which means strength under control. For a man, that's the language he understands and will receive from a woman. Otherwise, you'll be faced with resistance and contempt.

Armed with this knowledge and wisdom, you can operate with understanding. He's processing the whirlwind of responsibilities in his head and your peaceful demeanor is a calmer physical reminder of who he needs to be. You are the beacon of light that helps him find his way home. God will anoint you to this task and give you the grace to endure. This is the test of true love. This is why he made you his wife and none of those other women. Let me be the first to tell you that the world will condemn you for being long-suffering because their philosophy is self-gratification. They think that if you're not happy, you should leave. However, the Word teaches us to lose ourselves in order to gain life.

> **Proverbs 25:11**
> *A word fitly spoken is like apples of gold in pictures of silver.*

> **Proverbs 25:15**
> *By long forbearing is a prince persuaded, and a soft tongue breaketh the bone.*

8. **Attract.** No matter how saved a man is, he is still and always will be a man. That means he is a visual creature. Do not let yourself go. Make it your business to make yourself appealing inside and out as often as possible. If you're overweight and don't feel attractive, then ten to one, he's not going to find you as attractive either. Do something about it! Work out with him or on your own. He would be more attracted to you for at least trying. Even if you decide to remain on the plus side, stay big and beautiful! Keep your hair and nails nice as often as possible. Smell nice and dress nice. As long as he has eyes for you, it is more difficult for him to have eyes for someone else. Now, you don't have to make an effort in this area if you don't want to but just know you'll run the risk of him being attracted to other women who do.

9. **Adapt.** (1 Co 11:8-9) You must mold yourself to your husband, not the other way around. This is a challenge for a lot of women. I've seen marriages destroyed because both husband and wife went into different direction as a result of

two different visions, ideas or opinion. I was watching a popular reality show where one of the wives had a thriving business in the state they lived in (both had businesses there in fact). Then the husband decided to expand and open a business in another state. That move put a tremendous strain on their marriage. There were accusations that he was cheating and she was hurt by the accusations. She also missed having her husband around. Because his business was thriving, he decided to get a place there so that he can manage the business better. This infuriated his wife. At this point, she had a choice, move to be with her husband at the expense of her business and comfortable lifestyle or remain where she was and try to make him move back. She decided to **not to follow her husband** and began talking about divorce. Wrong move! That's how the world operates! As a believer, it is the wife that has to adapt to the needs of her husband not the other way around. Being willing to lose yourself, comfort zone, and even a successful business could be the very seed that will change your marriage forever...FOR THE BETTER! That is a faith move! Of course, it's an extremely hard decision and even considered selfish on her husband's part. But the body follows the head, not the other way around. Whatever you lose being obedient to God, He will recompense. God knows your desire and He will fix things in time. You have to step out on faith and be obedient to God's way of doing things.

> Luke 17:33
>
> *Whosoever shall seek to save his life shall lose it; and whosoever shall lose his life shall preserve it.*

11. **Accommodate, appease, and satisfy your husband's need for food, sex, companionship, and admiration.** Yes, FEED HIM! If you don't know how to cook, learn.

The concept of soul food is real. Hearty meals are more than nourishment for his body but also to his soul. Again, you don't have to make this effort, however, you will be giving place to the enemy who has no problem cooking for your man.

12. **Sexually please him as well.** Don't hold back, have fun, learn new things. Get creative, take initiative and he will love you for it! Worldly women gain leverage because they are usually (sexually) down for whatever. That mindset is exciting to men. If his wife would have that same attitude and excitement, chances are less likely that he will wander (he would be too tired! lol).

13. **Be his peace.**

14. **Accept him.**

15. **Remember, men are won over.** That means you beat him at his own game. You play to win by *becoming* the living Word, which is the actual embodiment of Love Himself. Worldly women are predictable because they are governed by emotions and they are more sensual. When you apply the word of God to your being, the enemy who is trying to influence your husband will not see you coming. Just as you have to submit to your husband and honor him as king, your husband has to do the same in the presence of the Lord. When you speak and behave the way the Word tells you to, your husband (whether he realizes or not) is now in the presence of the Lord and before you know it, he will bow down! He's not bowing down to you (let's be clear). Both of you are bowing down to the will of God.

Almost as important as love, men NEED respect! Sometimes women feel like they do respect their husbands but consequently they don't actually really know what it means to respect a man. I happened to come across this acronym for respect that provides a great insight on respecting your husband. If you master this, he will be happy indeed!

R = RESPOND PHYSICALLY

Of all your husband's needs, this is the one that only you can legitimately address. *If you pour all your energies into being a good wife in every other way, but marginalize or neglect the area of physical intimacy, then you have failed.*

God designed this one-flesh union to be uniquely characteristic of marriage. **Your husband will never feel completely respected as long as you habitually turn him down or slap him away when he tries to get physically close.**

E = EXPRESS SINCERE THANKS

Be grateful for the many things — big and little — your husband does for you, and **thank him every time.** *Show him that you appreciate him in whatever way speaks most clearly to him.*

Don't take your husband for granted *and don't saddle him with expectations. Expectations lead only to discontent. If your husband preforms well, he'll get no special acknowledgement or show of gratitude, because he was only doing what you expected. If he doesn't, you'll feel slighted and angry, and he won't know why.*

"There is no such thing as gratitude unexpressed. If it is unexpressed, it is plain, old-fashioned ingratitude." – Robert Brault

S = SILENCE CAN BE GOLDEN

"If you can't say anything nice, don't say anything at all." I'm not advocating giving your husband a cold shoulder, but neither should you give him a piece of your mind. **Sometimes it's better to just keep your mouth shut.**

The ability to hold our tongue is an underutilized skill for many of us. Yet, the Bible tells us **we should "not let any unwholesome speech come out of [our] mouths, but only what is good for building others up, that it may benefit those who listen."** (*Ephesians 4:29*)

So next time you are tempted to nag, argue, gripe, or belittle, keep these verses in mind: Proverbs 21:19, Philippians 4:8, Colossians 3:8

"Often the difference between a successful marriage and a mediocre one consists of leaving about three or four things a day unsaid." ~ Harlan Miller

P = PRAY WITH AND FOR HIM

Prayer is key to a strong marriage. **Don't wait until your marriage is in trouble to pray.** *By faithfully bringing your husband to the Throne of Grace — even when things are going well — you can head off a lot of problems before they ever arise.*

Don't just stop at praying for your husband. If he is willing, make it a daily habit to pray with him, as well. Couples who regularly pray together are far less likely to divorce.

E = EMPHASIZE HIS GOOD POINTS

Just as you would rather he dwell on your most praiseworthy attributes than to focus his attention on all your flaws, **your husband will also feel better loved and respected when you are**

expressing admiration instead of fault-finding and nit-picking.

Focus your attention on those traits that first attracted you to your husband. *Emphasize his most noble features.*

If you will make your default attitude one of warm approval and respect, then on the rare occasion you do need to discuss a concern, your husband will be far more likely to take it to heart.

C = CHOOSE JOY

What does being joyful have to do with communicating respect?

More than you might think!

A smiling, jovial wife announces to the world, "My husband knows how to make me happy!" But a sour, malcontent wife broadcasts the opposite message. **A wife who shames her husband "is as rottenness in his bones."** (Proverbs 12:24)

Choose to cultivate a happy, joyful attitude, regardless of your circumstances. In fact, the Bible tells us we should rejoice, even in the midst of trials and tribulations, knowing that God uses difficult circumstances to teach us patience, to build our endurance, and to mold us into the character of Christ. (James 1:2-3; Matthew 5:11-12)

T = TAKE HIS ADVICE

Undoubtedly you've already noticed that **your husband tends to look at things differently than you.** *His unique perspective, together with the way most men's brains are wired for problem solving, offers you a unique opportunity to get "outside the box" when looking at problems or challenges.*

Listen to your husband. Hear what he is saying to you. **Don't get defensive or discount his opinion**, *but try to see things from his perspective and honor his wishes. God will greatly bless you when you do. *Jennifer Flanders.*

CHAPTER 15

Strange Women

I'M SURE WE all have that one friend or know someone who has engaged in an adulterous affair. It's never a good thing or good feeling. I often wonder how a couple could be so in love with each other at the wedding, then next thing you know…bam, they (so called) fell out of love because someone cheated. Did they fall out of love? Didn't their spouse treat them right? What did that other person do that was so powerful it made them leave their family and estate? Inquiring minds want to know.

I had an interesting experience where someone very close to me had an affair with a married man. My friend was smart, beautiful, had a great job, and claimed to be a Christian. So I never would have thought in a million years that she would ever do such a thing as commit adultery. Like watching a bad movie, I saw it coming. She met the guy at work as a client. He was very charismatic, confident, and a straight genius when it came to business; even more intriguing was his style, which wasn't your typical suit and tie kind of guy. He was a self-proclaimed thug, very urban with the baggy jeans, timberland boots, body tattooed up all over and the ability to turn his hood lingo on and off at will.

To me, this guy wasn't much of a looker at all. *But* I could see why my friend was attracted. It was his charismatic, confident personality that melted most people, including my friend. I remember the day she met him. There was a spark in her eye (that I was oh too familiar with when she liked a guy) as she described him. She went on and on about how easy he was to talk to, how smart he was with his business and how much she learned from him etc. Since I knew her well, I knew there was a reason for all of these adjectives without the close (a date). Then I said, well that's awesome, are you guys going to go out? That's when she dropped the bomb… no, because he's married.

I told her right away, "Don't go down this road, and don't open yourself up." She assured me that she just wanted to be friends and nothing was going to happen. One phone call led to another, one meeting turned into a bunch, one seemingly harmless touch turned into a spontaneous kiss and before you know it, they had an affair.

Knowing my friend and watching the evolution of their relationship, I honestly believe she never *intended* on having an affair. It was her own lust that led her astray. Contrary to what one might think, it wasn't her lust *for him* that was the attraction but the lust for power and prestige. She thought that he could give that to her. In business, she was successful but not 7-figure successful like her "mentor." Her nature was very aggressive, partially because she always had a sense of entitlement.

Where did she get this attitude from? Why did she think it was okay to entertain another woman's husband? The answer is she was a strange woman, with strange doctrine, following a strange god.

She was strange because she governed her life according to her *own rules*, which is not of the covenant. Honestly, she didn't think she was doing anything wrong because she felt they loved each other and they didn't plan it. I couldn't understand this until I thought about her family history. Her father cheated on her mother, her mother cheated on her father. In fact, her father stayed with his mistress after he divorced her mom and later on, at one point they all lived together and got along. I'm only referencing her parents so you can understand how adultery ran in her bloodline.

Your bloodline, inheritance, even your DNA are considered territory. Our bodies are made from the dust of the ground; therefore, your very body is land. Your spouse and children are considered land, territory, and property—of course, not your own but for the Lord.

When we get born again, Jesus has purchased your spirit for Himself. As far as your mind and body are concerned, you have to *give* them to Him through living righteously according to the Word, which is your covenant (agreement) and governing body. It is through the Word that we learn the way to do things and protect ourselves from the evil one and strange women.

Strange women are conscious and unconscious assassins the enemy uses as a wrecking ball to not only destroy your family but also to annihilate, rob, and destroy you. This woman will inevitably not only take the husband from the family, she will try to take him from God through sensuality and strange doctrine. That doctrine declares what is right in her own eyes (which goes against the will of God), which is why the Word tells us that, when He brings you into the land He promises (marriage) you, do not go into covenant with strange gods, women, and doctrine.

The enemy always shows up when you arrive at success because if he can make you give in to temptation, you will lose it all.

> ### Deuteronomy 7
> *When the LORD thy God shall bring thee into the land whither thou goest to possess it, and hath cast out many nations before thee, the Hittites, and the Girgashites, and the Amorites, and the Canaanites, and the Perizzites, and the Hivites, and the Jebusites, seven nations greater and mightier than thou; And when the LORD thy God shall deliver them before thee; thou shalt smite them, and utterly destroy them; thou shalt make no covenant with them, nor shew mercy unto them: Neither shalt thou make marriages with them; thy daughter thou shalt not give unto his son, nor his daughter shalt thou take unto thy son. For they will turn away thy son from following me, that they may serve other gods: so will the anger of the LORD be kindled against you, and destroy thee suddenly.*

When the Word refers to sex and intimacy between spouses, it says "he knew her." The implication of the word *knowing* is that your spouse is a major part of your family who understands you, your history, culture, and nation on a deeper spiritual level. Intimacy between husband and wife is a form of worship unto God. It is a joining of mind, body, and spirit; two have become one.

Now, when someone or something unauthorized enters the marital covenant, they're considered a stranger (foreign, outsider, unusual). Strange gods, women, ideas, and doctrines are all outside of the covenant of marriage.

Adulterers are also considered thieves. They come like the enemy to steal, kill, and destroy. It doesn't matter if they're nice with SO-CALLED good intentions (I don't understand how that is possible), they are still thieves because they are trespassing onto a land that's not theirs, taking what doesn't belong to them. The adulterer is taking away a spouse, parent, covering, peace, stability, and love from another person's nation. If the king goes down, the entire NATION falls apart.

CHAPTER 15 | STRANGE WOMEN

We saw this happen to King Solomon. God blessed him beyond measure. The Bible declares that he was the wisest man that ever lived and ever shall be. He was so wealthy that when the Queen of Sheba came to visit him, she passed out from being so overwhelmed of the majesty of the kingdom. His soldiers had gold shields, and they used silver for decorative stones just to give you an idea of his wealth. He was like a billionaire during that time. People visited Solomon from all over the world just to hear his wisdom. If that wasn't enough, his father was David, the man that knew how to please God.

How can you have it all like that, money, wealth, health, and divine wisdom and still lose the kingdom? He allowed strange women, with strange doctrine and strange gods, into his house.

An interesting fact to note is when he was young and in his prime, he did not succumb to their strange ways. However, because he did not listen to God's instruction, he still allowed these strangers in his house.

Remember, God said when He brings you into the land to possess it, you should not go into covenant with these women because they will turn you away from following Him. Sometimes, when we do our dirt, it doesn't bite us until later on. Complacency tends to settle in because judgment and consequences haven't caught up yet. Nevertheless, sooner or later, if you join covenant with the world, you will suffer death (separation).

With Solomon, the enemy bided his time until he was old. As people get older, sometimes they tend not to be as sharp as when they were younger. They're more tired and just want to retire. Solomon was weary and it's at this juncture the enemy seduced and infiltrated his covenant.

> ### 1 Kings 11
> *But king Solomon loved many strange women, together with the daughter of Pharaoh, women of the Moabites, Ammonites, Edomites, Zidonians, and Hittites; Of the nations concerning which the LORD said unto the children of Israel, Ye shall not go in to them, neither shall they come in unto you: for surely they will turn away your heart after their gods: Solomon clave unto these in love. And he had seven hundred wives, princesses, and three hundred concubines: and his wives turned away his heart. For it came to pass, when Solomon was old, that his wives turned away his heart after other gods: and his heart was not perfect with the LORD his God, as was the heart of David his father. For Solomon went after Ashtoreth the goddess of the Zidonians, and after Milcom the abomination of the Ammonites. And Solomon did evil in the sight of the LORD, and went not fully after the LORD, as did David his father. Then did Solomon build an high place for Chemosh, the abomination of Moab, in the hill that is before Jerusalem, and for Molech, the abomination of the children of Ammon. And likewise did he for all his strange wives, which burnt incense and sacrificed unto their gods. And the LORD was angry with Solomon, because his heart was turned from the LORD God of Israel, which had appeared unto him twice, And had commanded him concerning this thing, that he should not go after other gods: but he kept not that which the LORD commanded. Wherefore the LORD said unto Solomon, Forasmuch as this is done of thee, and <u>thou hast not kept my covenant and my statutes</u>, which I have commanded thee, I will surely rend the kingdom from thee, and will give it to thy servant.*

You may have been the model spouse for years but we all get tired and fatigued sometimes…tired of fighting, tired of waiting, hoping, and tarrying. You may have been married so long that you're bored to death. Your spouse may have aesthetically let himself/herself go, taking little to no time and care with his appearance, and not making much effort to please you. Maybe it seems like just the same ole, same ole ritual of living day in and day out; no sex or intimacy, you both are like roommates and you're tired of it! In the end, we all just want what we want when we want it. Even if what you desire is a good, righteous endeavor, like praying and believing for the health of a loved one or your child's need for deliverance, God may still allow this unpleasant *season* to go on for longer than you would like. You have faith in God knowing He will come through but you just don't know when. It's during this **mean**time that the enemy will attack your vulnerability. The key is for someone to be on guard, always. Pay attention to the needs of your spouse. If one falls, the other can pick him up.

> Ecclesiastes 4:9,10
>
> *Two are better than one; because they have a good reward for their labour. For if they fall, the one will lift up his fellow: but woe to him that is alone when he falleth; for he hath not another to help him up.*

A wife may get tired too, waiting for her husband to pay more attention to her and spend more time with her. If she feels alone too long, she can begin to feel neglected and unattractive. This can happen to a husband as well. Times of weariness are prime soil for the enemy's attack. His strategy and tactics never change: he still uses lust of the eyes, lust of the flesh, and the pride of life. These spiritual doors give way to strange women, strange gods, strange ideas, strange language, and strange doctrine.

Some of the greatest men of God and most powerful of nations have been brought down by strange women. I witnessed the terrible fall of the man that my friend had an affair with. He lost everything as a result of **his decision** to have an illicit sexual affair. He was arrested, lost all of his money, freedom, and respect. He also lost his wife, children, and eventually lost my friend! It's just not worth it!

PURPOSE PRINCIPLE

All affairs start with a conversation.

> ### Proverbs 5:1-10
>
> *My son, attend unto my wisdom, and bow thine ear to my understanding: That thou mayest regard discretion, and that thy lips may keep knowledge. For the lips of a strange woman drop as an honeycomb, and her mouth is smoother than oil: But her end is bitter as wormwood, sharp as a two edged sword. Her feet go down to death; her steps take hold on hell. Lest thou shouldest ponder the path of life, her ways are moveable, that thou canst not know them. Hear me now therefore, O ye children, and depart not from the words of my mouth. Remove thy way far from her, and come not nigh the door of her house: Lest thou give thine honour unto others, and thy years unto the cruel: Lest strangers be filled with thy wealth; and thy labours be in the house of a stranger.*

Primarily, the goal of the enemy is to try to steal back the territory (your spouse, home, peace, and joy) you took from him by any means necessary. One classic maneuver he uses is the art of conversation. Strange women are manipulative, savvy, and seductive master communicators. From words spoken, suggestion, and body language, they are very persuasive and alluring. Most people think that they're too smart and loyal to be seduced by strange women and doctrine. Unbeknownst to them, this is not a natural attack but a spiritual one. The enemy is challenging you to see how much Word you really know and how committed to God you really are. Notice I said committed to God and not your spouse. Not that you shouldn't be committed to your spouse, you most certainly should be, but there are times that you may not like them at all, they may have betrayed you in some way and at the moment, you don't have the fortitude to believe in them again. Your commitment to God should be so strong that your *fear of him* is the strength that anchors you to stay committed to your vow and marriage.

> 1 Corinthians 10:13
>
> *There hath no temptation taken you but such as is common to man: but God is faithful, who will not suffer you to be tempted above that ye are able; but will with the temptation also make a way to escape, that ye may be able to bear it.*

If you're paying attention, the Holy Spirit will ALWAYS give you discernment and a way of escape. However, the reason most take the bait is that they don't have enough Word/God in them. They want what they want and are led astray by it. Adam and Eve are a perfect example of this. When the serpent approached Eve, he asked her, "Did God really say...?" Right there, he opened up a conversation with strange doctrine that challenged the Word she was supposed to have known and lived by. But she was not sure of the Word, and *wanted* to taste the fruit. She was weaker than she realized. Adam then listened to her, which means there was a part of him that also wanted something else outside of the Word he knew. Basically, neither of them probably would have engaged in this sin if they never engaged in strange conversation.

Adultery should NEVER be an option... *even if you are separated.* Beware also of women who claim to be women of God that have affairs with married men. They're ravenous wolves in sheep clothing sitting right in the church. These are strange wives; they are born-again women who were once in covenant with God but have left their estate. They too come with strange doctrine, led astray by a strange god. Women who have become strange usually justify their action according to how they feel and what they perceive. They are the ones who feel sorry for you because they think your wife is not treating you right (in their opinion). Or they've developed such a strong connection with the man to the point where she thinks they are best friends. She believes she is the one who really understands him. In her mind, somewhere along the line, the man she loves is trapped in a bad mistake called *your marriage*. This demonic assassin thinks she's doing the world good and her assignment is to save the husband from the wicked wife.

This strange woman has been deceived and the Bible says that out of the abundance of the heart, the mouth speaks. She would do just about anything to have you. She doesn't see it as breaking up your family and nation. In her mind, she wants to simply replace your wife. Although it may be true that the wife has been negligent with her husband, the mistress never gets the full story. She doesn't really know what's true or not, nor does she know all the ramifications contributing to your situation or the reasons *why* the wife treats him that way. This is not to justify the wife's negligence. Regardless of what anyone thinks, the covenant stands, til death do them part.

Generally, the husband is the one susceptible to this strange woman with strange conversation because he *feels* justified as well. He thinks, finally, someone sees what he's been saying and going through. Finally, he thinks he has found *someone who really cares, respects, believes in, and understands him*. That is where the crack in the armor is. Wives, please pay attention here, read and re-read the previous sentence in italics. These are the reasons why most men cheat. If your husband steps out on your marriage, before you completely condemn him, check and see if you were a co-conspirator to your own demise. Under no circumstance should he cheat, but sometimes wives practically push their husbands into the hands of strange women who will pay more attention to him and his needs. Why do you think when a man cheats on his wife, the mistress is usually less attractive (in almost every way) or seems like she's not even his type? He chose her not because of what she looked like but because of convenience, comfort, and conversation. It's through conversation the strange woman gets her foothold because she listened and got 'intel' about your man in order to make him happy, and then applied it. It's ironic that God has informed wives that *your husband* will be *won over* by **chaste conversation**.

Chaste defined:

- Morally pure or decent: not sinful
- Simple or plain

The Word of God is your marital foundation and doctrine. It is the law of your land, the pillars to your government. When you got married, your covenant with God and your wife has been establish along with the purpose of your union. What is forgotten is the responsibility of governing and protecting your nation. Your feelings, even if they are justifiable, cannot override purpose. Infidelity by the husband is like inviting an invading army over for dinner and then allowing them to kick your spouse out and take over everything. The husband is supposed to be a protector and covering, king, and ruler of his house. Understand that strange women are sent from hell to destroy your kingdom. You are not cheating on your wife alone, but also you are cheating yourself when you engage.

> Ezra 10:10
>
> *And Ezra the priest stood up, and said unto them, Ye have transgressed, and have taken strange wives, to increase the trespass of Israel.*

Satan has studied man for centuries and knows that most people are weakest when tired and unsatisfied. Make the *effort* daily to satisfy your spouse for the entire duration of your marriage. Make it your lifestyle. Husbands love your wife; and wives, love and respect your husband. Obedience to that commandment is literally a spiritual border and boundary to keep the enemy out.

Dissatisfaction is a doorway. The main reason why people are often dissatisfied is that they're ungrateful and don't even realize it. They have forgotten what God *has done for them*, their oath, and purpose, by focusing on what they don't have. You may have forgotten how beautiful your wife is or handsome your husband is or that this is the person you swore to love. Robert Greene, author of *The 48 Laws of Power* says, "It's virtually impossible to seduce a satisfied person." If you're satisfied with your spouse, when the enemy tries to seduce you, you have no need or desire for what the devil is offering. The enemy plays on dissatisfied, worn-out emotions and sends in the strange woman. The Bible says that we are led astray by our own lust.

> ### James 1:13-15
> *Let no man say when he is tempted, I am tempted of God: for God cannot be tempted with evil, neither tempteth he any man: But every man is tempted, when he is drawn away of his own lust, and enticed. Then when lust hath conceived, it bringeth forth sin: and sin, when it is finished, bringeth forth death.*

Samson, a judge in the Bible, was attracted to strange, foreign women. The Hebrew women were too plain and boring to him (they would be considered Christian women today). His parents pleaded with him to stay with women of his nation but he insisted on doing things his way. Consequently, every time he got with a strange woman she betrayed him.

Like you, God anointed him with supernatural strength to overcome his enemies. Before Samson was born, an angel of the Lord visited his mother and told him that he was to be a Nazarite to God until he died.

> ### Judges 13
> *But he said unto me, Behold, thou shalt conceive, and bear a son; and now drink no wine nor strong drink, neither eat any unclean thing: for the child shall be a Nazarite to God from the womb to the day of his death.*

The marriage covenant is similar to the Nazarite vow because our oath as a believer is to serve the Lord. Nazarite comes from the Hebrew word *nazir*, which means consecrated and set apart. That's what you and your spouse really are—set apart from the world for the special purpose of birthing a nation. The Nazarite vow however is very specific in this respect:

- No wine or strong drink must be taken.
- You cannot eat any unclean thing.
- You cannot touch the dead.

Each instruction is something that we all should consider from the perspective of being consecrated to the Lord and for protection from strangers. Drinking strong wine and strong drink in excess opens up the door to strange forces. If you have struggled with addiction to alcohol or drugs, I bet you will see that Proverbs 23:29 is a picture of things going on in your life.

> Proverbs 23:29-33
>
> *Who hath woe? Who hath sorrow? Who hath contentions? Who hath babbling? Who hath wounds without cause? Who hath redness of eyes?*
> *They that tarry long at the wine; they that go to seek mixed wine. Look not thou upon the wine when it is red, when it giveth his colour in the cup, when it moveth itself aright. At the last it biteth like a serpent, and stingeth like an adder. Thine eyes shall behold strange women, and thine heart shall utter perverse things.*

> Numbers 6:3
>
> *He shall separate himself from wine and strong drink, and shall drink no vinegar of wine, or vinegar of strong drink, neither shall he drink any liquor of grapes, nor eat moist grapes, or dried.*

According to Scripture, it is clear to see that when you're intoxicated, your attention will be redirected to behold strange women and utter perverse things (cursing people out). In other words, under normal circumstances you would be spiritually stronger and your focus would be in the right place. When intoxicated, you're UNDER THE INFLUENCE! He begins to mess with your emotions by making you feel strange and observe strangers. The enemy then enters your *heart*, with lustful thoughts gaining control of your body. Whoever controls the mind controls the body.

> ### Proverbs 6:23
> *For the commandment is a lamp; and the law is light; and reproofs of instruction are the way of life: To keep thee from the evil woman, from the flattery of the tongue of a strange woman. Lust not after her beauty in thine heart; neither let her take thee with her eyelids. For by means of a whorish woman a man is brought to a piece of bread: and the adulteress will hunt for the precious life.*

There is no account in the scriptures that Samson drank. That wasn't his weakness. His proclivity to strange women caused Samson to lose his strength and more importantly, his *vision*.

CHAPTER 16

Evil Men

YOU MAY BE wondering, well what about women who cheat on their husbands? Most certainly, there are wives who cheat on their husbands. As a matter of fact, women are notorious for being better cheaters. It could be years before they get caught. However, the reason why they have such a long run is that a lot of time their husbands don't know their wives.

Not knowing your wife through careful consideration as the Bible instructs opens the door to evil men. They don't care about you or your family. They are carnivorous men who look for weak women to prey on. Again, the objective of the enemy is to reclaim your territory. If the husband is too strong to conquer directly, the enemy will attack from a different vantage point. You may have resisted the strange woman and her doctrine but have you neglected to know your wife enough to know that she was unhappy or unsatisfied?

Evil men are predators that lurk at your wife's job, church, supermarket, school—basically everywhere. It could even be a lingering ex-boyfriend. You may be so used to neglecting and ignoring your wife that you don't find her beautiful or interesting at all. Just because you've taken your wife for granted doesn't mean that what you feel is true. Other men may still find her attractive and *very interesting*. For the evil man, he is waiting for the opportunity to have a conversation with your wife and make her feel special because that's usually all it takes to get her.

> Proverbs 24:1, 2
>
> *1Be not thou envious against evil men, neither desire to be with them.2For their heart studieth destruction, and their lips talk of mischief.*

What makes such a man so evil is that he doesn't really want to *be* with your wife. For him, it's just a conquest...a narcissist looking for another worshiper that he doesn't have to commit to. He can have the excitement of the forbidden fruit, secret rendezvous, a loyal subject without any responsibility, and all the good your wife has to offer without commitment. Upon close examination, you will see the enemy. He's coming for you and, if he takes your wife, it was your fault because you weren't watching.

> Romans 1:18
>
> *For the wrath of God is revealed from heaven against all ungodliness and unrighteousness of men, who hold the truth in unrighteousness; Because <u>that which may be known of God is manifest in them; for God hath shewed it unto them.</u>*

You may not have all the facts or proof that your wife is cheating or that an evil man is seducing her but your spirit will inform you that something's not right (according to Romans 1:18). Although your wife should not be indulging or even considering another, it is your job to cover her because she is the weaker vessel. As the husband, a part of your assignment is to dwell with her with consideration. If she is unhappy, you already know it. She probably already expressed to you what she needed from you. Loving and considering her is a preventative measure and divine strategy to block her from the enemy.

Your physical body would go completely out of wack and sync if you lost your mind. When the husband sends mixed signal, ignores, or doesn't nourish his wife (body), the body starts feeding on itself, thus operating in dysfunction. In other words, you wife will begin to act silly. Her behavior will become unseemly, whereas she will be open to entertain evil men because she was lacking inside. She began to want, and that emptiness deceived her, changing the truth of God into a lie and as Romans 1:24 says, she worshipped the creature more than the Creator, being led astray by her own lust.

> Romans 1:24,24
>
> *Wherefore God also gave them up to uncleanness through the lusts of their own hearts, to dishonour their own bodies between themselves: Who changed the truth of God into a lie, and worshipped and served the creature more than the Creator, who is blessed forever. Amen.*

Evil men are described as:

> 2 Timothy 3:1-7
>
> *This know also, that in the last days perilous times shall come. For men shall be lovers of their own selves, covetous, boasters, proud, blasphemers, disobedient to parents, unthankful, unholy, Without natural affection, trucebreakers, false accusers, incontinent, fierce, despisers of those that are good, Traitors, heady, highminded, lovers of pleasures more than lovers of God;*
>
> *cont/d...*

> *Having a form of godliness, but denying the power thereof: from such turn away. For of this sort are they which creep into houses, and lead captive silly women laden with sins, led away with divers lusts, Ever learning, and never able to come to the knowledge of the truth.*

You may be saying, isn't my wife accountable for her own actions? Why does it sound like it's all my fault? The answer is yes, she is accountable for her own actions as a believer. But the husband is accountable for the actions of his wife because you both are one and you are the head. A physical body can survive for a while if the heart stops; but if you are brain dead, there is no recovery. God holds you accountable for how you manage your nation.

We see this accountability with Adam and Eve. When Eve ate the fruit, nothing happened. It wasn't until Adam ate the fruit that God came and pronounced judgment. Why? Because the Word came directly to Adam. Eve was close enough in proximity to Adam to offer him the fruit; therefore, he was close enough to observe an inappropriate conversation. He could have addressed her behavior right there and taken the issue to God. God appointed him to be the strongman of the house. It was his job to consider his wife with discernment and protect her from the enemy.

2 Timothy 3 states that this evil man "creeps into houses and lead captive silly women laden in sins and lead away with divers lust." An evil man cannot creep into your house and steal anything unless he binds the strongman first. Are you strong? Examine your strength levels and if they are low, you must recharge. You recharge spiritually by praise and worship, studying the Word, and prayer. Naturally, you recharge by a healthy diet, exercise, and work. Finally, sex recharges you physically and spiritually.

The enemy has to bind the strongman (you) first in order to take over your home and territory. Husbands, guard your wife with your life! Sobriety is of utmost importance because if you are intoxicated in any way, you're not going to be cognizant of what's really going on around you. Your response to things won't be quick and sharp, rather sluggish and easy to defeat. Your discernment as to what is going on with your body (wife) will be off. Matter of fact, her displeasure and disappointment with you being drunk or high could be the catalyst to her wanting another man or out of your marriage altogether.

Your choice to be *under the influence* makes your nation an easy target. It also shows how weak you are because you have given control over to another entity outside of covenant to govern you. I say that because over-indulgence is a sign of overcompensation for dissatisfaction somewhere within. If you were stronger, you wouldn't need superficial stimulants. Of course, the enemy will be happy to assist your dysfunction by providing confusion, lies, and opportunities to keep you under the *influence*. Whoever controls the mind controls the body. He understands that as long as you facilitate the school of thought that drugs and alcohol, pornography, or whatever sin you have opened yourself up to is what you need to make you feel better, he got you in a stronghold. Thus, if he binds the strong man—you—then your wife, house and everything you own and love is up for grabs.

PURPOSE PRINCIPLE

Whoever controls the mind controls the body.

Remaining faithful to your spouse; and covenant takes work and courage. You may fear losing your wife to another man because of your insecurities. If this is the case, you are in a weakened state. The only way to defeat the evil man in this case is to walk in faith and truth with the only fear being the fear of the Lord. The truth is, she is your wife, and he can't have her unless you allow it. However, if you do all God has told you to do, being sober, vigilant and faithful, and yet she leaves, let her. God can replace her with better. In the meantime, your job is to always man your post and never let the enemy bind you with his lies and influence.

> ### 1 Peter 5
> *Be sober, be vigilant; because your adversary the devil, as a roaring lion, walketh about, seeking whom he may devour: Whom resist steadfast in the faith, knowing that the same afflictions are accomplished in your brethren that are in the world.*

Wives, if you are not recharging your husband with affirmative words, submission, and sex, you are weakening him and yourself. You are creating a breach in your wall of protection. This is silly behavior. Disobedience to God's word and way is sin and in time will weigh on you, to the point of deception and delusion. Evil men will come for you and lead you astray by your own lust. This is foolishness. A strong marriage is not built on feelings. Just because you feel lonely and abandoned doesn't give you a pass to avert your vow to God and your husband. An evil man will lie to you and wreck your marriage, home, and entire nation, and then leave you!

> ### Proverbs 14:1
> *Every wise woman buildeth her house: but the foolish plucketh it down with her hands.*

Tearing down your husband with disrespectful words, insubordination, and disrespect allows the enemy to come and bind him up. It may feel good to release your frustration, you may even feel like you've done better by creeping off with an evil man, but there are serious consequences to this choice. Your house is not just the physical building but it is your entire nation. Children are affected; the man you married, whom you loved, is affected; and your friends and family will be affected. By your one act of selfishness, you will pluck down your own house!

To be clear, ANY MAN (no matter how nice he may be to you) that tries to seduce you into an affair or are willing to indulge in one with you is an evil man. Don't be silly or deceived, God is not mocked.

> Mark 10:9
> *What therefore God hath joined together, let not man put asunder.*

SECTION FOUR

The truth about love

CHAPTER 17

Love Language

ONE OF MY favorite movies is 300. In this movie, King Leonidas and a handful of 300 soldiers fought against Xerxes, a tyrant and his massive innumerable army. As the 300 were on the road to go to the "hot gates," (a narrow passage that would funnel their opponent right into their hands), they ran into a severely deformed Spartan man by the name of Ephialtes. This man desperately wanted to join forces with the king and fight against Xerxes. However, the king reminded the man about how their failings work. He told them that the soldiers were to operate as *one impenetrable unit*. Each soldier was to protect the man beside him from thigh to neck. Unfortunately, Ephialtes was so deformed that he could not raise his shield high enough to protect a man on his left or right. As much as the king could use help, and as much as the man wanted to help, he could not use him.

Ephialtes FEELINGS were hurt and you could tell that the King wished he could have told him what he wanted to hear. However, the king's decision couldn't be based on *emotions*. All of his decisions had to be practical because his kingdom, soldiers, families, and children's lives were on the line. He understood that his strength and ability to withstand the enemy resided in unity and the eradication of any weak spots.

Unfortunately, (like many of us do in life and relationships) King Leonidas was wise in his decision but failed to notice a bigger problem. He neglected to notice how deep Ephialtes' need to feel important and accepted was. Neglecting deep-rooted needs of your spouse can lead to major problems and disaster. We must listen with both ears, natural and spiritual. Address issues in love and head on…don't ignore them. King Xerxes took advantage of Ephialtes' weakness and used it against King Leonidas. Very much like how a strange woman or evil man would take advantage of the lonely wife or neglected husband simply by making them feel loved, accepted and important.

Ephialtes was so bitter, self-centered, and hurt that he gave up *the entire nation* to the enemy for material, superficial gain (money, women, and a uniform) and it cost King Leonidas the battle and his life. All because the King neglected to see and hear the real need. That lack is an invitation and strategy of the enemy; lust of the eyes, lust of the flesh, and the pride of life.

Weak spots to look out for:

- Loneliness
- Depression
- Confusion
- Division
- Fear
- Insubordination
- Lust

- Greed
- Gluttony
- Laziness
- Anger
- Selfishness
- Idolatry
- Control
- Manipulation

All of the above weak spots are stored in the heart and mind. Upon deeper introspection, these deficiencies are cries for help. If these shortcomings go unaddressed, that spouse is likely to become like the crippled man who wanted to go to battle but was incapable of defending the person fighting by his side. What you see, perceive, and understand is translated in your mind and that message is stored in your heart. If what you're thinking is carnal (self-centered), then what you see, believe, and understand will be also. And, you guessed it, out of the *abundance* of the heart, the mouth speaks. We're not talking about a passing thought or feeling. It's an overflow of messages that are sent to the heart that you *actually* believe.

Language and speech are not inexplicably the same. When you speak, there's a dual language spoken at the same time. There's your native language, i.e. English, Spanish, French, etc., and then you have a spiritual language. The spiritual language is heard and received by your spirit man and translated by your mind. These are the words that are not spoken with the mouth per se, but from your soul.

Oftentimes, we observe this spiritual sound, if you will, through undertones and body language. It's all the things you express underneath as to what you've actually said verbally or haven't said. Yet, whether the messages we're sending are words out of our mouth, body language, or manifested through action, it comes from our heart. This leads to the question, what's really in the mind of your heart? The answer to this question will help you understand your husband or wife.

King Leonidas pointed out that Ephialtes' parents should have taught him about the soldier failings system. Just because he was *born* a Spartan and had his *father's uniform*, wasn't enough to qualify him for this assignment. The army could not risk a weak link and neither can your marriage. Unity...being one impenetrable unit, is actually a military strategy employed to protect you and defeat the enemy. It's also a strategy to successfully build just about anything. Therefore, it should come as no surprise *when* the enemy attempts to divide and conquer. He does so by confusing your language. God, too, utilized this strategy of divide and conquer by confusing the language to prevent unauthorized building:

> ### Genesis 11:1-9
>
> *And the whole earth was of one language, and of one speech. And it came to pass, as they journeyed from the east, that they found a plain in the land of Shinar; and they dwelt there. And they said one to another, Go to, let us make brick, and burn them thoroughly. And they had brick for stone, and slime had they for morter. And they said, Go to, let us build us a city and a tower, whose top may reach unto heaven; and let us make us a name, lest we be scattered abroad upon the face of the whole earth. And the LORD came down to see the city and the tower, which the children of men builded. And the LORD said, Behold, the people is one, and they have all one language; and this they begin to do: and now nothing will be restrained from them, which they have imagined to do. Go to, let us go down, and there confound their language, that they may not understand one another's speech. So the LORD scattered them abroad from thence upon the face of all the earth: and they left off to build the city. Therefore is the name of it called Babel; because the LORD did there confound the language of all the earth: and from thence did the LORD scatter them abroad upon the face of all the earth.*

PURPOSE PRINCIPLE

When the enemy tries to destroy your marriage, he confuses your language. Guard your heart, and watch your words.

God employed this strategy because they were trying to *build a nation without Him*. Nimrod, (the father of rebellion) began his unauthorized building project because he was a self-proclaimed king who wanted to outshine all other nations. He also desired to be worshiped as a deity. He rebelled against the patriarchal way that God established and decided only to consult with self. We see Nimrod doing things *his way* by substituting standard procedures like using brick instead of stone. He begins separating his nation from God by saying, "let us make us a name" by reaching heaven according to his own efforts.

PURPOSE PRINCIPLE

Selfishness and self-centeredness are a manifestation of lust. Selfless behavior is a manifestation of love. Love gives, but lust takes.

The moment we rebel against God's word and way, it becomes a mission of self-gratification, which excludes God. Ironically, it's amazing how quickly people forget that God *is Love*. Therefore, if the language spoken is not love, your marriage will have a lot of misunderstanding and confusion because you are speaking a foreign language. Carnal living, decisions, attitudes, and behavior is a strange language that you cannot build upon. Every marriage must live by, speak, and understand LOVE LANGUAGE. Love language is learned as you become the embodiment of love.

LANGUAGE DEFINED:

1. the words, their pronunciation, and the methods of combining them used and understood by a community : audible, articulate, meaningful sound as produced by the action of the vocal organs 2. a systematic means of communicating ideas or feelings by the use of conventionalized signs, sounds, gestures, or marks having understood meanings 3. the suggestion by objects, actions, or conditions of associated ideas or feelings <*language* in their very gesture — Shakespeare> 4. the means by which animals communicate 5. a formal system of signs and symbols (as FORTRAN or a calculus in logic) including rules for the formation and transformation of admissible expressions

LOVE DEFINED: (according to the word of God)

Charity suffereth long, *and* is kind; charity envieth not; charity vaunteth not itself, is not puffed up, Doth not behave itself unseemly, seeketh not her own, is not easily provoked, thinketh no evil; Rejoiceth not in iniquity, but rejoiceth in the truth; Beareth all things, believeth all things, hopeth all things, endureth all things.

It's interesting to note how the absence of love is compared in this scripture with an uncomfortable sound:

> 1 Corinthians 13:1
>
> *Though I speak with the tongues of men and of angels, and have not charity, I am become as sounding brass, or a tinkling cymbal.*

Love language is a manifestation of God in the flesh, mind, body and soul. It is a uniform that we wear and become. Anytime you see something in uniform, it is consistent, identifiable and in order.

When you notice confusion in your marriage, something is out of order, and communication is off. Generally, when communication gets intense and scrambled, people are not being loving. I'm not talking about love in the dimension of affection but of character.

If your spouse falls out of love with you, you can feel it in your spirit. Oftentimes, the unloved spouse will respond to the other with frustration or anger (either overt or covert). The way to get your marriage back in love is through the following:

Anchor *yourself* in love: The way that you anchor yourself in love is by putting on the mind of Christ. I AM NOT TALKING ABOUT RELIGION! Putting on the mind of Christ is learning God's word, commands, instructions, precepts and applying them to your life! Notice, this is part of your individual covenant and walk with God. Getting in line and uniformity with the Word is about YOUR ADJUSTMENT, not you ADJUSTING ANYTHING ABOUT YOUR SPOUSE! You must *become love* in everything you do by doing things God's way. God denied His flesh, He laid down His life and most of all He did THE WILL OF THE FATHER.

Prayer, by far, is your best weapon against the enemy. And remember, your spouse is not the enemy. If anything, it is the demonic spirits that may be influencing them or you. The Bible tells us what we are actually in spiritual battle:

> ### Ephesians 6:12 ~King James Version (KJV)
> *For we wrestle not against flesh and blood, but against principalities, against powers, against the rulers of the darkness of this world, against spiritual wickedness in high places.*

We understand that within marriage, there is a hierarchy. Whether he's treating you right or not, you are to submit to him and respect him. HOWEVER, although he is your head, God is his head! Prayer goes over his head! Through prayer, God intervenes on your behalf.

That is how you get on the same page so you can once again speak the same language.

Husbands, if you are speaking outside of the love language to your wife, the Bible says your prayers will be hindered! Whether she is a boring nag, or you don't find her attractive anymore, God commands you to love her.

> *You husbands in the same way, live with your wives in an understanding way, as with someone weaker, since she is a woman; and show her honor as a fellow heir of the grace of life, so that your prayers will not be hindered.*

You must once again become unified with the proper language, the word of God. That's the only way God will hear you. He's looking to hear His voice through you because you're the head.

Wives, with Agape love coming through you, you will help him become one with his body (you) again. Nagging won't conquer him. You don't have a right to nag him. That's actually out of order. No one argues with the King. Always speak in a loving soft manner to him…and through *prayer*… go over his head! God will begin to speak to him in a way he can understand.

1. Wait and listen
2. Speak with love
3. Allow. Here's the BIGGEST CHALLENGE—letting that person go. Here's what the Bible says:

> *For the unbelieving husband is sanctified through his wife, and the unbelieving wife is sanctified through her believing husband; for otherwise your children are unclean, but now they are holy. Yet if the unbelieving one leaves, let him leave; the brother or the sister is not under bondage in such cases, but God has*
>
> *cont/d …*

> *called us to peace. For how do you know, O wife, whether you will save your husband? Or how do you know, O husband, whether you will save your wife?*

If you are speaking love into your spouse, never stop. If they decide to leave let them, God doesn't hold you accountable if they do so. He also says this:

> **1 John 2:19**
> *They went out from us, but they were not of us; for if they had been of us, they would no doubt have continued with us: but they went out, that they might be made manifest that they were not all of us.*

CHAPTER 18

Love On Purpose

> Matthew 7:12
> *Therefore all things whatsoever ye would that men should do to you do ye even so to them: for this is the law and the prophets.*

A FRIEND TOLD me something so simple yet so profound that it changed my life. She said, "If you change *you*, you change your surroundings." As obvious as that sounds, it took a while to grasp the concept because I would often respond defensively to circumstances around me. Almost as if I was helpless or had no choice about my finances, relationships, etc.

Sometimes we love people who are set in their ways. Ten to one, they are never going to change. How do you live with someone who has a hurtful, disturbing or abusive attitude or behavior? Especially, when you don't believe they will ever change? First, understand that there is nothing too hard for God. He has a way of getting our attention if he wants to. No one is so set in their ways that God cannot change them.

Secondly, it's not always about God changing *them*. Sometimes God uses them to change *you*. He uses that adversity to make you spiritually stronger. Perhaps God is teaching you how to love *for real*. It's easy to love loveable people. The challenge is loving people who are difficult and seemingly unloving. scriptures tells us that it's the anointing that destroys the yoke (bondage). The anointing is power from God. Therefore, you cannot love a person that's hurting you by your own power. What it takes is a conscious decision to obey the Word of God by loving them no matter what. In order to do that, you have to die to self because your flesh is going to want to fight or leave.

Most spouses who are being treated unfairly (if they decide to stay) arrive at the point where they feel helpless. They're depressed, angry, and unhappy. Unfortunately, they will more than likely remain in that state until they come to the realization that they can change their *perception* of the situation. They could change their *attitude* about what's happening, gladly do whatever she asked and choose not to allow themselves to get angry. The problem is a lot of people take the victim stance instead of taking ownership and responsibility for **their own thoughts, actions and decisions!**

PURPOSE PRINCIPLE

If you change you, you can change your surroundings.

Unbeknownst to me, my thoughts and perceptions of certain situations at times fostered responses I didn't like. Sometimes unconsciously we're co-conspirators to our own demise. Once I decided to change *me*, I was no longer susceptible to the actions of others. By allowing my spirit to govern my feelings, I could stabilize how I felt about my environment.

In marriage, there may be times you feel as if you're helpless and vulnerable to a spouse that is, consciously or unconsciously, treating you in an unfair, unkind and unloving manner. Even so, God *STILL* holds *YOU* accountable for your actions! Why? Because God wants you to know that if you change you, you can change your surroundings.

There's only one answer or key you need to access a great marriage. Although it's one word, it opens up many doors; doors to peace, joy, satisfaction, contentment, health, wealth and the list goes on. With this key, your marriage will stand the test of time. The key is for **YOU** to become LOVE.

Love has characteristics, love is a spirit, and God is love. When you *become l*ove, your attitude will change as well. What's interesting about becoming the embodiment of love in your marriage is you no longer depend on your partner's reciprocity (or lack thereof). Both parties should be loving at all times but we know that is not always the case. Regardless of where your feelings land, your position as husband or wife never changes. God is always looking at your covenant, your word/vow. Therefore, HIS expectation should be yours. He requires you to fulfill your oath.

Being the embodiment of Love, you are God in the flesh. God is love, nothing can stand in His way or defeat Him. He is an all-consuming fire and you have this fire residing in you. In other words, if your spouse is wicked, treats you or your children badly, neglects you or whatever negative form of behavior shown towards you, in the presence of God, they will eventually *have to* cease.

> Ephesiansm5:22
>
> *But the fruit of the Spirit is love, joy, peace, longsuffering, gentleness, goodness, faith, Meekness, temperance: against such there is no law. And they that are Christ's have crucified the flesh with the affections and lusts.*

Sowing love into an unfruitful marriage is a *process*, oftentimes a painful one. Loving your spouse through trials, tribulation and allowing God to come in and fix it is challenging. And there are times where fixing it means divorce. Not that God will tell you to get a divorce because He hates divorce. However, He may *allow* it.

In the Bible, there was a story of a woman named Abigail of whom the Bible says was married to a fool. Some of you may be married to a fool (male or female) and feel trapped. Abigail had the spirit of a virtuous wife and helped her husband even though he made foolish decisions. Then one day, she met King David. There was an obvious attraction between them but Abigail and David could not indulge in unlawful affairs due to their circumstances. Abigail did not entertain the idea of leaving her foolish husband just because she met a king that was attracted to her. She (Agape) loved her husband until the end. And that is in fact what happened… his *end* came sooner than later. Some days after she met King David, Nabal died of a heart attack.

The moral of the story is your assignment and purpose is to honor your *covenant* and love until the end, no matter what. If you believe the person you're married to is not the one meant for you, more than likely eventually they will leave you. The reason why they will leave is that they have not become one with you. In order to become one, first you must leave and cleave. Some people never *leave* their past (mother, father, neighborhood, the way things were when they grew up) to cleave to their future (you).

Secondly, they are not of the same kind. In order for two to become one, they must be the same being. You cannot be Holy and your spouse unholy. That will never work. Over time, something will have to give.

Let me be clear, I'm not talking about religion here where you have to church goers. You can have two saved people where one is living righteously and the other is not. There can be a form of rebellion in that partner. Either way, the opposing spouse will ultimately be won over and sanctified by the saved spouse or they will leave because there is nothing in common, no spiritual agreement.

Nevertheless, God honors position, so if you chose to be unequally yoked, God still expects you to perform as a husband or wife as long as you're married. The key to endure that kind of torture is through love.

> ### Mark 2:21
> *No one sews a patch of unshrunk cloth on an old garment. If he does, the new piece will pull away from the old, and a worse tear will result.*

If in fact you're in that situation, continue to man your position and *get into character*. Doing so will require you to faith it until you make it. In due time, you will become one or there will be a separation because all faith will be tried by fire. If you or your spouse is living a lie, the fire of truth will eventually expose it. They will leave because living a lie will become unbearable and you will be exonerated.

God does not expect you to suffer forever. Remember, you cannot blame God in this situation because he told you from the beginning not to be unequally yoked with an unbeliever. And this time when they leave, let them go. Here's what the Word says about it:

> **1 Corinthians 7:15**
> *But if the unbelieving depart, <u>let him depart</u>. A brother or a sister is not under bondage in such cases: but God hath called us to peace.*

> **1 John 2:19**
> *They went out from us, but they were not of us; for if they had been of us, they would no doubt have continued with us: but they went out, that they might be made manifest that they were not all of us.*

So you see, the command to love is not contingent on how you are being treated. It's based on your response to your covenant agreement with God. When you obey His word and stand on it, God is now compelled to move on your behalf and however things go, it will be His will. If you do things your way and only love your spouse when convenient, you remove the sovereign *power of God* to act within your marriage. That power of God hits the point of contact to your problem only when you are in alignment with His word and in position. You are to *BE* a loving spouse even if it's NOT BEING RECIPROCATED.

PURPOSE PRINCIPLE

The truth and proof of your love will stand trial by your trials.

Now you say you love your spouse, right? Well let's see! If you have become love, this is what you should look and sound like:

1. **Patient**: Are you patient with your spouse according to the Word and your position? Patience is the first characteristic and requirement of love. It's easy to be patient when your spouse is communicating the way that you like and

understand, or if they're treating you the way you want to be treated. But what about when they are immature, mean, inconsiderate, negligent or make mistakes? Have you been patient? If not, this is the first key.

2. **Kindness**: What is your disposition like? Are you kind to your spouse on a regular basis? Do you place them in high esteem and cater to them with kindness? This very simple key unlocks, disarms, and facilitates the best in everyone. Make this attribute part of your being and watch how your relationships change for the better.
*Remember, your behavior is NOT contingent on whether they are nice to you or not.

3. **Longsuffering**: I must admit that this characteristic has to be one of the hardest. Sure, it's easy to be patient and kind for a little while. But there are times where you get tired of taking the high road when it seems like your spouse is not making any effort or won't take you and your needs seriously. After a while, you get tired of trying. I totally understand, heck anybody could understand that. But when you've done all to stand you need to *just stand*. We were never created to endure the institution of marriage alone. You cannot be long suffering without God helping you. God is a Spirit and His power transcends our understanding, emotions and defies all logic. You endure in spite of the pain and suffering because the purpose of your love is greater. Notwithstanding, you love by faith and your faith will be tried. The truth and proof of your love will stand trial by your trials. Longsuffering and faithfulness gives glory to God and He will reward you with real Love.

> **1 Peter 4:12-16**
>
> *Beloved, think it not strange concerning the fiery trial which is to try you, as though some strange thing happened unto you: But rejoice, inasmuch as ye are partakers of Christ's sufferings; that, when his glory shall be revealed, ye may be glad also with exceeding joy. If ye be reproached for the name of Christ, happy are ye; for the spirit of glory and of God resteth upon you: on their part he is evil spoken of, but on your part he is glorified. But let none of you suffer as a murderer, or as a thief, or as an evildoer, or as a busybody in other men's matters. Yet if any man suffer as a Christian, let him not be ashamed; but let him glorify God on this behalf.*

You see, love is internal with an external manifestation. Therefore, like a seed planted in the ground, for a season, you may find yourself in a dark place, crushed and left for dead. The process of that season is called long-suffering. However, never lose sight of the purpose of the process. That individual seed (you) have to die in order to release, multiply and produce what's inside of you (Love).

4. **Hold no record of wrong**: Mastering this aspect of love will yield countless rewards, love, joy, peace, and happiness. You have the power to change your own thoughts, which can change how you feel, which will change your behavior and perception. Forgiveness is at the core of this characteristic. How many relationships fail to have peace and be restored because one or both spouse is holding record of wrong? If your spouse has hurt you or violated your trust, the fact is it has already been done and cannot be undone. The power behind this love is really about empathy. When you've wronged someone you love and want to be forgiven, you just want everyone to forgive and forget. That is what your

spouse expects from you, can't you understand that? If you have empathy, it is easier to forgive AND forget. When you really love someone, it actually takes an effort to STAY MAD. We often hold record of wrong with the ones we love because we feel they should pay for hurting us or violating our trust. But isn't that equally unloving? Don't lose your peace or your marriage by holding records of wrong. Even if you apply all of the other characteristics, this one can unravel everything!

5. **Do not envy.**
6. **Do not boast.**
7. **Do not be proud.** Here is another biggie! If you really love someone, your character should manifest a degree of humility, because of who you are. Genuinely loving someone is of a lowly estate that propels you to the highest of esteem. Contrary to our society that tells us to take pride in ourselves, the Bible says that love is *not proud*. Consider yourself in your marriage. Are you manifesting pride when you exalt yourself beyond your spouse? Pride can be very subtle and virtually undetected by the proud but strongly felt by the recipient. Do you find it hard to humble yourself before your spouse when you are wrong? Do you find it hard to humble yourself when you are right? When you love someone, your bottom line will be peace. Strive for peace through humility not pride, for that is a divine strategy of God. He will fix the rest.

> **Proverbs 11:2**
> *When pride cometh, then cometh shame: but with the lowly is wisdom.*

> **Proverbs 16:18**
> *Pride goes before destruction, And a haughty spirit before stumbling.*

> **Proverbs 18:12**
> *Before destruction the heart of man is haughty, But humility goes before honor.*

> **Proverbs 29:23**
> *A man's pride will bring him low, But a humble spirit will obtain honor.*

CHAPTER 19

How To Stay In LOVE

BEING *IN* LOVE is actually a geographical location. Whenever you're inside of something that means you are positioned somewhere. Better translated, to say that you are *in* love, what you're really saying is, "I'm in God" or "I'm in the Word." In order to meet someone anywhere, there has to be a point of contact. There must be a distinct time and place for two or more to come together.

Our being is clothed with a suit of flesh, trapping our eternal spirits in time. Therefore, even though our being is spirit, our flesh makes us subject to time and place. God is a Spirit. He is not bound by time or place, He is infinite, omniscient and omnipresent.

This poses a challenge for us then when we desire to be in alignment with God because we're temporarily trapped in this thing called time and place, while God is everywhere. How do we as human beings meet with Love? We have to meet God where *He is*. He inhabits the praises of His people. That doesn't mean you have to walk around speaking in tongues all day. Rather, you meet God in your *being*...authentically expressing the love of Christ through everything you do. The meeting takes place inside of you. Your body is a temple.

> ### 1 Corinthians 6:19
> *What? know ye not that your body is the temple of the Holy Ghost which is in you, which ye have of God, and ye are not your own?*

He says that those that worship Him must worship Him in spirit (remember, your spirit is the person you really are) and *in truth*. No one said you had to be perfect but he does require us to be *righteous*. Obedience to God's Word is your truth and righteousness. **Obedience** *is the place.*

> ### Psalm 22:3
> *But thou art holy, O thou that inhabitest the praises of Israel.*

> ### Matthew 18:19, 20
> *Again I say unto you, That if two of you shall agree on earth as touching anything that they shall ask, it shall be done for them of my Father which is in heaven. For where two or three are gathered together in my name, there am I in the midst of them.*

The Word of God IS YOUR INSTRUCTION MANUAL on how to love and be in love for real! Actual OBEDIENCE to God's Word is the distinct point of contact. Why? Because your faith is the substance that God touches in the spirit. Believing God right now for what you've asked Him for according to His Word provokes Him to action because *God looks for His Word to perform it.* **God cannot**

fail. So when you pray for your spouse/marriage/finances/health or anything for that matter and you believe God, your mouth and behavior is praise unto God. He is in the midst of whatever you're going through because He inhabits praise. His Word is light and it is life. When you obey God's Word, the wisdom of God is built in you. No matter what the situation is, or what your spouse or children are doing, if you continue to do things God's way and obey His Word, God has to come do what He says. Obedience is the place that God meets you.

Staying in love requires you to reside in God because God is love. Our idea of love in most cases is more about affection which is *Eros* love. Eros does not keep marriages together, *Agape* does (because God is Love). Therefore, if you want to have love *reside* in your marriage, you must learn how to locate God. He resides in **you**. He is present and involved when both of you agree and ask of Him. That means, you have to agree to live how the Word tells you to regardless of how you *feel* towards your spouse.

Some people have wonderful, peaceful marriages. Oftentimes those marriages lack passion because there's no purpose. When you live on purpose, you will be challenged and stretched because God will bless you with more capacity to **receive**. In order to enlarge something, it has to be made bigger. If you want more love in your marriage, God will stretch and destroy your need to be selfish. The more you give up what you want to give what your spouse need you will reap what you need. Having all you need is a state of contentment and satisfaction. It's virtually impossible to seduce a satisfied person.

When people are hurt, angry, disappointed or lack, they have the proclivity to withhold. As tempting as that may be, (because in your mind they don't deserve anything) don't take the bait. Notice, those feelings are…feelings; they change. The good thing about that is you can be proactive in that change. The enemy is banking on your predictability. Your spouse, if they make you angry, hurt your feelings or have been ignoring you, they know it. If you indulge in your feelings, more of the same ill will perpetuate through your marriage. You can stop this by out-loving them. Love them more than they expect and more than they deserve. Before you know it, the body will come together again.

PURPOSE PRINCIPLE

Always love your spouse more than they expect and more than they deserve.

It takes courage and faith to love someone for real. The return may be slow and long but rewarding. Although you may be longsuffering in love with your spouse, what is instant is the peace of God and righteousness, knowing you have done all that you could do. God takes care of the rest.

PURPOSE PRINCIPLE

Give your spouse what they need and they will give you what you want!

Philippians 4

But I rejoiced in the Lord greatly, that now at the last your care of me hath flourished again; wherein ye were also careful, but ye lacked opportunity. Not that I speak in respect of want: for I have learned, in whatsoever state I am, therewith to be content. I know both how to be abased, and I know how to abound: everywhere and in all things I am instructed both to be full and to be hungry, both to abound and to suffer need. I can do all things through Christ which strengthens me. Notwithstanding ye have well done, that ye did communicate with my affliction.

It's also possible to be satisfied and still have a need. However, God said that *He* would supply all of your need according to His riches in glory. That's interesting because the scripture doesn't say that your spouse will provide your need. God may use your spouse but that doesn't necessarily mean your spouse will always be the answer to what you need. Understand, God leaves a place inside each one of us for Him to be a part of us. Aside your natural love for the Father, your need causes you to seek Him. Sometimes, God will allow a dry period within your marriage if you both have become so consumed with your *selves* that you've forgotten about Him.

PURPOSE PRINCIPLE

Don't divorce your spouse because they cannot supply ALL of your needs. That's God's job. Know who your source is.

If you want love and passion in your marriage, you have to find Love first. Romance and affection is an outward manifestation of the love you have for another inside. You can only give what you have. Love is the tree, while romance and affection are the branches. Please, please, please, don't confuse what I'm saying with religion. Some people believe because they know how to theatrically and skillfully pray or go to church more than the other person—that doesn't mean you have more God residing in you. That just means you go to church. The Bible says that you will know a tree by its fruit. It doesn't matter how much you go to church if the church is not *in you*, you will not change in character. Love is not something you do, it's the person you become.

PURPOSE PRINCIPLE

Love is not just something you do; it's the person you become.

You must ask yourself, if your spouse/children/job/health whatever is bothering you or causing problems, have you obeyed God's word on how to handle these situations?

- Did you seek God first?
- Husbands:
  - Did you love your wife like Christ loves the church?
  - Did you provide for your family?
  - Did you provoke your children to wrath?
  - Do you tithe?
- Wives, did you submit?
  - Did you respect your husband?
  - Have you been foolish, contentious, and clamorous?
  - Do you stay home?
  - Do you actually believe that God's Word and way works? Have you been faithful to your faith?

Questions like these (amongst others) are what you need to ask **yourself** when things go wrong. Do you realize that in most cases when there are marital issues or scenarios, people generally accuse, question or blame their spouse. It's rare that people look at themselves objectively and judge themselves. As a result, no progress is made because the problem is perpetuated through you. Even when you realize you're wrong, you don't want to confess it voluntarily. That bad habit alone has caused many people to stay out of love and into divorce court. The scriptures clearly states:

> ### James 5:16
> *Confess your faults one to another, and pray one for another, that ye may be healed. The effectual fervent prayer of a righteous man availeth much.*

God has given you the power and authority over these things, so why is it having dominion over you? Do you know what God says about things? If you don't know, then you must go into prayer and ASK God to show you in His Word what to do and how to be. Then do what He tells you do to! Live the principles of the Word. Performing God's will in your body is God performing His word. That is the meeting place. Inside of you, through the place of obedience, you are worshipping God in spirit and in truth. That is how God gets the glory out of your life. This is the place where you make love!

Prayer is where you have a conversation with God. It's also an act of faith because you're acknowledging God's presence and sovereignty. Prayer is a powerful tool that one must learn how to wield. We are to pray according to God's will and word. It's necessary for you to pray for your spouse because you can see what they need. Prayer is the place where you make your request known unto God.

I've heard people say they've done all that they can do, so all they can do at this point is pray. That's out of order, they should have prayed first.

God wants you and your spouse to make it a habit to pray together because when you agree in the spirit as touching anything, God will do it for you. He also is in the midst. When God starts moving and answering prayer, you and your spouse will fall deeper in love because you'll see how effective you are together. Success is very attractive.

Agreement is a meeting place where two minds and opinions become one. When you and your spouse decide to do and be what God tells you in HIS WORD, you meet God. Did you hear what I just said? I'm telling you how to fall in love! God is telling you, if you just treat your spouse and people the way that I tell you, I will meet you there!

In other words, God is Love. And the key to that statement is this, He said if YOU LOVE ME, KEEP MY COMMANDMENTS. Obedience is the proof of love because you have to completely lay down your life in order to love to the fullest.

PURPOSE PRINCIPLE
Obedience is the proof of love.

Have you ever watched one of those action movies where there's a major underground deal going down? You have one person with the product (something of high value, money, diamonds, secret weapons, etc.), the other person is the buyer. Both stand to win big but everyone proceeds with caution because there's so much on the line. Everyone has their guns drawn, with bodyguards ready for war. Although both parties are expecting a positive exchange, the fear of an ambush looms in the air. Someone has to take initiative and make a move. Eventually one opens the briefcase and shows the money, the dealer shows the goods. Then they both slide the briefcases over, make the exchange, and the deal is done. The fear of sabotage, loss, or theft was present as long as each party fearfully clung to what they perceived as value. Ironically, in order to get what they needed from the other party they had to release what they were holding onto. They had to risk dying in order to gain. When the exchange was finally made, the fear of loss disappeared because they realized that the other party was trustworthy.

If you examine your marriage, you and your spouse are (emotionally) like the dealer and the buyer. Both bring value to the table but because the worth of your feelings, ideas, dreams, goals, etc. are so priceless to you, there's a looming fear and apprehension that if you make the first move, you may be taken advantage of. Although that's a very real concern, you cannot get what you need from your spouse until you give them what they need. Progress is held up as long as each person clings to what they hold dear (including a dreadful past, molestation, rape, financial devastation, health challenges, you name it) being afraid to be ambushed or shot down when they've decided to be vulnerable and transparent. Your spouse has LOVE to give but what happens to the one who moves first? Consequently, the transaction of removing hurt and replacing it with love can only occur when both parties release. You may say, I was vulnerable before and I got shot down, I'm not going to expose myself until they expose themselves. The goal in your marriage is for both of you to be naked and NOT ASHAMED.

PURPOSE PRINCIPLE

One of the goals in marriage should be for both of you to be spiritually naked and NOT ASHAMED.
It's okay to be transparent and vulnerable with your spouse.

One of the principles in the Word we are to live by is sowing and reaping. Remember, when you plant something, it doesn't grow instantly it's a process over time. Humbly listening to, considering and meeting the need of your spouse is the will of God because God loves and touches your spouse through you. Surrendering your will, desire, and emotions is the same as dying to the flesh. When you die to self, Christ is exalted in you. The Bible says that if I (God/love) be lifted up (exalted), I will draw all men unto me.

You are the seed. When you surrender to your spouse, you risk your life. Since you did what the Word told you to do, you died to self and exalted God in your life. You sowed love into your spouse by giving up what you wanted to fulfill the need of THE OTHER PART OF YOU (your spouse). God is promising you that if you SOW YOURSELF in LOVE, you will REAP LOVE in your life. Obeying God's Word and principles is where you always want to be. But you have to be WILLING to die first, just like in the high stakes deals in the movies.

PURPOSE PRINCIPLE

You cannot get what you need from your spouse until you give them what they need. Consequently, that need could be different from yours.

The Bible declares, *I shall provide all of your need according to my riches in glory*. He also says, *The Lord is my shepherd, I shall not want*. The word "want" is defined as lack, destitute, needy; lust. Want is what leads us astray. God doesn't give us what we *want* because when you want something, you position yourself in a stance that is telling God what *you think* you need (remember the body doesn't govern the head). God said that He knew what we needed before we ask of it. *Wanting* comes from your carnal perspective, it's not spiritual. You see something and you want it. That is carnal. When God gives you something, it comes from within first because God gives you desires. A desire is a request. God instructs us to make our petition known. The Lord is our shepherd and we shall not want. That is also a command to not wanting. God has all you need and He will give it to you.

When you want something, you are summoning to yourself something that God hasn't given you. It's as if you are trying to bless yourself by taking what wasn't given. Every good gift comes from above, which means God will GIVE it to you and He does so by faith. Faith is the substance of things hoped for and the evidence of things not seen. When something is already yours, there's no need to want it. We only want things that we don't have.

What does this have to do with my marriage? Well, people *want* what they don't have. If it belonged to them already, then there is no need to want it. If you desire a good marriage and it isn't working for you, then you don't have enough faith. If you really, truly (just between you and God) believe your spouse is *your* spouse, YOU KNOW THAT THEY'RE NOT GOING ANYWHERE. If you don't believe your spouse is committed, you are sowing fear because you don't believe that they are yours. The Bible says, "When you stand praying, *believe*." You need *now* faith. Believe with your whole heart. When you do that, you are able to stop wanting and start focusing on sowing and reaping love.

Physics says that work is done when a force hits an object and displaces it, causing the object to move in the direction of the force. The Bible says that faith without works is dead. In other words, faith (substance of things hoped for) is just the substance, but what makes that substance a reality is the force hitting the body. That force is the Holy Spirit, moving you in the direction you need to go. God (being the force) comes and breathes life into the substance making it a reality. If you know (in your heart of hearts) that your spouse is one with you, walk in that faith until God manifests your desire. God does the work, NOT YOU! Work is done when a force hits a body. You are a body, your marriage is a body but you are NOT the force! When you pursue what you want *without* the force, you summon AND allow the enemy to illegally become that force to manifest a lie to you. The truth is not in him. If God did not give you what you wanted, then it wasn't yours. God will not withhold any good thing from the upright.

PURPOSE PRINCIPLE

Sex is physical; making love is spiritual.

When you try to force a relationship, you're only doing so because you're living a lie. That's not walking by faith. You can't make anybody love you, obey God or do anything! But God can, and prayer initiates the force to action. Making love IS SPIRITUAL! When each person is totally focused on what the other person wants and need, that very act ignites a passion in the other that you wouldn't believe! But you must remember that falling in love is a process because all parties (you, your spouse and God) have to meet in agreement. In other words, you may arrive at the place of obedience before your spouse. If you do, continue loving them until your harvest of love manifests. That's how you *make love*. Sometimes, the thing that is holding your spouse back is a demonic stronghold, which has nothing to do with how they actually feel about you. The

Bible says LOVE conquers all! Love is what makes your spouse lower their guns and slide over that briefcase!

Don't fight your spouse, when you do, you're working against yourself, and a house divided cannot stand. Love your spouse as you love yourself. Why? God is the one that can change a man's heart. The wife is a vessel. If she has become love, she is a priceless golden vessel...a treasure. Where your treasure is, *there will your heart be also.* Obeying God's Word, becoming love is how you stay in Love. "The king's heart *is* in the hand of the LORD, *as* the rivers of water: he turneth it whithersoever he will."

CHAPTER 20

Money Matters

> Proverbs 3:9
> *Honour the LORD with thy substance, and with the firstfruits of all thine increase: So shall thy barns be filled with plenty, and thy presses shall burst out with new wine.*

P ART OF BEING married on purpose is to understand God has joined you and your spouse to produce and multiply; not just physically and spiritually but also financially because the Bible says, "Money answers all things." Faith is the substance of things hoped for (which is spiritual) but money is the currency used in the natural realm.

Aside from sex, I believe finances are one of the biggest challenges faced in most marriages. Again, in marriage, you are bringing two people with separate mindsets together, where each person believes their perspective is the correct reality. Society (or I should say the carnal mindset) suggests that whomever makes the most money is the one who is in charge. There are some men who may feel because they're the breadwinner; they don't have to discuss how the money is managed. There are some women who primarily make more financially leading them to believe they are the head of the house. Others are taught to save money for a rainy day or just in case is the way to go, while the other spouse feels like you should live now and in the moment. Variances in attitudes regarding money along with difference of opinions on how money should be managed can cause a major rift in a marriage.

First, we must understand who we are. We have a body of flesh but our being is spirit. Your body has feelings/emotions but our mind has the spirit, which governs our emotions. In other words, many people manage and spend money emotionally instead of practically. Some may be a spendthrift because when they purchase something, it makes them feel better about themselves even though their circumstances haven't changed. Unfortunately, monetary, emotional outbursts are the very holes plaguing their financial pockets. In this case and all other, potential emotional decisions should be held under subjection to the Holy Spirit, knowledge of the Word, and discipline. Acknowledging the fact that your financial behaviors are governed by emotional spending or compulsive saving (because you're afraid of loss) is the first step. The second step is to be governed/ruled by God's principles for prosperity and wealth.

Regarding money and finances in marriage and the roles we are to play in that capacity, the Bible seems to be silent. Instead of saying "here are the explicit rules on money in marriage," God leaves us with principles that if applied, would work for anyone. Interestingly, those principles are not one-dimensional chauvinistic concepts regarding who does what. On the contrary, it's more focused on the spiritual principles that reveal the way we should *perceive the purpose of money*; how to increase it, what it's for and the spirit behind it. This brings us back to the patriarchal order, faith, sowing and reaping, working and tithing.

The patriarchal order is the foundational outline to begin with. No matter who brings in the money, the decisions end with the husband. The overall vision of the marriage of the family begins and ends with him. However, this does not negate the mandate for the husband to meet with his wife. It's his job to communicate and conference with her, get her opinion and insight because she lends another point of view. No one has eyes behind their head. Therefore, it is nice to have someone watch your back. If you will always look at your spouse as such, you would have greater chance at coming into agreement with respect and love.

Secular society would vehemently disagree with the theocratic system and patriarchal system because the world is taught differently—you have to pay the cost to be the boss. Thus, whoever makes the most or is the most educated, is the one to be in charge. The mere idea of the term "boss" and "in charge" is condescending and mean. God did not come to condemn us but to save us through Himself. In other words, He's saying for us to do things His way and everything will be alright. The husband is not the boss because there is no boss. He is the head of the body, and the head and body are one. Everything the head does should be in agreement with the body.

PURPOSE PRINCIPLE

Order creates a positive flow.

Order is key. You can have a good cash flow along with material things but if things are out of order, there will always be something wrong. Having a marriage out of order clogs up the flow that should come from the head, down the beard, and onto the skirts. Wives, the scripture never says the anointing flows from the skirt to the head. It doesn't matter if you are making more money or even if at this time you are solely financially providing for the household, you are not the head. Serve your husband humbly until God deals with the matter.

PURPOSE PRINCIPLE

Things begin to work when you are in agreement.

Husbands, the Bible says that a man that doesn't provide for his family is worse than an infidel. Everyone goes through challenging times and in the beginning, it may be hard to find your way but you must find a way. This is where your faith kicks in. Your wife is there to help you but if you mess up the dynamic of the household by not providing for your family, you will be unhappy and no one will respect you. Each person is held accountable to their covenant. We all are held to the standard of the Word of God and if you don't come into alignment with God's way of doing things, then you miss being a partaker of HIS POWER, MIRACLES, FAVOR, BLESSINGS AND MOST OF ALL…WISDOM.

STRATEGY

No matter how deep in debt you are or how much money you have, you will need a strategy and plan. The scriptures say that wisdom is the principle thing. It really is! When creating a strategy, you and your spouse must come together as one…naked. I don't mean come to the table with no clothes on! You need transparency in EXACTLY how much money each person has, assets, interest, and debt. This is one of the most vulnerable places for anyone to be because so much can be said or perceived by how you manage or don't manage money.

Your meeting is not about condemning your partner for past poor financial choices. Rather, it's a question or picture of where you are now, what you collectively have to work with and how are you going to work together to be fruitful, multiply, replenish, and subdue. Don't forget, that's your marital purpose and assignment. No one successfully wages war without a strategy.

It is wise to select a day every month that you both agree on to be your financial meeting day. Initially, the first meeting or two will be the most emotional because you will be financially vulnerable. Pray first and agree to go into this meeting with Love and the mind of Christ. No matter how bad you may be in debt, remember that there is nothing that you can't do if you be agreed. God is also in your covenant working with you, giving you ideas, strategy, and favor to get out of the stronghold and move into prosperity. But if you never go through the fire of the first step, you will never get out of the hole. You must be honest, transparent, and loving. You are in this together for life, it is important that you figure out a long-term plan.

> Ecclesiastes 7:12
> *For wisdom is protection just as money is protection, But the advantage of knowledge is that wisdom preserves the lives of its possessors.*

LEADERSHIP

Husbands, leadership are your mandate. It's natural for you to lead your wife and family through life. Whatever you may not know regarding finances, you must learn or learn how to employ the services of those who know. Perhaps your wife is better at managing money. It would be wise for you to enlist her services in this area. Doing so is not a negative implication on you; on the contrary, it actually highlights your wisdom in managing your entire nation and kingdom. It shows that you know how to wisely delegate responsibilities. There are a lot of things that a husband has to manage and your wife is there to help. Whatever she's better at, it is wise to let her do it. She's on your team.

> ### Genesis 2:20
> *And Adam gave names to all cattle, and to the fowl of the air, and to every beast of the field; but for Adam there was not found an help meet for him.*

Both your wife and children are watching and should follow your lead but if you don't lead, how can they follow? You cannot get mad at your wife for not having a plan. As the head of the house, you are supposed to be the brains, eyes, ears, and mouth of the body. There are times you may be frustrated because you haven't figured it out yet. It's at this moment where men are prone to being mean to their wives because she may be asking questions about what you're going to do and you're not prepared to answer. Please understand, just as men NEED respect, women need a SENSE OF STABILITY. Even if you don't actually have what you need at the moment to provide, it is soothing to your wife when you can at least discuss options. She is at your mercy, and she has a right to ask questions. The key is to always look at her as yourself. Know that she loves you and her concern is for your well-being. Who knows, you may find an answer to the problem through talking to her or listening to her suggestions. She's not asking questions because she doesn't believe in you, she's asking because she is scared or nervous (emotional).

Wives understand that when a man doesn't have the answer, he is not going to want to talk. Do not bother him with questions unless you absolutely have to. Let wisdom guide you, not your emotions. Don't make him feel less than a man because he hasn't figured it out. Pray for God's intervention and God will answer!

Husbands, show your family how to manage finances and a nation by presenting a clear, concise vision. A vision is not a plan, it's an idea. Share your idea with your spouse, then *together* make a plan. Allow your spouse to spot and share with you any holes in your idea because you are not egotistic and emotionally driven. Rather, take the constructive criticism to avoid pitfalls in the future. Constructively listening to your partner can save you from financial calamity.

If the husband has a plan that he believes in strongly and the wife doesn't agree, she must submit her thoughts and feelings to her husband's direction! However, the wife should pray about her concerns. Pray, pray, pray!

Notwithstanding, the scriptures suggest that when you're dealing with financial or business planning, it's good to talk to counselors. Great leaders know when they're in over their head or something is out of their league. It's wise to get advice from someone who knows better.

However, proceed with caution when getting advice. Proverbs 11:13 suggests that you consult with people who have a FAITHFUL SPIRIT because they will keep your business private and give you good honest advice. It is imperative that when you consulting with someone outside your marriage (of whom you and your spouse are in agreement with) ensure they have a proven track record of faithful credibility. Just because they're your frat brother/soror or you've known them for 20 years doesn't automatically qualify them as a faithful spirit. They could have been a busy body, hater all of those 20 years! So use discernment and honest assessment.

> ### Proverbs 11:13, 14
> *A talebearer revealeth secrets: but he that is of a faithful spirit concealeth the matter. Where no counsel is, the people fall: but in the multitude of counsellers there is safety.*

> **Proverbs 15:22**
> *Without consultation, plans are frustrated, But with many counselors they succeed.*

> **Proverbs 20:18**
> *Prepare plans by consultation, And make war by wise guidance.*

As a leader, risk will be taken. Both spouses need to understand this. Just because you have all your ducks in a row, it doesn't guarantee that it will turn out the way you expected. Either way, in order for anything to be accomplished, you must take risk. And almost always, there will be challenges. When your husband takes a risk, it is scary for everyone. No matter how it goes, always be supportive.

Dynamics between husband and wife according to the Word of God is interesting because, at times, it defies logic and at the same time makes complete sense when you see the correlation between our natural proclivities. A man is created to be a leader. Although there are women who are natural born leaders, sometimes those gifts become misconstrued within the marriage structure. It should be understood by all that her leadership value is a contributing asset in subjection to her husband (never to usurp his authority). I cannot emphasize this enough because our success is not based on our work alone but according to God's work, favor, and blessing. He cannot bless disobedience. If you are out of order, you are out of position, which leaves you vulnerable to the attack of the enemy. Which means you can have financial success at the detriment of your marriage. Of course, I understand that many will disagree with this because women have been carnally brainwashed to believe that their monetary value adds up to absolute, sovereign power. Submission is a surrendered power. Yes, you may have more money/education but a wife's covenant duty is to submit under the authority of her husband.

DISCIPLINE/ORDER/PRIORITIES

Once you have order in your marriage as to who does what and you've created a plan, you must prioritize. Many financial crisis and setbacks are created simply from not having your priorities in order. God is a God of order, structure, and discipline. He gives us instructions through His Word on how to do the same. You see, it's not so much how much you make but the decision you make with what you have. So what comes first? God always comes first. From the very beginning in the Garden of Eden, we see God set the tree of the knowledge of good and evil aside for Himself. Then Cain and Abel were to make an offering to the Lord, and so on and so on. The practice of putting God first is really the beginning of a prosperity principle, flow, and order. You give God His 10 percent and you keep the ninety. It's a liberating feeling when you get your responsibilities out of the way first and knowing what you have left is yours to do as you please.

God is teaching us through the practice of tithing to take care of our responsibilities first. He also says in the scriptures that before you build, count the cost. If you pay attention to His direction, you will see a budget system of percentages instead of dollar amounts. The only actual percent number we see in Scripture is 10 percent as to what God set aside for Himself. You and your spouse are the king and queen of your nation, so you will decide your financial structure and priorities. However, God has set the tone so that you can have an idea of how to structure your financial profile.

- Tithe: 10% of your gross income to God
- Pay yourself 20%. For the scripture saith, Thou shalt not muzzle the ox that treadeth out the corn. And, ***The labourer is worthy of his reward*** (1 Timothy 5:18). In

other words, you earned your portion. All of your money should not go to just paying bills. You should have a portion for yourself as well. Since God has set 10% for Himself and we are a reflection of Him, it is fair to conclude that you take at least 10% for yourself and 10% for your spouse. It is important that you pay yourself. If you don't, overtime you could develop resentment towards work and all the people you provide for.

- Count the cost required to build. Financial planning and management is a process of building over time. Many marriages fall apart because both parties fail to see the light at the end of the tunnel. No woman can follow a man that doesn't have a plan. The plan lets everyone see the end game. There must be a written plan so that you both can take it and run with it.

> **Habakkuk 2:2**
> *And the LORD answered me, and said, Write the vision, and make it plain upon tables, that he may run that readeth it.*

> **Luke 14:28**
> *For which of you, intending to build a tower, sitteth not down first, and counteth the cost, whether he have sufficient to finish it?*

Building example includes (but not limited to):

- Tithes/offering — 10%
- Housing — 30%
    - One major financial problem a lot of marriages face is living beyond their means. Having the appearance of wealth without the wealth to the detriment of your actual well-being is poverty. No matter where you are

right now, (if at all possible) once you've established the percent that you will commit to housing, live within that means. You can increase the value of this percent by owning property and renting it out. You can downsize to a home or apartment that meets your needs.
- When meeting with your spouse to discuss your financial portfolio, be honest with yourself regarding your spiritual perception and attitude. Are you full of pride and ego? Don't let those demonic spirits prevent you from making wise decisions for your family. On the forefront, it may seem like downsizing is taking a step backwards but it's actually a power move God can use to propel you and your family forward. It's not a permanent situation, rather a strategy.
- Now you don't have to do the things that I'm mentioning, they're merely suggestions. The idea is more so about understanding the spiritual and psychological ramifications of applied principles or the consequences of violating them. Many people are impoverished and stuck in their situations because they refuse to sacrifice, discipline, and plan. And for the ones that are able to do those things, oftentimes they cannot reach their highest potentials because they fail to address the pride and ego within. The place to begin these new habits is with self, at home first. Again, your children/nation are watching how you manage the family affairs. They will pass on to the next generation your teachings and behaviors.

- Food — 15%
  - Wisdom is the principle thing. Many times, we don't really sit down and consider our day-to-day habits and how much it may cost us. Eating out can cost you a tremendous amount of money annually. In one day, I

can go to a fast food restaurant and purchase breakfast (sandwich, coffee, and hasbrown meal) for $5. Lunch, no matter where I go, will at least be $6. Dinner, no matter where I go, seemed to be no less than $7. That's $18 for one person (trust me, my numbers are on the low end). Multiply that by 5 days a week, you have $90. So easily within a month, that's approximately $400. That's not wise.

- If you manage 15% of combined earnings or single earnings of your income to feed your family, you will save thousands of dollars. Use coupons, MAKE A LIST and go grocery shopping. Prepare your food at home. If you don't have a lot of time, set aside a day when you make food for the week and freeze it. You may have to invest into a deep freezer but it will be well worth it. This frees up our time, your family will be taken care of whether you are home or not. They can just heat up what's already made.
- If you like going out to dinner, plan that as well. Be creative and stick within your budget. Again, overtime, you will see the amount of money stored in that percentage will increase and your restaurant options will get better and better.

• Transportation — 15%
- When you have a spouse and family, transportation is a huge consideration. Whether it's just a car to get around, to flights and vacations, you need to provide for this area as well. As challenging as it may be, when you build up each category of your budget and stick to it, you can have it all. Carpooling can cut expenses; park and drive to public transportation. Purchase flights months in advance. Try your best annually to plan for all trips and transportation needs. Overtime, you will see that you've built up this category where

your trips will get better and better, and you will be able to afford more and better vehicles. But be careful to not live beyond your means. If you discipline yourself, in time, you will have it all.

- Savings — 10%
  - When you save money, it also spiritually gives you a sense of security and fulfillment. There's nothing worse than having absolutely nothing when you really need it. Having money gives you a feeling of empowerment and confidence. The scriptures says:

> Ecclesiastes 10:19
>
> *A feast is made for laughter, and wine makes merry: but money answers all things.*

> Proverbs 18:3
>
> *The poor useth intreaties; but the rich answereth roughly.*

  - Proverbs 18:3 says that the poor uses *intreaties*. In other words, poor people can't be bold and say how they really feel because they cannot afford to. That same attitude also plagues marriages. When the husband doesn't have money, he can feel powerless, especially if the wife makes more money and lords it over him. She controls the system because her money is answering family needs. However, poverty is a spirit. Therefore, when you always have money in the bank and your bills paid, you begin to have a prosperity consciousness. Saving money helps to develop that spirit even if it's not a large amount. 10% is not much but overtime, it will grow like you wouldn't believe! Some will say that they cannot afford to save. I say you cannot afford not to. And when you think about it, you probably regularly waste way more than 10% on things you don't need.

Everyone benefits when there's money in the bank.

- Debt — 20%
    - As much as we would all like to be free from debt, most of us have to work our way out. If you can afford to just pay it all at once and be done with it, I encourage you do so. Most people do not have that available cash. Many people are stressed and struggling because of the pressure to pay off what they owe. Lenders obviously want their money back but they also understand most people struggle to pay their debt in its entirety. Therefore, once you've created your budget plan and have allotted your 20% value for debt, between you and your spouse, divide your bills under the 20% value and communicate with your debtors what you will consistently pay. Put that 20% dollar amount in a separate account and have your debtors automatically withdraw. This will increase your credit rating, and release you from stress and worry. With this plan, you can do the math and see exactly when the debt will be fulfilled.
    - Also, practice using cash for purchases instead of credit. Credit is actually for people who don't need it.
- Taxes — 10%
    - If you're self-employed, you have to make sure that your taxes are covered at the end of the year. You can prepare for this by having a separate account where you put away 10% of your earning and at the end of the year you won't be caught by surprise with this expense. You will also have negotiating power.

- Self-improvement — 10%
    - This category includes education, books, seminars, just about anything educational that will add value and knowledge to help you increase personal enrichment. Overtime, that 10% will increase significantly and you will be able to afford the enhancement that you couldn't previously.

Of course, you can adjust your budget according to your needs but it's important to set your income/expense budget according to percentage instead of dollar amounts. When you do that, you can manage your life necessities accordingly no matter how much you make. Everyone and everything gets what it needs. Initially, it may be a challengeing getting your finances in alignment but once you do, it will run like clockwork. It is incumbent on you to make sure that you have the discipline to stick to the program.

Again, you and your spouse are managers to the kingdom/nation that God has given you. You must work what you have. Once you see where you are financially as a couple, develop a strategy, system, and plan. Regardless if it seems like it will take a lifetime, it won't. That's why God wants you to write out the vision.

PURPOSE

The purpose of money is to answer all *things* here on earth. It is a tangible method for exchange of goods and services. Money also serves as a fortress and platform to be heard. When you have money, you feel more confident and people are more inclined to talk to you. It's not the ultimate power but it's definitely a form of power.

HARD WORK PAYS OFF

There are some cold, hard facts that some people ignore because they don't want to acknowledge their faults. The Bible instructs us to cleanse ourselves. We cleanse ourselves with the water of the Word, which is also known as the Truth. The fact is, many people are poor or haven't acquired wealth because they're lazy. It's not the system that's not working, it's you that's not working. Sometimes it's hard to see ourselves because we don't generally consider our daily habits. We all have 24 hours in a day, what do you do with those hours? Are you maximizing your gifts and talents?

The Bible says that if you don't work, you don't eat. This is not to be confused with having a job. Rather, it's about providing an income for you and your household. Provision doesn't have to come from having a job. It comes from work.

The husband is to be like Christ, loving his wife like Christ loves the church. He worked for us and provided salvation. The husband IS THE SAVIOR OF THE BODY. It is your job to provide, if you don't, God doesn't honor that nor can He bless you. If you work within your gifts, the Bible says that your gift will make room for you. Working to provide for your family, whether you feel like it or not, is an act of faith. You trust that God will provide all of your need.

> **1 Timothy 5:8**
>
> *But if any provide not for his own, and specially for those of his own house, he hath denied the faith, and is worse than an infidel.*

There is also a misconception that wives don't have to work. I'm not saying that a wife has to work a job either. What I'm saying is that it is okay and scripturally sound for a wife to work and financially contribute to the household.

The wife described in Proverbs 31 bought and sold real estate and goods, and provided for her family and staff. It said that her candle did not go out day or night and her family was clothed with scarlet and purple. This virtuous woman worked hard to help build wealth, prosperity, and good well-being for her husband who, as the scriptures reveals, "sits with the elders."

> ### Proverbs 31:10-31
>
> *Who can find a virtuous woman? for her price is far above rubies. The heart of her husband doth safely trust in her, so that he shall have no need of spoil. She will do him good and not evil all the days of her life. She seeketh wool, and flax, and worketh willingly with her hands. She is like the merchants' ships; she bringeth her food from afar. She riseth also while it is yet night, and giveth meat to her household, and a portion to her maidens. She considereth a field, and buyeth it: with the fruit of her hands she planteth a vineyard. She girdeth her loins with strength, and strengtheneth her arms. She perceiveth that her merchandise is good: her candle goeth not out by night. She layeth her hands to the spindle, and her hands hold the distaff. She stretcheth out her hand to the poor; yea, she reacheth forth her hands to the needy. She is not afraid of the snow for her household: for all her household are clothed with scarlet. She maketh herself coverings of tapestry; her clothing is silk and purple. Her husband is known in the gates, when he sitteth among the elders of the land. She maketh fine linen, and selleth it; and delivereth girdles unto the merchant. Strength and honour are her clothing; and she shall rejoice in time to come. She openeth her mouth with wisdom; and in her tongue is the law of kindness. She looketh well to the ways of her household, and eateth not the bread of idleness. Her children arise up, and call her blessed; her husband also, and he praiseth her. Many daughters have done virtuously, but thou excellest them all. Favour is deceitful, and beauty is vain: but a woman that feareth the LORD, she shall be praised. Give her of the fruit of her hands; and let her own works praise her in the gates.*

Laziness is a cancer to prosperity and productivity, making it a sin. God instructs us to be fruitful, multiply, replenish and subdue. You cannot conquer anything without movement. You cannot complete anything without satisfying the work required. God rewards the diligent.

Husbands and wives are rulers. You rule the kingdom on earth that God has given you until He returns and the Bible says that the ***diligent shall bear rule***. Some couples are stuck in a powerless rut because they refuse to work, discipline themselves to diligently execute the plan.

God meets you at the point of obedience. He's the one who gives the increase. If you're lazy, you're in disobedience. Check yourself.

THE POWER SOURCE

Another challenge people face financially is the fear of poverty. There's a certain bondage that's associated with fear, especially in the work environment.

When people/corporations perceive you need them, a real sadistic, demonic force seems to arise in them causing them to withhold what they *believe* you need. So you take abuse and hard labor because you feel like you have to.

The *fear* of job loss and poverty mindset is a stronghold that YOU unconsciously established within yourself. Whatever you believe will be your reality. If you believe your job is your source, that will be a self-fulfilling prophecy, thereby giving the enemy spiritual, legal right to torment you. This fear is not limited to your job; it could actually be your spouse or a parent withholding a trust fund or inheritance. As long as you believe these people hold your fate in their hands that will be true.

In order to break this stronghold, you must identify your true source. If you don't tithe, you are making the unsaid statement that you and your job is the source. When you tithe, you're declaring to yourself, spouse and the world that God is your source. By faith you're believing that all of the blessings and protection promised the tither and those who obey God, belong to you. This is your security blanket. God promises to bless and protect you! Malachi 3 is the only place in the Bible where God says to "prove Me!" He's promising you that if you obey His Word, he guarantees it!

> Malachi 3
>
> *10Bring ye all the tithes into the storehouse, that there may be meat in mine house, and <u>prove me now herewith, saith the LORD of hosts</u>, if I will not open you the windows of heaven, and pour you out a blessing, that there shall not be room enough to receive it. <u>11</u>And I will rebuke the devourer for your sakes, and he shall not destroy the fruits of your ground; neither shall your vine cast her fruit before the time in the field, saith the LORD of hosts. <u>12</u>And all nations shall call you blessed: for ye shall be a delightsome land, saith the LORD of hosts.*

You don't have to take unnecessary abuse just to provide (unless God has you in a certain season for your development). God has given you the power to bind and loose things here on earth. That power is yours when you are in right standing with God, operating in His principles. God always comes for and helps the righteous. Therefore, if you continue to do the right thing and remain faithful, God will deliver you and give you wisdom for all the moves you need to make to prosper. He will protect you from the devourer. People and problems will arise to challenge you but they will not be victorious over you.

ONE MIND

Once you're married, we all understand that the two of you become one. It's super important that you live your life that way…including financially. Some people will argue that married couples should not have joint accounts. I understand why they would say that.

Notwithstanding, having a joint account is a great and healthy idea to have as the foundation (regardless who makes more money or not). When you join all incomes into one account and break it down into an agreed budget according to percentage, everyone will get what they need. Let's say you and your spouse agree that after combining all monies, each spouse gets 10% for themselves. That 10% can go into that spouse's personal account to do as they please without question. The reason they can spend without question is that you've already had a discussion before you dispersed the money. This system is a great way to operate because as an adult, each person would like to be able to spend money sometimes on things that they desire without question or guilt.

Most men cannot understand women's fascination with shoes and expensive handbags. Likewise, some women can't understand what the big deal is about an expensive watch or a good car! Everybody has their own personal thing that others may not understand, which may be considered a waste by another. If both spouses agree to this system, everyone gets what they need and want, making their entire well-being better, fulfilled and more at ease.

PLAN TO INVEST

The Bible says that the earth is the Lord's and the fullness thereof. God is an owner and investor. That makes you the same thing. God has invested life and love into us and He's expecting a return. When you own something, you have the power and authority (in general) to do what you want with it. For that reason, God wants you to be an owner. He expects you to be the head and take the lead. The way to get ahead is to live and work righteously, and then invest.

You and your spouse need to work towards owning EVERYTHING! Ownership provides freedom, power, and authority. Once something is paid for, you can move on to the next thing. Working towards ownership is scripturally sound and is a building strategy for your nation and the Kingdom of God.

God shows us investing with the principles of sowing and reaping. Understanding the principles of sowing and reaping will give you a reasonable idea of timing and expectancy. This scripture here describes a 5-year plan.

#1 WORK AND INVEST (PLANT)

> ### Leviticus 19:23-25
> *'When you enter the land and plant all kinds of trees for food, then you shall count their fruit as forbidden. Three years it shall be forbidden to you; it shall not be eaten. 'But in the fourth year all its fruit shall be holy, an offering of praise to the LORD. 'In the fifth year you are to eat of its fruit, that its yield may increase for you; I am the LORD your God.*

#2 DON'T BE GREEDY, GIVE. GENEROSITY CREATES A FLOW OF PROSPERITY. IF YOU JUST THINK FOR YOU AND YOUR FAMILY, YOU MINIMIZE YOUR MULTIPLICATION.

> ### Leviticus 19:9-10
> *'Now when you reap the harvest of your land, you shall not reap to the very corners of your field, nor shall you gather the gleanings of your harvest. 'Nor shall you glean your vineyard, nor shall you gather the fallen fruit of your vineyard; you shall leave them for the needy and for the stranger. I am the LORD your God.*

#3 DON'T WASTE TIME FIGHTING OVER SMALL LOSSES. REMEMBER, GOD IS YOUR SOURCE, NOT THE MONEY OR THE JOB. GOD SAID IT HIMSELF THAT HE WILL BLESS YOU IN ALL THE WORKS OF YOUR HANDS!

> Deuteronomy 24:19
>
> *"When you reap your harvest in your field and have forgotten a sheaf in the field, you shall not go back to get it; it shall be for the alien, for the orphan, and for the widow, in order that the LORD your God may bless you in all the work of your hands.*

#4 DO THINGS GOD'S WAY

> Leviticus 25:18-22
>
> *'You shall thus observe My statutes and keep My judgments, so as to carry them out, that you may live securely on the land. 'Then the land will yield its produce, so that you can eat your fill and live securely on it. 'But if you say, "What are we going to eat on the seventh year if we do not sow or gather in our crops?" then I will so order My blessing for you in the sixth year that it will bring forth the crop for three years. 'When you are sowing the eighth year, you can still eat old things from the crop, eating the old until the ninth year when its crop comes in.*

OPEN COMMUNICATION, NO SECRETS

Secrets destroy marriages. Do not withhold information about your finances—no hidden bank accounts investments, transactions, nothing! The enemy uses these secrets and insecurities to cause division in homes today. Never forget your spouse is YOU. They're your life partner. If you can't be vulnerable with them, then whom can you be vulnerable with? When you consider your spouse as you would yourself, you will not withhold information or keep secrets from yourself. You are patient, forgiving, and understanding of yourself. That is what your spouse will need in all areas, especially in the highly sensitive area of financial transparency.

Never make a public spectacle of your spouse's poor financial mistakes. Put your heads together and pray for wisdom on how to work it out. Whatever your spouse does is a reflection on you and directly affects you, which is why it's so important to love (AGAPE LOVE) your spouse deeply in this area. In time, YOU WILL PROSPER! The kingdom of God and future generations depend on the good management decision you make today!

> Proverbs 9:1
>
> *Wisdom has built her house, She has hewn out her seven pillars.*

> Proverbs 14:1
>
> *The wise woman builds her house, But the foolish tears it down with her own hands.*

> Proverbs 24:3
>
> *Through wisdom is an house builded; and by understanding it is established:4 And by knowledge shall the chambers be filled with all precious and pleasant riches.*

CHAPTER 21

Prayer Changes Things

MANY MARRIAGES ARE strained and with discouragement because they're believing God for certain things that haven't come to pass yet. Matter of fact, you don't have to be married to experience that kind of frustration. However, there are some reasons why some prayers are answered and others are hindered.

A few are:

- Husbands not treating their wife right
- Motives, play a rather large part of whether or not your request is granted.

> James 4:3
> *Ye ask, and receive not, because ye ask amiss, that ye may consume it upon your lusts.*

In other words, your prayers are not about doing Gods will, because God said he will supply all of your needs. What you're asking for are things that you want and do not need. Those request are purely to satisfy the flesh. Lust is not designed to be satisfied because it is a lure to destruction. Love gives, lust takes. If what you're asking was for you, you wouldn't have to lust after it. God will give it to you.

- Pride. God RESISTS the proud!
- Sin. Separates you from God.
- Lack of faith
- Disobedience

James 4:1-10

WARNING AGAINST PRIDE

From whence come wars and fighting among you? come they not hence, even of your lusts that war in your members? Ye lust, and have not: ye kill, and desire to have, and cannot obtain: ye fight and war, yet ye have not, because ye ask not. Ye ask, and receive not, because ye ask amiss, that ye may consume it upon your lusts. Ye adulterers and adulteresses, know ye not that the friendship of the world is enmity with God? whosoever therefore will be a friend of the world is the enemy of God. Do ye think that the scripture saith in vain, The spirit that dwelleth in us lusteth to envy? But he giveth more grace. Wherefore he saith, God resisteth the proud, but giveth grace unto the humble.

DRAWING NEAR TO GOD

Submit yourselves therefore to God. Resist the devil, and he will flee from you. Draw nigh to God, and he will draw nigh to you. Cleanse your hands, ye sinners; and purify your hearts, ye double minded. Be afflicted, and mourn, and weep: let your laughter be turned to mourning, and your joy to heaviness. Humble yourselves in the sight of the Lord, and he shall lift you up.

Sometimes, we're not cognizant of our own motives, attitudes or how we may be sabotaging spiritual progress. Therefore, it's a good thing to read the Lord's prayer every day, with conscious thought so that you cover all bases (self, others, problems, etc.) . Of course, when we read the Bible, God speaks to us and reveals himself in a unique/special way. I've found that the Lord's prayer is so complete and thorough that he lets you know who he is and who he is to you. If at all possible, you and your spouse should read this prayer *together* at some point every day. If not, at least read it yourself every day, it will certainly help your marriage. Below is a breakdown of the prayer as God has shared with me:

Our Father - This very first line is a salutation letting you know who God is to you and how to approach him. You're coming to God as you would a Father because that's who he is to you. There should be a reverential fear, respect and honor of him. Knowing that God is your father, it's a safe place to be transparent and vulnerable. He loves you.

Who art in heaven— Jesus is giving His geographical location to indicate God's superiority over all. The heavenly father resides above us. He is above all in power and authority. Acknowledgement of His elevated sovereignty should give us peace of mind, knowing that He sits high and looks low. He sees everything and knows all.

Hallowed be thy name— God's name is above every name, He is King of Kings, Lord of Lords. The name of Jesus is all powerful and has full authority under all. God has given you power and authority on earth in His name...*not your name*. Every knee shall bow and every tongue shall confess that *Jesus* is Lord. Praying to God with reverential fear and respect is essential and fitting to the Most High God. It's critical to understand the sovereignty of Jesus's name because, when you pray to God about something, you are coming to Him asking for His help. In order for what you're praying for to happen there has to be an authority greater than the barrier. The name of Jesus is that all powerful, final ultimate authority. God gives us the authority to use His name but he's also letting you know that it is sacred. Do not use His name in vain. He is Holy.

Thy Kingdom Come—Remember, God is looking for a Holy Nation and Godly offspring. God uses our bodies to do His will on earth. We can do nothing without Him successfully because every good gift comes from above. We need His kingdom (power, authority, and government) to come. We're reclaiming territory for the Kingdom of God here on earth. This is part of your marital purpose. When we understand first what God wants, it may compel us to change our prayer because what we want may be contrary to what the Kingdom requires. In order for your prayers to be effective they have to be in alignment with His Word and will. Sometimes we are so self centered that we become blind, deaf, and insensitive to what others need and God's purpose in our lives. When you ask God's Kingdom to come, you are asking God's government to come into the earth realm and take sovereign rule over your situation. Requesting God's kingdom to come is saying, "God I need Your provision and guidance". You are opening yourself up to wisdom, knowledge, and possibilities that you may not have considered. It is God's desire that we request this.

Your will **be done in earth as it is in heaven.** – The statement, "Your will" eliminates whatever it is you want, think, or feel that is outside of God's desire. Our bodies were made from the dust of the earth, therefore our physical bodies are earthen vessels as well. So when we say "Your will be done in earth, as it is in heaven", get ready for God to do something amazing in you! Praying, "Your will be done in earth as it is in heaven" spiritually, legally gives God access to your body and your life to do what He wants to do through you. Although God cares about your feelings, he is not limited by them. Which is why in order for Him to accomplish some things through you, it may be a painful process. If your impregnate your wife, that is a blessing. However, after conception, the woman goes through months of being uncomfortable and when it's time to deliver the baby, she goes through the awful pains of labor. We can understand that natural concept but if you understand this in prayer, regarding your marriage (or anything else for that matter) you can endure God's process. Committing yourself to living according to God Word is allowing God to not only be God in heaven but to be God in your life. Limitless and infinitely perfect.

Give us this day our daily bread—This verse is so powerful because God is talking about order, relationship, stability, trust, patience, and discipline. Praying for God's daily provision acknowledges Him as your source and provider. Here is where you will get what you need from the Lord for the day. God doesn't want us to worry about what's going to happen tomorrow because He will meet us daily with the provisions for that day. Only He knows what tomorrow holds, even when we think something will happen one way, God can do it in another. That's why worry is futile and trust in God for your daily sustenance is vital.

This prayer is relational because your request invites God to participate in your life and, when He does, you get to see His character and feel His presence. It is a bonding process with you, your spouse, and God because daily bread is not just tangible food but also spiritual nourishment that preserves and edifies the body. Your marriage will endure to the end if you take it day by day.

Forgive us our debts as we forgive our debtors—There are times that we are praying for God's intervention or provision and it seems as if He doesn't hear us because it may take a long time or doesn't happen at all. When we experience delays, it is wise to consider potential spiritual blockages. What is hindering the blessing? A debt is an outstanding balance you borrowed and failed to give back according to the terms rendered. A debtor is someone who owes you. In marriage, both parties fluctuate between being in debt and being debtors because your covenant vow swore certain things that you have reaped the benefit from but failed to give in return. When we are the ones in debt, we want grace to be granted to us. If you are the one that hasn't gotten a return on their investment, you may be bitter and angry because by right you are owed but the other party has not fulfilled their obligation.

What's frustrating about debt is that you cannot make people do what they don't want to do and you can't squeeze blood from a stone. Sometimes, people just don't have the means to fulfill the obligation at the time when the balance is due. So what do you do? You forgive the debt. We forget how much we consciously and unconsciously violate God's will. How can you expect God to forgive your sins, trespasses, and iniquities if you won't forgive your spouse? Remember, God doesn't see you and your spouse. He only sees one person. Not forgiving your spouse is like not forgiving yourself. Unforgiveness is a blessing blocker. This verse, *Forgive us our debts as we forgive our debtors*, is the application of the law and principle of sowing and reaping. Perhaps if you forgive your spouse daily for their debts, they will build up better character and fortitude to be able to satisfy all debts against you in the future. Again, your marriage is about you and God. Don't hold unforgiveness against your spouse. You don't want to block your blessings because you need God to forgive you.

Lead us not into temptation but deliver us from evil—After Jesus was baptized by John the Baptist, He was led into the wilderness by the Holy Spirit to be tempted by the devil. If you read that entire story, it is important to note that, when Jesus was baptized, God the Father said, "This is My son in whom I'm well pleased". God at that point declared to Jesus and the world who He is, then He was led to be tempted by the devil. The Word of God had been declared and Jesus received the Word of who He was, along with His purpose (He died to self and set out to do the will of God). Thus the wilderness was the beginning of a fiery trial. The temptation was an attempt by the enemy to get Jesus to move out of His sovereign position of God by waiting until He was hungry and physically weak. Because Satan is carnal minded, he did not anticipate that when his body is weak, his spiritual man was heightened. Inside Jesus knew who He was so He couldn't be fooled or tempted to do anything but the will of God.

I believe that God is praying and He wants us to pray according to this verse with the understanding of the power of who He is in us. It wasn't through angels that Jesus was delivered out of temptation - knowledge of who He was and the Word was what did it. You can only be tempted by what you want. The Lord commands us not to want (the Lord is my shepherd, I shall not want). You must put your wants in subjection to the Word and Will of God. The Holy Spirit did not lead Jesus into temptation, he lead him into the wilderness. When you are in a wilderness season with your marriage, family, finances, personal issues, etc... REMEMBER WHO YOU ARE. The Word and the Holy Spirit reside in you. Your will is to do the will of God. When you remember your vow to your spouse and God, you will have the power and strength to resist the enemy and he will flee from you.

For thine is the Power and the Glory forever amen—This verse sums it all up. God is your source for everything that you need. God is not going to give you what you want but what you need. If you delight yourself in Him He will give you the desires of your heart. His name and blood is your authority to overcome any obstacle. Every victory you have through Him gives God the glory. It is about Him, everything is about God's glory!

WARFARE

The Lord's Prayer is *how* Jesus says you should pray daily. But warfare is a different kind of prayer. It's more strategic in its applications. Certain strongholds won't be released except through prayer and fasting. Other times people may be so bound that they need intercession. The Bible instructs us that if there is any sick among you to let him call for the elders. Sometimes you'll need to call on the elders for them to pray over you.

Every sickness is not physical. Your marriage can be sick and toxic. You may be in over your head. In that case, call on the elders to intercede for your marriage.

> James 5:14
>
> *Is any sick among you? let him call for the elders of the church; and let them pray over him, anointing him with oil in the name of the Lord.*

> Mark 9:29
>
> *After Jesus had gone into the house, His disciples asked Him privately, "Why couldn't we drive it out?" Jesus answered, "This kind cannot come out, except by prayer."*

One thing you must remember; people are not your enemies. We wrestle not with flesh and blood! Every day we must put on the whole armor of God. Each spouse needs to pray for each other and together. Prayer is where you have a conversation with God. This is the place where He meets with you. Don't get so caught up in your problems that you are too stressed or hurt to pray. Do it when you feel like it and *ESPECIALLY* when you don't.

The Bible says the unbelieving husband is sanctified by the wife and the unbelieving wife is sanctified through her *believing* husband; else were your children unclean; but now are holy. ~1 Corinthians 7:14

Coverage in prayer by believing spouses extends all the way to the children, your holy nation. God doesn't want you to worry about your marriage, children, finances or anything. He created you in his image and likeness; He created you to be gods on earth (god with a little "g"). Prayer keeps you connected to the voice of the Lord that will guide you to all truth, health, wealth, and prosperity.

CHAPTER 21 | PRAYER CHANGES THINGS 305

PRAYING FOR YOUR HUSBAND FROM HEAD TO TOE

Pray for His Brain:
Ask that God would keep it sharp and focused and that his thoughts would not be conformed to this world, but would be transformed and renewed by the power of God. (Romans 12:2)

Pray for His Eyes:
Ask that he would guard them diligently and would set no worthless thing before them. (Psalm 101:3)

Pray for His Ears:
Ask that they'd be tuned to hear God's still, small voice and that your husband would always remain attentive to the Holy Spirit's promptings. (1 Thessalonians 5:19; Isaiah 30:9)

Pray for His Mouth:
Ask that no unwholesome talk would proceed from it, but only what is good for building others up. Pray that your husband would always and only speak the truth in love. (Ephesians 4:15, 29)

Pray for His Heart:
Ask that Christ would sit enthroned upon it, that your husband would love God with all his heart and soul and might, that he'd love his neighbor as himself. (Mark 12:30-31) Pray for his heart to remain soft toward you (Proverbs 5:18-19), and to be knitted to the hearts of his children. (Malachi 4:6)

Pray for His Arms:
Ask that God would strengthen them and make them firm. Pray that your husband would take delight in his labor and that God would bless the work of his hands. (Psalm 90:17, Ecclesiastes 3:22)

Pray for His Legs:
Ask that God would give him strength and stamina, that your husband might run with endurance the race that is set before him, without growing weary or fainting along the way (Hebrews 12:1; Isaiah 40:31)

Pray for His Feet:
Ask that they'd be quick to flee from temptation, to turn away from evil, and to faithfully pursue wisdom, righteousness, peace, love, and truth. (2 Timothy 2:22; Psalm 34:14; Proverbs 4:5-7)

Praying for Your Wife
From Head to Toe

Pray for Her Brain:
Pray that God would mold her into a capable, intelligent, and virtuous woman and would keep her thoughts centered on whatever is true, lovely, right, pure, noble, and worthy of praise. (Proverbs 31:10; Philippians 4:8)

Pray for Her Eyes:
Ask God to give her eyes of compassion, so she could see others as He sees them. (Matthew 9:36; 1 Samuel 16:7b)

Pray for Her Ears:
Pray that she would listen for God's still, small voice and would remain ever attentive to the His promptings. (Isaiah 30:9; 1 Thessalonians 5:19)

Pray for Her Mouth:
Ask that God would fill her mouth with skillful and godly wisdom, that the law of kindness would remain on her tongue, and that she would only and always speak the truth in love. (Proverbs 31:26; Ephesians 4:15)

Pray for Her Heart:
Pray that God would fill your wife's heart with love and respect for you and with tender patience toward your children. (Ephesians 5:33; 1 Thessalonians 2:7)

Pray for Her Arms:
Ask God to gird your wife with strength, making her arms strong and firm. Pray that He would bless the work of her hands and that she would do her work cheerfully, as unto Him. (Proverbs 31:17, 31; Colossians 3:23)

Pray for Her Womb:
Pray that God would bless the fruit of her womb by giving her children who walk in truth. (Psalm 127:3; 3 John 1:4)

Pray for Her Legs:
Ask God to strengthen and sustain your wife, so that she can walk and not faint and will not tire of doing good. (Isaiah 40:31; 2 Thessalonians 3:13)

Pray for Her Feet:
Pray that her feet would be shod with the preparation of the gospel of peace so that she might faithfully pursue righteousness and love. Ask God to lead her in the path of wisdom and truth and to keep her foot from stumbling. (Ephesians 6:15; Proverbs 21:21; Proverbs 4:11-12)

CHAPTER 22

Moving Forward: The Purpose & Power Of Forgiveness

> James 5:16
> *Confess your faults one to another, and pray one for another, that ye may be healed.*
> *The effectual fervent prayer of a righteous man availeth much.*

WHEN THERE IS crisis, loss, tragedy, and pain, the first thing we want to know is whose fault it is. Why is that? The damage is already done, so why bother pointing fingers? The Bible gives a very simple, yet poignant reason as to why we need to take responsibility for our faults…THAT YE MAY BE HEALED! Much of what is wrong in marriages today is because no one wants to take responsibility for the things that have gone wrong in the marriage. The husband blames the wife, and the wife blames the husband. As the scales continue to tip, people get tired of the same ole crap, get fed up, and off to divorce court you go.

God's plan is much simpler than that. Remember, in the beginning of this book, I talked about your individual covenant within the marriage covenant. Here's where that principle applies. For example, your husband travels the majority of time for work, pays all the bills and when, he's not working, he spends all his time with you. The only thing that he requires for you to do is keep the house clean and have a home-cooked meal when he gets home.

Husband comes home the majority of the time to a half-cleaned house, his wife looking a mess, no groceries in the refrigerator, and no dinner prepared. Her argument is that he's not home most of the time so she feels neglected. Therefore, she's not cooking anything—he should take her out to a nice dinner! Furthermore, he knows that she doesn't like to cook, that's how he met her so why is he expecting it now?

The husband is so tired from traveling that he doesn't even have the energy to fight. He gives in and they all go to dinner. She's happy, but he's ticked off (but doesn't show it). Next, the husband takes more and more work on the road, comes in later and later; and before you know it, he's in an affair. Whose fault is it? Automatically, the wife would be crying and screaming, "How could you do this to me?" etc. Yet she never saw that, to some degree, this was her fault.

Consequently, the same story can be flipped the other way around. The wife is expressing her needs but they were either denied or ignored so she got what she needed by FORCING his hand. Technically, she gets what she wants but what she really wants is her husband to love her through sacrifice.

The point here is we all are at fault in one way or another. In order to heal your marriage relationship, you must *confess* your faults one to another. This is so important! To confess something is to voluntarily reveal in detail what you've done wrong. For some people who are introverted or private, this could be excruciating. This personality type vehemently resist exposure by justifying within themselves that confession to God inwardly is sufficient. However, that is not scripturally accurate. So sorry introverts, you have to be transparent to your spouse directly, verbally, and with detail! On the contrary, to the more talkative extrovert, just because you're comfortable communicating, doesn't mean you're actually admitting your fault in the midst of clever word play.

Confessing of faults is a form of purging for the one that has done wrong, which is extremely liberating once done (regardless of how the other responds). However I must say that, before you confess, pray to set the atmosphere with love and peace. Also consider you may be the only willing party at the time that's willing to be honest. By right, the scriptures say, "Confess your faults one to another," but not everyone is always willing to be the first to be that vulnerable. Again, God is within your covenant and if you do your part, He comes in and does His part. This is the spiritual move of God that we don't see with the naked eye.

In other words, according to Scripture, when we confess our faults one to another, *healing* takes place. For the one whose spiritual cut is small, it's easier to be transparent. But for the spouse that has been deeply wounded, more healing is needed. Understanding that, God comes in and goes to work on our behalf, healing the hurts we cannot reach.

The enemy wants to keep you and your spouse at war with hidden resentments, bitterness, rage, etc. Satan is well aware of the later part of the scripture, "The effectual fervent prayer of a righteous man availeth much." That's key! If you don't confess your sins, you're not being righteous, which makes your prayer ineffective! God does not respond to disobedience and unrighteousness, nor is He impressed by it. When you do confess (voluntarily with detail), healing immediately enters the room. Now that doesn't make you exempt from taking responsibility for your actions. On the contrary, if you are sincerely confessing your faults, you're doing so to make amends.

YOU'RE BOTH RIGHT AND YOU'RE BOTH WRONG

Are you having a hard time believing that you may have contributed to the problems in your marriage? If the answer is yes, you need to visit a counselor. The counselor that I'm referring to is the Holy Spirit, the Word of God. God is no respecter of persons, for He tries and weighs the heart. To put things in practical perspective, align yourself with the Word and you'll see just how righteous you are…or not. A few questions you need to consider:

- Do you love your neighbor as you love yourself?
- Husbands, are you loving your wife like Christ loves the church?
- Husbands, are you managing your house?
- Wives, are you submitting and respecting your husband?
- Are you withholding your body from your spouse?
- Do you ALWAYS put your spouse first?
- Do you care more about other people, places, or things more than your spouse?
- Do you put on the mind of Christ?
- Do you tithe?
- Do you help each other?
- Do you confess your faults and pray one for another?
- Are you training your children together?

It's not about who is right and who is wrong, it's about overall righteousness. When both spouses focus on what's right, everyone will get what they need and grow together. God anointed you for your spouse and for the nation the two of you will birth together. Know this—marital challenges are normal. Don't feel or assume that because you may be unhappy at the moment, that it will always be this way. Be faithful to God and in time, things will get better.

If things are going well, enjoy it and don't sabotage it with fear. It is a blessing when God allows you to enjoy the fruit of your labor. God wants you to have life and have it more abundantly. He wants you to STAY MARRIED ON PURPOSE!

PURPOSE PRINCIPLES

PURPOSE PRINCIPLE #1
Whomever you listen to and believe will be the one who governs the body.

PURPOSE PRINCIPLE #2
Money, power, and sex can form a bond but it's your word and spirit that makes you one.

PURPOSE PRINCIPLE #3
The marriage covenant overrides feelings and what you think about your spouse, be it good, bad, or indifferent

PURPOSE PRINCIPLE #4
God expects you to become one with Him in order to become one with each other.

PURPOSE PRINCIPLE #5
You will feel good about your spouse when you handle the business of your marriage and they will feel good about you.

PURPOSE PRINCIPLE #6
Contract thinking says, "I love you until you tick me off, then I'm out." *Covenant* mindset says, "I don't like you right now but I love you so I'm not going anywhere."

PURPOSE PRINCIPLE #7
Change your vision/perspective/perception by putting on the mind of Christ.

PURPOSE PRINCIPLE #8
Your husband will do his job when you stop doing it for him.

PURPOSE PRINCIPLE #9
Your husband will listen to you more when you talk low and say less.

PURPOSE PRINCIPLE #10
You already are who you are going to be, as you're becoming it.

PURPOSE PRINCIPLE #11
He will treat you more like a queen when you address him like a King.

PURPOSE PRINCIPLE #12
Your wife is priceless. You can *produce* a seed but you cannot *reproduce* without her!

PURPOSE PRINCIPLE #13
Your wife is your God-given help.

PURPOSE PRINCIPLE #14
When you love your wife more than yourself, that's when you know you've adopted the *character* of Christ.

PURPOSE PRINCIPLE #15
If you touch her soul, she will give you her body.

PURPOSE PRINCIPLE #16
Married couples, don't withhold sex from your spouse. Have sex…lots of it and have fun doing it! God has given you the green light!

PURPOSE PRINCIPLE #17
Nothing works right when it's out of order.

PURPOSE PRINCIPLE
Common Law marriage is a contract that requires no sacrifice or promise. Marriage is a covenant sealed by an oath and blood. Real love *cuts* covenant voluntarily, not forced by law.

PURPOSE PRINCIPLE #18
In order to defeat your enemy, you must know who it is.

PURPOSE PRINCIPLES #19
Whomever you choose to obey is your God because your thoughts control your actions.

PURPOSE PRINCIPLE #20
When each spouse crucifies their flesh by sacrificing their will for the will of God, they unleash the undefeatable power of God in their life and nation.

PURPOSE PRINCIPLE #21
Dying to self for your wife is the greatest act of love she can witness!

PURPOSE PRINCIPLE #22
It is imperative that a wife witness her husband die to self.

PURPOSE PRINCIPLE #23
When you die to self, no one can kill your spirit.

PURPOSE PRINCIPLE #24
If you're not willing to lay down your life for your wife, you cannot be her savior.

PURPOSE PRINCIPLE #25
Wives: Do not try to *CHANGE* his mind, *INSPIRE* change with godly behavior and conversation.

PURPOSE PRINCIPLE #26
When a spouse listens attentively without interruption, the other spouse will feel like they've been heard and in some cases understood.

PURPOSE PRINCIPLE #27
Mastery of the mouth creates a happy wife and happy life!

PURPOSE PRINCIPLE #28
All affairs start with a conversation.

PURPOSE PRINCIPLE #29
Whoever controls the mind controls the body.

PURPOSE PRINCIPLE #30
When the enemy tries to destroy your marriage, he confuses your language. Guard your heart, and watch your words.

PURPOSE PRINCIPLE #31
Selfishness and self-centeredness are a manifestation of lust. *Selfless* behavior is a manifestation of love.
Love gives, but lust takes.

PURPOSE PRINCIPLE #32
If you change you, you can change your surroundings.

PURPOSE PRINCIPLE #33
The truth and proof of your love will stand trial by your trials.

PURPOSE PRINCIPLE #34
Always love your spouse more than they expect and more than they deserve.

PURPOSE PRINCIPLE #35
Give your spouse what they need and they will give you what you want!

PURPOSE PRINCIPLE #36
Don't divorce your spouse because they cannot supply ALL of your needs. That's God's job. Know who your source is.

PURPOSE PRINCIPLE #37
Love is not just something you do; it's the person you become.

PURPOSE PRINCIPLES #38
Obedience is the proof of love.

PURPOSE PRINCIPLE #39

One of the goals in marriage should be for both of you to be spiritually naked and NOT ASHAMED. It's okay to be transparent and vulnerable with your spouse.

PURPOSE PRINCIPLE #40

You cannot get what you need from your spouse until you give them what they need. Consequently, that need could be different from yours.

PURPOSE PRINCIPLE #41

Sex is physical; making love is spiritual.

PURPOSE PRINCIPLE #42

Order creates a positive flow.

PURPOSE PRINCIPLE #43

Things begin to work when you are in agreement.

INDEX

A

Abigail 9, 254
Abraham 32, 88, 144, 150, 189, 190
adulterers 220
adultery .... x, 67, 217, 225
ambition 147, 201
anointing 98

B

boredom 147, 222

C

commandments, ten 107
communication 4, 75, 247, 294
complacency 221
confession 309
consummation 67, 72

Covenant:
    marriage .... vii, 3, 13–22
    mindset 17
    with God 2
covering, of husband ... 33, 59, 101, 192
creation 18
Curses:
    Adam 121, 122, 137
    generational 76, 94, 126, 131, 168, 172
    marriage 184
    tithing 120, 122, 170
    violation 10

D

Daniel [book] 162
David [King] 151

debt 116, 276, 286, 301–2
deception 163
democracy 102
discouragement 297
Divorce:
    divine order 102
    finances 116
    Moses xi

E

energy 75, 79
Esther [Queen] .. 37–38, 103, 104, 114
evil, men 231–37

F

failure, allowed by God 31
familiarity 27
Finances:
    money chapter 273–95
    problems ix
flesh, conquering 156
Forgiveness:
    God's presence 91
    purpose & power 307–11
    record of wrong 258

G

Goliath 157
    See Also .... David [King]

H

healing, sexual 65–83
helper 43, 60, 62, 188

hindrances 32, 76, 77
Holy of Holies 90–94, 105
husband, definition 29, 30
husbands, unbelieving 304

I

idolatry 23, 171
incompetence 40
infidelity .... x, 147
Isaac 88, 150, 190

J

Jacob 9, 88, 129, 136, 150

K

king, definition 34
Knowledge:
    definition 74
    God's truth 163
    husbands 71, 72
    lack of 103
    love 6
    spiritual 2

L

law, common 14
Leah 9, 150
Love:
    Agape ... 132, 248, 254, 263, 295
    embodiment 9
    Eros .... vii, 7
    God 161
    language 154, 241–49

Love *cont/d*:
   on purpose 251–59
   real 147
   staying in love 261–72

M

manna 107
Marriage
   covenant......................... 13–22
   purpose 1, 8, 9
   unhappy................................... 9
materialism 163
Mind:
   carnal..................................... 28
   of Christ 17–22, 247, 277, 314
   one 291
ministry 90, 92, 95, 114
Moses .... xi, 88

N

nagging 248
nation, becoming 141–52

O

obedience..................................... 4
offspring, Godly 8
order, divine 105

P

perfection 19
power, abuse of 21

Prayer:
   Lord's- 299–303
   warfare 303
Pride
   demonic............................... 201
   of life.....163, 166, 192, 223, 242
   warning................................ 298
priesthood, royal 87–98
promiscuity.............................. 130
Purpose Principles 313–18

R

role reversal............................... 30
rule, husband over wife............. 28

S

seduction 221
seed, godly.................................. 9
sex, health benefits 80–83
sexual healing 65–83
Solomon 221
spirit, location of........................ 20
stewardship 30
strongholds................. 76, 168, 303
submission................................ 33
submission, to the Word 24
superwoman complex 31

T

temptation.........219, 225, 302, 303
territory 159–61
theocracy................................. 102

tithing 120–23

U

unbelieving husband 304
unity.......................... 111, 114, 244

W

warfare 303
warfare, spiritual 161, 165
will, God's 10
words, importance of 127–29

www.ingramcontent.com/pod-product-compliance
Lightning Source LLC
Chambersburg PA
CBHW071300110426
42743CB00042B/1125